DESCRIPTION OF BEARER
SIGNALEMENT DU TITULAIRE

No 922422

NAME - NOM
JOSEPH EARL HARRIS

BIRTHDATE - DATE DE NAISSANCE
13 DEC 1951

BIRT...
WI

HEIGHT - TAILLE
5 FEET / PIED   10 INCHES / POUCES   1.77 METRES / METRES

HAIR
BRO

PASSPORT ISSUED AT - LE PASSEPORT DÉLIVRÉ À
OTTAWA

CHILD...

ON - LE
23 MAR 1977

PASSPORT EXPIRES - CE PASSEPORT EXPIRE
23 MAR 1982

S051844

SEE PAGE 5, 12

See information on page 32 and inside back cover.    Voir l'Avis à la page 32 et en troisième page de couverture.

The bearer is
Le titulaire est

Photograph of bearer
Photographie du titulaire

(Signature of bearer - Signature du titulaire)

3

# The Houseguests:

# A Memoir of Canadian Courage and CIA Sorcery

**Mark J. Lijek**

Dedicated To Richard Sewell,
Chris Beebe, Richard Queen
and all other
"Absent Friends"

# Acknowledgments

This book began as a jumble of notes written in the middle of 1980 as I was settling into Hong Kong. Had it not been for the need to keep the CIA role secret, I might have written it earlier. When the agency went public in 1997, I began to think about the book again. In particular, I was concerned the actions of the Canadians were being relegated to a secondary status they did not deserve. Still, it took the production of the film *Argo* to convince me it was necessary to have a factual account of the rescue to help insure Hollywood fiction, no matter how well done, did not become a substitute for fact.

Many people helped with this project. Among those who read the first draft were many friends and relatives. It is dangerous to list them because someone will be left out, but Michael Bricker, Tom Larsen, my sisters Mary and Joann and my daughter Krys offered important encouragement. Tom Larsen and Michael Bricker in particular provided detailed comments that helped me improve subsequent drafts while Michael was my primary cheerleader. Robert Wright, author of Our Man in Tehran, provided a critical boost to my confidence as his positive judgment of my initial draft was that of a historian and published author. Bob Anders and Tony Mendez agreed to be interviewed and provided important details.

The original plan was to publish a traditional paper book, but the editor and I were unable to come together on a time line. My daughter had all along been promoting the e-book option, and her encouragement led me in that direction. I was fortunate to find a friend, Annie Lastar, who was willing to give several large blocks of time to editing the manuscript. Other aspects of creating an e-book became a family project, with my son Mike helping with graphics (including the Canadian passport) and taking charge of the website and my daughter Krys also doing graphics and serving as the marketing consultant. My sisters were involved with the artwork also. My wife Cora lived this experience with me and offered useful substantive comments on the manuscript. She also generously overlooked the deterioration of the level of housework for which I am usually responsible that resulted from my focus on this project.

I reserve special thanks to Roger Lucy and his wife Susan. Susan's encouragement was important. Roger's substantive knowledge was critical. He provided numerous corrections as well as additional details that enhanced the narrative. He also saved me from a number of embarrassing mistakes. I can't feel too bad about that, however, as thirty plus years earlier he saved the CIA from an embarrassing mistake: a dating error on our forged visas showed us arriving after we departed and could have derailed the exfiltration completely. He is a true renaissance man.

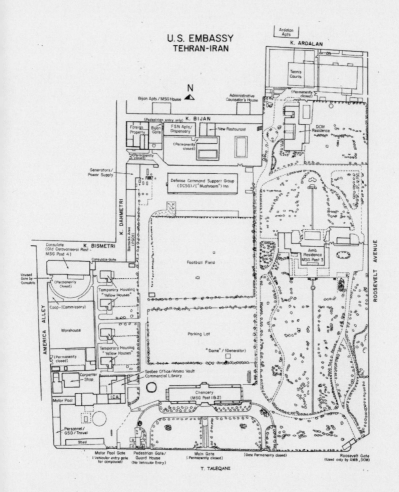

U.S. EMBASSY
TEHRAN-IRAN

# Contents

# Foreword

This is a story about heroes. It is often said heroes don't exist anymore, except for caped crusaders in films or comic books. I disagree. I still believe ordinary people in extraordinary circumstances can prove heroic. That was my experience after I became embroiled in the 1979 Iranian revolution. Although this book tells my story, I am not one of the heroes, just someone who was in the wrong place at the wrong time. The heroes are the people who helped me, often risking their safety and well-being and possibly their lives, in order to help assure my companions and I remained free and ultimately escaped from Iran.

Their actions deserve recognition. Over the thirty plus years since these events took place, many articles, documentaries, books and even films have told parts of the story and recognized to one degree or another the heroism of these individuals. But no one has provided a direct account from the perspective of one of the six Americans who came to be known collectively as the "houseguests." While I make no claim to speak for the others, I believe telling the story in full detail is enough to make clear who the true heroes are and why their roles should be celebrated.

This is also a story of adventures, big and small. Iran was my first assignment for the Department of State so I have included some background on the assignment process, training and other factors that collectively put me into the consulate building on the embassy compound the day it was attacked. I hope that makes the story more readable and understandable. I have also described what it was like to live and work in Tehran during the early days following the revolution. This again serves to put the story into context, and if I have done my job correctly, will be interesting in its own right. For those who remember the hostage drama it provides perspective on our lives before the takeover, something that has received relatively little attention in other accounts of these events.

A writer whose work I enjoy once referred to a former politician as a dot in the rear view mirror of history. Our story too is a dot, but before we disappear entirely in the distant haze I wanted to record the facts as I remember them. Part of my motivation is to correct some errors. Of greatest concern is the controversy regarding the relative roles of the Canadians, both in Tehran and Ottawa, and the US Central Intelligence Agency (CIA). It has been disheartening to read the criticism directed at the Canadian side for allegedly overstating the importance of its help to us. Worse still are versions that mention the Canadians only in passing. It is as if we were somehow in suspended animation while waiting for the US government to decide our situation warranted the CIA's attention. I hope to provide some balance to this debate primarily by laying out the facts and letting the reader decide.

On a more personal level, I was motivated by minor but erroneous information in other accounts. For example, in Mark Bowden's excellent <u>Guests of the Ayatollah</u>, Mr. Bowden alleged I gave a briefcase to one of the people in the consular section, subsequently a hostage, having falsely told him it contained sensitive information. I did not and would never have considered such a "joke" in the circumstances. Another example is Jean Pelletier's assertion in <u>The Canadian Caper</u> that I am short. I am of average height; he confused me with another of the houseguests who was several inches shorter than me. I mention these issues not because I care that a book published thirty years ago called me short (okay, I will admit it was irritating at the time), but to illustrate how easy it is for an author who was not part of the story to get things wrong.

This is not to say my version is without errors. More than thirty years have passed since the actual events and while I made notes in the months following our escape and have consulted with other participants on some topics, I admit there may be errors both of omission and commission. I have sparingly used other published accounts in order to supplement my recollections, sourced as appropriate. When in doubt, however, I have trusted to memory and there are some conflicts between this and other versions of these events. I have tried to be honest with the reader by using terms such as "my best recollection" or "as I recall" to qualify information about which I am not absolutely confident but which deserves inclusion because of its importance to the overall story.

Though our adventure is a mere footnote in the history of US-Iran relations, a footnote in this sense is by definition an elaboration of details in a bigger story. So while this is primarily a memoir I have included some history so readers unfamiliar with the broader story will be able to understand the circumstances. I have done my best to get the facts straight, but this book is not intended as a substitute for a more detailed and expert account of US-Iran relations. There are good books available. I have listed a few in the afterword on the assumption anyone interested in further information will know better which books to consider when they have finished mine.

In the text I alternate between "I" and "we." This is not a "royal we," but rather recognition I believe the opinion or attitude I express was shared by other people in whatever group makes sense in the context. I realize this may seem to contradict my earlier statement I do not want to speak for the others, but I have tried carefully to use "we" only in situations where it is not controversial. For example, I might write "we had a great dinner." While it is possible one or more of the diners may not have shared this opinion, if I were to write "I had a great dinner," the implication might be the others did not eat or were fed less well. Please accept my assurance I have used "we" with deliberation.

I have used Farsi (Persian) terms from time to time. The spellings are phonetic and based on the Lijek system, which may not correspond to any other system. I have tried to make the word sound like what I remember from Farsi language training or the way I learned it in Tehran. Most of the Farsi words used in the book are ones without good English equivalents and were routinely used in conversations that were otherwise in English.

Lastly, a note on names. Since this is a factual account, I have a preference for real names. The primary exceptions are Iranians who helped us and may not be known to authorities in Iran. Even though more than thirty years have passed it is not possible to rule out reprisals even now. So they have been given false names.

# Prologue: Rain on Our Parade

There was a time, remembered best by those of us who were born before 1960, when Iran and the United States were close allies. Former President Jimmy Carter went to Iran in 1977 and said to its ruler: "There is no leader with whom I have a deeper sense of personal gratitude and personal friendship." He went on to describe Iran as an "island of stability in one of the more troubled areas of the world." [1]

Less than two years later, that man, Shah Mohammad Reza Pahlavi, was in a New York hospital undergoing treatment for cancer. His successor, the Ayatollah Ruhollah Khomeini, was an anti-Western theocrat intent on turning Iran into an Islamic state. The revolution that drove the shah from power had shaken the Iranian nation to its core. The American Embassy in Tehran remained ensconced in a walled twenty-six acre compound, a reminder of the close relations the two countries had once enjoyed. Although in people terms a shadow of its former self, the embassy retained seventy-five American employees, engaged largely in the difficult task of trying to build a relationship with the new Iran. That process came to an abrupt, total and dramatic halt on November 4, 1979 and has yet to resume in any significant way.

Certain dates in history stand out. While I admit to a personal interest that may color my judgment, I would argue this was the day the long-simmering volcano of Islamic discontent against the West finally erupted. The eruptions have continued, some more dramatic than others. In the years since the West has experienced numerous attacks by Islamist radicals, and the US and its allies have engaged in two large wars and many small ones in an effort to protect against further attacks. Regardless of one's beliefs about the politics of the conflict or the rightness of any particular policy, there can be no

---

1. Doyle McManus, Free at Last (New York, New American Library, 1981), 22

disagreement November 4 marked an irrevocable shift in the nature of the relationship between Islam and the Western world.

Of course none of this was known to us on that November morning. It was the start of another work week; routine except for the temporary closure of the tourist visa section. It was a small protest against the anti-American graffiti and posters plastered on the embassy's walls over the weekend. At the time there was no US ambassador because the Iranians had rejected our candidate. Our boss, the chargé (technically chargé d'affaires ad interim) was at the foreign ministry to demand more security.

The shah had been in exile for nine months, moving from place to place as his various local hosts found him inconvenient. The pressure mounted to admit him to the US. The Carter administration initially resisted, recognizing that allowing the shah into the States would vastly complicate the task of building relations with the new Iranian leadership and could potentially endanger embassy employees. But when the shah's illness became publicly known and his supporters argued the medical expertise available exclusively in the US was all that could save him, Carter surrendered. In the two weeks since the shah had flown to New York we had been told to expect trouble. The security officer did not have any specific threat data or warnings of things we should or should not do. Realistically we had no choice except to carry on as before. Still, the chargé concluded the heavy barrage of posters and graffiti was a good excuse to remind the Iranians of their responsibility for our security.

The morning was exceptional in one other respect. It looked like it might rain for the first time since my arrival in Iran four months earlier. My wife, Cora, and I drove to work, arriving in time for the usual 7:30am start. She would have a paperwork only day, a welcome break from the usual 200 tourist visa interviews. My day would be normal since my responsibilities only occasionally involved tourist visas. We joined the nine Americans whose workplace was the consular building in the middle of the west side wall of the compound. The majority of Americans worked in the chancery, the traditional name for the main embassy office building. My first project of the day, after getting a cup of coffee, was to meet

5

with a transient American who had lost his passport and was having trouble getting an exit visa. I reviewed the telegrams from the State Department that came in over the weekend and was happy to tell him his family had arranged airline tickets home. I suggested he wait until my senior local employee returned from an unplanned run to the airport so the three of us could talk about next steps regarding the exit visa.

Around 9:00am there was a commotion in the outer office. People were saying demonstrators had climbed over the main gate and were running loose in the compound. The duty Marine locked down our building. We waited. There were sixty or so Iranians in the building, employees and clients, primarily for the immigrant visa unit next door to my office. People huddled in groups. They spoke quietly. Then they told us to prepare to leave the building. We were to walk to the chancery. Why or how we were to navigate through the demonstrators roaming the compound wasn't clear, but fortunately no order to move came. A half-hearted effort to break into the building was followed by footsteps on the roof. Some people claimed to smell smoke. I did not.

The power went off. Still we waited. We huddled in the few areas where natural light filtered into the building. The Marine told us again to prepare for the move. Then our immediate boss, the consul general, said we were going to try to leave the building and make our way to the British Embassy, a twenty minute walk. We were given no details. It seemed the attackers had breached the chancery's defenses.

We were lucky our building had a direct entrance to a back street, normally mobbed by applicants for tourist visas. Today there was no crowd. The only window overlooking the street was a tiny slit in my office. The view was so restricted we didn't know whether there were people outside who would prevent our leaving. The bosses decided it was worth the risk. We opened the doors. One American went out.

He returned a few minutes later. The Iranians posted outside the door would not stop us from leaving.

We were told to break up into groups of eight or ten. There should be a couple of minutes space between the groups as they left. We wanted to look as inconspicuous as possible. The Iranians, customers and most employees, went first. The Americans settled into two groups. My wife and I were in the first. An Iranian employee had volunteered to guide us to the British compound. Although we tried to create some separation between ourselves and the Iranians who had just left it did little to minimize the appearance of a long parade. Of course it was pouring rain. My wife shared an umbrella with a co-worker. I wondered, *"Won't a man wearing a nice suit, no coat, without an umbrella look odd walking in the rain?"* But there was no alternative. Our group exited past the guards and turned left. We followed our guide on the most direct route toward the British Embassy.

It was uncomfortable. I felt many eyes watching me. But with each step we were further away from the compound and closer to refuge. The Brits were not far. They had already agreed to take us in. I was hopeful in an hour or two the takeover would be over and we'd be back at work. Maybe we'd get the rest of the day off.

Just a few more blocks.

Cora now walked with our guide at the head of our group. We had allowed ourselves to form clusters and string out, so perhaps 150 yards separated the head from the tail.

Suddenly Cora and her co-worker made a u-turn. The look on their faces said enough.

# Part I

How to Visit

a Really Rotten Place

and

Drag Your Wife Along Too

# 1. Exceptional or Expendable

So how does a shy young man from Seattle end up scared and wet, wandering the streets amid the turmoil of post-revolutionary Tehran? More than once during our weeks as refugees, I found myself wondering how I had gotten myself, and especially my wife, into this situation. As comedian Oliver Hardy said to Stan Laurel, "Here's another nice mess you've gotten me into." Who was my Stan Laurel?

I decided I wanted to join the Foreign Service in my junior year of high school. An older acquaintance told me there was such a thing as the Foreign Service. I knew there were people engaged in diplomatic activity on behalf of the United States but had never given any thought to who their employer might be. I had never traveled, except to Canada from Seattle and to Mexican border towns when we lived in Tucson. The idea of getting paid to live in exotic foreign lands sounded exciting. My friend also told me about the Foreign Service school at Georgetown University. The information gave me a concrete idea of what I might do to turn the dream into reality. When senior year came I applied to the Foreign Service school on an early decision basis and was accepted. I never considered any alternatives.

Georgetown was expensive. I hadn't figured out how to pay for it when the opportunity to apply for an Army Reserve Officers' Training Corps scholarship was brought to my attention. I applied, was accepted and Georgetown here I come. Although I knew the scholarship entailed a four year active duty commitment following graduation, I didn't give that part of the deal much attention. As it turned out, I was able to spend my time in Washington, most of it as either an aide to one of the deputy commanders or as the speechwriter for the commanding general. These were unusual assignments for a lieutenant, but the heavily civilian Army Materiel Command was a unique organization within the Army, and in most cases I got the job because no one else wanted it. I surprised myself by enjoying my four years and it was a tough call to leave the Army.

I met Cora at Georgetown. She was three years behind me, majoring initially in Japanese but later in history. We met through a college club. Her mother was Japanese and Cora used to joke she had inherited the worst genetic traits from each of her parents. She was short, not 4'11" like her mother but just three inches taller and had the round face typical of many Japanese women. From her father she inherited her thick dark brown hair. In Tehran days she wore it shoulder length and I thought it looked just fine, but she has always complained it was difficult to manage. The combination worked for me. We started going out in 1972 and that she was still in school was one of the reasons I requested a Washington assignment after entering active duty with the Army. In 1976 we got married for the best of reasons: the Army paid higher allowances to married officers.

I had never lost the desire to join the Foreign Service, and Cora, as an Army brat who lived in many places over the years, had no objection. While I was on active duty she obtained a master's degree in English as a Second Language, thinking it would be relatively marketable while we were abroad. I took the dreaded six-hour Foreign Service written examination while still an undergraduate; I passed but failed the follow-on oral interview. I was asked to trace the development of American literature and floundered. I considered this a dry run. Since my scholarship came with an active duty commitment, even had I passed the entire process it is unlikely I could have accepted an appointment offer.

While still on active duty I decided to try again, this time passing both the written and the oral exams. I was fully prepared to discuss the development of American literature, but the examination panel fooled me and wanted to talk about theater instead. In the mold of generals fighting the last war, I was busily studying theater when I was surprised by a letter informing me I had passed the oral. I was pathetic but apparently I did well enough overall.

In those days it took a long time to get through the hiring process. Even though I held all sorts of security clearances from the Department of Defense, the State Department wouldn't accept them. I had to redo everything. In the end, that worked to my advantage because the employment offer came just as I was leaving active duty.

I finished with the Army in September and joined State on October 10, 1978. The timing could hardly have been better, although all my work almost came to nothing. I told the recruitment people I would be away for the month of September on terminal leave from the Army and they should contact me at my parents' home in California. I knew I was on the list of people eligible for employment but State refused to predict if and when they would go far enough down the list to reach me. As it was, I returned home from leave and found a letter offering me the appointment; it had been sitting at the post office for two weeks and I had one day remaining to confirm my interest before the offer was automatically withdrawn. In hindsight, maybe this was the first of a number of the close calls that got me into Iran and out again.

New Foreign Service officers were put through an orientation program, known informally as A100. The classes were numbered sequentially, and we were the 138th class since the "new" system had come into use around 1950. We called ourselves the "Fighting 138th," for reasons which eluded me then and now. Our assignment list later gave it some credibility. We were a varied group. At twenty-seven I was younger than all but one man. Some of the other students were starting second careers. We had a brilliant Harvard PHD who would eventually make several unsuccessful runs for the presidency. We also had a geology major with no work experience. What we all had in common was we had passed a grueling written exam, the oral interview, a security screening included a complete background check and a medical examination which found us to have no physical limitations precluding assignment anywhere in the world.

The course was five weeks long. The sixth week to which spouses were invited was dedicated to diplomatic protocol. We learned the basics of how the Department was organized, how an embassy operated, how to write telegrams (cables in State-speak), which at the time were the primary means of communication between embassies and Washington. As the class progressed we were given an opportunity to express our assignment preferences. State had a bad reputation as an undisciplined organization. The critical positions went begging while officers fought for the plum postings. I learned how true this was as a personnel officer for the European bureau later in my career. A big exception to the rule was new hires. Offices representing the different regional areas pleaded with personnel to include their most critical junior level vacancies and ultimately the system came up with a list of positions suitable for new hires; it matched exactly the number of employees in the class. So if the regional bureau succeeded in getting personnel to put a job on the list it was probably going to be filled.

There were twenty-seven recruits in the class and twenty-seven jobs. All the positions were abroad and virtually all were consular. Our class was composed of employees selected to spend the majority of their careers working in political, economic and administrative jobs as well as the consular area. At the time State offered an appointment it was in one of those four functional areas. They were called "cones" for reasons no one has ever been able to explain to me. The candidate decided to accept or reject the appointment in part with the knowledge he or she would likely spend the bulk of their career doing that type of work. I was selected for administration, no surprise since I had done occasional administrative work in the Army and completed a Masters in Business Administration at American University. The MBA came with a specialty in international marketing. It had been my hope to do commercial work. Shortly before I joined the Department, then Secretary of State Henry Kissinger reached an agreement with the Department of Commerce to transfer the function to a newly established Foreign Commercial Service. Although its representatives would be stationed in embassies abroad just like "real" Foreign Service officers, they were civil servants working for the Commerce Department. That did not fit with my plan so administration was an acceptable fallback.

We were each allowed to select (the process was called bidding) six positions. I chose six in Latin America, having studied Spanish in college. I had no particular interest in any other available countries. Generally speaking, the jobs were in "visa mills," Mexico City was the outstanding example. They entailed primarily interviewing visa applicants, some of whom attempted to perpetrate fraud. It was unpleasant but necessary work and at State it was considered a ritual baptism of fire. Virtually every new hire had to spend his or her first or second tour in a job of this type.

Perhaps the most interesting position on our list was in Beirut. That poor city was already a basket case and one man volunteered to go. There was at least one other bidder, Richard Queen, who was soon to join us on the Iran list, but for whatever reason he wasn't selected. Soon we learned the alleged volunteer didn't intend to go. He had friends at State and expected they would pull strings and get him reassigned. At first it didn't make sense to the rest of us. If he didn't want the job, why ask for it? I guessed it was an attempt to beat the system for new hire assignments. His friends would rescue him from Beirut. By the time this was done, he would no longer be limited to one of the twenty-seven positions open to our class and could compete for more desirable positions. It was at a minimum unethical, I thought, and ultimately a dumb thing to do. I was pleased the assignments system did not allow itself to be so easily manipulated: he resigned prior to the completion of the orientation class. Americans appreciate a level playing field. On general principles alone I was more respectful of my new employer after this stunt failed. As the situation in Tehran deteriorated, it became even more important to me that we remaining twenty-six were all playing by the same rules.

Second to Beirut in terms of risk were three positions in Tehran and one at the consulate in Isfahan, an important city to the south of Tehran. Iran was in the process of moving from friend to foe. The US had enjoyed good relations with Iran and its ruler Shah Reza Pahlavi for many years. The shah was a tyrant, but successive American administrations considered he was an important ally, a bulwark against Soviet influence in the region. And while his human rights record was hardly perfect it was at least somewhat better than those of many of his neighbors. Furthermore, he was moving Iran in the direction of becoming a modern nation. He abolished the chador, the Iranian version of the head-to-toe covering for women, that is again increasingly mandatory in the Islamic world. He also provided women with equal access to education. From a broader perspective one could argue his human rights record was mixed. While some of his opposition came from western-educated democrats who wanted political liberalization, at least as much came from Islamic zealots who objected to secularization of government as well as education and equal rights for women.

Jimmy Carter campaigned for president in part on an agenda stressing human rights as an integral part of our foreign affairs agenda. He promised America would no longer accept human rights abuses just because the dictator in question happened to be an ally. Iran was where the "rubber hit the road" as far as this policy was concerned. When decision time came, Carter followed the tradition of previous administrations and embraced the shah. Nevertheless, a variety of factors worked against him. Carter's zigs and zags, even though they ended ultimately in our supporting the dictator, had emboldened the opposition. For the first time the thought the US might not support the shah under some circumstances gained a tiny wisp of credibility, not just with the opposition, but with the shah himself. He became concerned too much repression might affect US support so was increasingly hesitant in his responses. The opposition also benefited from poor economic conditions in Iran. The shah's efforts to westernize Iran antagonized Islamic fundamentalists, in particular the Ayatollah Ruhollah Khomeini. Ayatollah is a title used in Shia Islam (the smaller of the two main branches of Islam, the other being Sunni). Shia is very dominant in Iran. The title denotes a religious leader or teacher of high standing, At times it seemed there were more ayatollahs than taxi drivers in Iran, but when someone said "*the* ayatollah" they meant Khomeini. He was the most respected and therefore most feared by the shah. Exiled to France, Khomeini's sermons were widely circulated on cassette tapes. Meanwhile, the secular opposition wanted more political freedom and an end to the rampant corruption that was increasingly visible against the background of a bad economy.

This is not intended as history and entire books have been written about the reasons for the Iranian revolution. In order to make what happened to us understandable, however, I summarize the progress of the revolution at various points. This capsule summary tells you what I understood about the situation in Iran as I studied the assignment list. Most of this information was public, some I picked up while still on active duty. The Army Materiel Command was responsible for developing weapons systems, many of which were sold abroad. Iran was a good customer so events there were a frequent part of the daily intelligence summaries I read each morning.

Had I known I would be trying to decide whether to volunteer for a Tehran assignment, I would have paid more attention to the classified Iran reports. Even so, no one knew what was to happen. In early November of 1978, the shah was still holding on to power, but just barely. American civilians had not yet been evacuated; family members were still permitted at the post. The embassy itself had been significantly downsized but remained large compared to most. The private American community also was relatively large. The close relationship between the US and Iran could not dissolve overnight, even though many observers were convinced the shah's days were numbered.

Another element of the assignment process was taking the MLAT, Modern Language Aptitude Test. Rather than evaluate a candidate's ability to learn foreign languages before offering an appointment, State waited until after hiring. A new officer had a certain period to develop acceptable fluency in a language. The amount of training and the required level of success depended on whether the language was considered hard or normal. I scored a seventy-two out of a possible eighty points on the MLAT. I don't remember the system, but it was a good score, high enough to qualify me for assignment to a post requiring hard language training. My Spanish was not good enough to allow me to test out of the fluency requirement, but part of my reasoning in bidding on jobs in Latin America was the thought that with a couple of months of full-time language training, I would be able to get off probation in Spanish.

Against this background, our class anxiously awaited the attention of the personnel types so we would finally learn where we were going. Around the fourth week we were each scheduled to meet with the officers who were in charge of managing our careers. All junior officers were the responsibility of Richard Masters. He headed a special section in personnel focused entirely on making sure the new people received assignments designed to give them the wherewithal to succeed in the service, as well as to allow the system to evaluate their ability to do so. In addition, we each had an officer responsible for everyone in a particular cone. In my case it was Bill Hudson, the chief of assignments for administrative officers.

I don't remember Masters well. My main interaction with him was a phone call, when he asked me to consider volunteering for

Tehran. I asked why. He said there were no bidders and I had one of the higher MLAT scores so was a good candidate for Farsi (Persian) language training. I then met with Bill. He was on the tall side, leaning toward stocky, with short blondish hair, and a knack for putting people at ease. In my case, however, the ease lasted only a minute as Hudson advised I go along with the suggestion and hinted I could get the American citizen services position in Tehran.

Bill pointed out there were some pluses. This would not be a visa job. I would therefore be able to fulfill my consular requirement without suffering through the ordeal of interviewing hundreds of applicants every day. Furthermore, he'd talked with the new administrative counselor (chiefs of section at larger embassies were given the title counselor) heading to Tehran and there was a chance I could transfer to an administrative position after just one year. No guarantees, of course.

At this point in time the shah was still in charge and Washington was backing him. His survival in power was not a sure thing, but a good bet. I had not bid on any of those positions because I suspected the rise of the Islamic movement in Iran, even if it did not unseat the shah, would make life difficult for Western women. Unlike me, Cora had traveled extensively, including to Iran when her father worked there a few years earlier. She had already experienced some of the difficulties Western women faced there. Also, I wanted to get the language fluency requirement out of the way. Doing so in Spanish was certainly a safer bet than Farsi.

On the other hand, I had joined the Foreign Service to see the world and there was more potential for adventure in Iran than, say, Maracaibo, Venezuela. So I talked to Cora and we agreed to go along. We also discussed the possibility saying "no" would not matter, so we might as well accept our fate. Personnel did its magic and soon I had a piece of paper assigning me to Tehran.

Two other officers received the same paper: Joe Stafford and Don Cooke. Joe was thin, about 5'7" with black hair and mustache. He and his wife, Kathy (Kathleen), had been living in Rome, although Joe's official state of residence on his Presidential commission was Crossville, Tennessee. Joe had no Tennessee accent, something I would have recognized since Cora's father's family was all from the Knoxville area. Like me, Joe had been selected for the administrative cone. Kathy was four inches taller than Joe, with dark hair combed back over her shoulders. She was a talented painter who looked forward to expanding her artistic perspectives as they traveled the world.

Don Cooke was our resident rebel as well as the youngest at age twenty-five. He was the one person in our class with a hard science background, geology. Though his father was a university professor, Don seemed most at home in jeans and cowboy boots. He had longish brown hair and a shaggy, medium length beard. He avoided suits, adding a jacket and tie to his usual jeans whenever this could substitute for a suit. In talking about his school days he was most enthusiastic about the time spent in the Utah desert digging for rocks. On the other hand, there was obviously something attracting him to the Foreign Service and he made it through the examination process. The Department in those days was just beginning to recognize scientific issues would become increasingly important in the future, and Don was appointed in the economic cone, of which science was a sub-specialty. Don was single.

Richard Queen, brought into the Department in the consular cone, got Isfahan. Rich was tall, 6'2", with brown hair and a mustache, both worn in military style. He tended to speak softly and laugh readily. Rich's undergraduate and master's degrees were in history with a particular interest in military history. He had just completed two years of active duty in the Army as part of his reserve commitment. Like me, he enjoyed his time in the service; he was a supply officer in charge of POL, the army term for gasoline, oil and other similar items. Rich too was single but made no secret of his desire to find someone to marry. Iran was probably not good from that perspective.

Other than having done well on the language aptitude test, there wasn't a pattern. Two of us were single, two married. Two had recently left military service; two had no military experience. We represented three of the four cones. With the Beirut position in limbo because of the bizarre actions of the person assigned there, we four were clearly going to the most dangerous posts on the list. Unable to come up with a real explanation, we decided, jokingly we hoped, that the personnel types must have gotten together and determined we were the most expendable new hires.

The A100 class drew to a close. Cora joined me for the one week follow-on course in diplomatic etiquette, which seemed strangely inconsistent with our assignment. I realized there was still a diplomatic community in Tehran and we would probably spend more time with other diplomats just because the political situation would make it harder to meet Iranians. Nevertheless, the news from Iran each day was worse than the day before, and it seemed to me a class in self-defense methods might be more useful in the short term anyway.

The first nominee for the Stan Laurel "Nice Mess" award would have to be Richard Masters. Since he asked me to volunteer and processed my assignment it would be unreasonable to exclude him. In fairness, he had no leeway in filling these positions. If not me, someone else from our class would have gone. Furthermore, the situation at the time was not yet critical. We thought the shah still had a chance.

# 2. From Chaos to Confusion

After we spent a week learning about fish forks, where to place soup spoons and other similar esoteric knowledge, the initial training program was over. I was given a week of consultation time, something to keep me on the payroll until the start of language training. This meant my place of duty was the Iran desk.

The chief of the operation was Henry Precht. Henry was a gentleman of the old Foreign Service school, with a soft southern accent and a gracious manner that complemented his dignified appearance. He was the first senior officer I came to know on a first name basis, and I liked him very much. Henry had two assistants. The senior man was older, about Henry's age, thin with a drawn face. I don't remember his name but he was very friendly and always had time for us. Like Henry he had served in Iran, though less recently as I recall. The other desk officer was Mark Johnson, a Georgetown grad not too much older than me and also very accommodating of our desire to learn. Most of my time that week was spent reading files, both historical and the daily cable traffic between the desk and the embassy. I also spent time learning what a country desk does and where it fits in the Department bureaucracy.

The policy-making apparatus at State is divided into bureaus, some functional such as the Bureau of Intelligence and Research, and others geographical such as the Bureau of Near Eastern Affairs. The geographical bureaus are in turn organized by country, with smaller countries clustered together and bigger ones with their own offices, known informally as a "desk." Probably at one time there was one person, sitting at one desk, who was responsible for tracking US relations with a given country. That was long ago, but the name, desk, stuck.

Henry knew Iran well. He had come to his present job after four years as the counselor for political affairs at the embassy. In a normal embassy, the head political officer comes immediately after the ambassador and the deputy chief of mission; effectively it is the number three position. At a huge embassy in a critical country like Iran, this was an important spot. I think he had served in Iran earlier still, either as a junior officer or perhaps in the Peace Corps. I believe he considered himself as knowledgeable as anyone at State when it came to Iran. He was probably right. Still, the cables made clear even to a novice like me there was a big disconnect between what the embassy was reporting and what Henry was telling us. This disconnect would become more pronounced in the coming months. In fairness, Henry was not alone in his optimism. The CIA issued a report in the summer of 1978 which stated Iran was not in a "revolutionary or even pre-revolutionary" situation.[1]

After a week at the desk learning about the policy issues surrounding Iran as well as the differing views of its future prospects, I was, perhaps perversely, energized and ready for language school. We were back at the site of our initial training, the Foreign Service Institute in Rosslyn, just across the Potomac River from the District of Columbia and a twenty minute shuttle bus ride from Main State. The institute had a well deserved reputation for the quality of its language instruction, but in the case of Farsi the circumstances were less than ideal. The senior instructor, Ferydoun, was nearing retirement and displayed a notable lack of enthusiasm for his work. His boss, the supervisory linguist Jim Stone, put the temporary contract teacher, Mehri, in charge of the four officers. We were required to learn Farsi not just because of the job requirements but because we needed to end our language probation status. The rules allowed a maximum of six months of language training to an untenured officer. In effect we were rolling the dice that we'd be able to get it done within the time allowed and Farsi is a tough language. So Rich Queen, Don Cooke, Joe Stafford and I were Mehri's pupils.

We soon learned Mehri and Ferydoun were barely on speaking terms. She was an attractive, stylish, mid-thirties woman married to a wealthy Iranian exile. She had hopes of returning to Iran someday if the political situation permitted. Her husband had the foresight to get his assets and his family out while it was still relatively easy. Ferydoun was from a peasant background. Mehri never missed an

1. Cited in Robert Wright, Our Man in Tehran (New York, Other Press, 2011), 42

opportunity to tell us he spoke Farsi like a peasant. No doubt the information reached him. All that aside, however, Mehri was the better teacher, so we got her, and the wives got Ferydoun. Cora complained he would chat with them in English rather than Farsi.

I know there is at least one company that advertises a program to help people learn languages the way diplomats do, implying there is some magic formula. Maybe they have discovered it since 1978, but for us it was simply dedication and memorization. We were in class six hours per day. I am reasonably sure the other students, like me, spent at least three hours every night reviewing vocabulary or visiting the language laboratory to practice pronunciation or do listening drills.

Within a few weeks, it was clear some of us were better than others. Joe was the star of the class. I was behind him, then Don and finally Rich. Rich was finding the pronunciation very difficult and after a while he developed a complex about Mehri. True, she did poke gentle fun when someone messed up, but Rich messed up more often than the rest of us combined and a more professional teacher would have known it was time to lay off the jokes. Mehri was a good teacher, but she did not have the sensitivity or training to realize Rich was struggling and needed encouragement rather than sarcasm, no matter how gentle or well-intentioned. As the class progressed, the relationship between the two continued to deteriorate, unfortunately to Rich's detriment. In the end, however, all four of us received a passing grade from the assessment panel. I could not help but think, at least in Rich's case, this was as much because State wanted him in Iran as because he had technically reached the level to get off probation. But two things are for certain: he had earned it through intense hard work and he had more than enough Farsi to do the job.

As language studies progressed and we reached the point where we could have meaningful conversations, both Don and Joe got on my nerves occasionally. They would take extreme positions on some issue or other. I realized later Joe was doing it just to keep the conversation going. Don's obsession was to bring every discussion around to his favorite topic, Bokononism. For those who are not fans of Kurt Vonnegut, this was a fictional religion from the book Cat's Cradle. I had earlier mentioned Don was a bit of a rebel. I think Bokononism appealed to him because it was based on the idea all religions are lies including Bokononism itself. There was something in this circular paradox that appealed to his sense of the absurd. Richard had too hard a time to focus on anything other than the language itself. The truth is, however, I really liked all three of these guys. This was very fortunate because we spent seven hours a day together for six months.

Part of language training was area studies. We looked forward to these occasional breaks from the stress of the endless memorization and repetition learning a language requires. The area studies were focused on the Middle East, and although there is a variety of cultures and languages within the region, the majority of people are Arabs and Arabic is the dominant language. Iran is what remains of the ancient Persian Empire. Farsi is a close cousin of Dari which is spoken in Afghanistan, but significantly different from Arabic, although for historical reasons (the conquest of Iran by Muslims) it uses the same writing system. Since Farsi has sounds which do not occur in Arabic the use of the Arabic script made it even harder for us to learn to read and we never got beyond the basics. Fortunately for us, the Department did not require anything more than rudimentary reading skills in certain languages like Farsi. Iranians are a proud people and do not appreciate being lumped in with their Arab neighbors, with whom they share a common religion despite significant cultural differences.

So while much of what we studied was not directly relevant to Iran, the instructor attempted to give us appropriate readings and commented on areas of difference. I came away from area studies with an appreciation of three things. First, never confuse Iranians with Arabs. Second, the Iranians have a conspiratorial view of history in which they are routinely the victims of manipulation by foreigners. How far back this trait goes is not clear to me, but there was certainly a basis for the belief during the 20th century. The British were the primary influence in Iran until World War II. After the war, as the government deliberately pulled back from its imperial commitments, the US took its place, at least in Iran.

Third, I learned the story of recent American involvement with Iran. Again, this is not a history book, but it is important to understand the US role in Iran during the 1950s was very much in the mind of Khomeini and his supporters. In 1953 the CIA and British intelligence (there is controversy as to which deserves the greater "credit") engineered a coup against the democratically elected prime minister, Mohammad Mossadeq and pressured the shah to name a replacement. He had tried to do this earlier but caved in to public demands to restore Mossadeq. Through bribery and careful manipulation of various factions in Iranian society, the CIA created an opposition movement that weakened Mossadeq's challenge to the shah. Most importantly, the Shia clerics abandoned Mossadeq. He was arrested and placed under house arrest. Many of his supporters were also arrested and some even executed. From this point until his abdication, the shah's authority was not seriously challenged.

Through the lens of the cold war, a left-leaning government intent on nationalizing Iran's oil assets was considered too great a danger to Western interests in the region. While I suppose one can argue the merits of this act, there is no denying many, perhaps most, Iranians from that point considered the shah an American puppet. We were therefore responsible for his actions and judged to have more influence over his policies than we in fact had. For example, we certainly did not support the shah's role as one of the founders of the Organization of Petroleum Exporting Countries, OPEC, the primary purpose of which was to jack up world oil prices. But the natural Iranian tendency to see conspiracies everywhere, combined with the actual history of our relationship with the shah, created a perspective that understandably subjected all American actions in Iran to intense and usually negative scrutiny.

In hindsight, it is worth noting there is more than a trace of irony in the coup against Prime Minister Mossadeq. Had Mossadeq been left in power and a tradition of secular democratic government taken root in Iran, how would Khomeini have brought his Islamic republic to life? It is difficult to avoid the suspicion Khomeini would not have much more use for a real democracy than he did for the shah. Certainly Mossadeq is not a celebrated figure in today's Iran. The nations that staged the coup, on the other hand, would today like nothing better than a secular democratic government running Iran. There is no question we paid a steep price for our meddling. Unfortunately, the people of Iran have paid a higher one.

During the twenty-four weeks we were in language training, the situation in Iran changed dramatically. When we started the shah was still in charge and family members were allowed at the embassy. The demonstrations got larger and more violent. It reached the point the shah told the army to fire on the demonstrators. Some did. People were killed but this did not quell the disturbances.

The anti-shah agitation had serious economic implications as well. Strikes paralyzed much of the economy. By late October of 1978, oil production had fallen to 28% of its former level.[2] Oil was the lifeblood of Iran and reduced oil revenues affected virtually every aspect of the economy. Political instability fed on economic weakness as the government was increasingly unable to provide jobs and housing for the urban poor, making them even more open to the appeal of revolution and dependent on the Islamic charities organized around the mosques.

As violence increased, the demonstrators championed the victims as martyrs and the military itself became less and less interested in worsening the bloodshed. Perhaps seeing the handwriting on the wall, the officers began to think about their situation in a post-shah Iran. Most of the enlisted personnel were from the peasantry and in many ways had more in common with the people they were shooting than with those who were ordering them to fire. It finally reached the point where the shah realized his orders might not be obeyed. Or perhaps he decided enough blood had been shed in defense of his government. Either way, it was time to leave.

Although we were reading newspapers as well as taking advantage of the occasional opportunity to shuttle over to the desk and read the cable traffic, most of our information came from Henry. He organized a weekly "brown bag" lunch for the four officers and two spouses. Over lunch Precht preached optimism. He was no fan of the shah. His departure of itself was not a strong negative in Henry's view. He did believe in the westernized democratic opposition, the people to whom the shah ceded power when he went into exile.

Prior to leaving Iran the shah named Shahpour Bakhtiar as prime minister. Bakhtiar was a long-time member of the National

---

2. Nikki Keddie, Roots of Revolution (New Haven, Yale University Press, 1981), 251

Front, an opposition group that favored a constitutional monarchy with primary power vested in the Majlis, as the Iranian parliament was known. The $64 question was how much power this government actually had. Two weeks after the shah's departure, on February 1st, the Ayatollah Khomeini returned in triumph from exile in France. He was greeted with huge demonstrations in the streets, a clear vote of confidence. The secular democratic opposition could produce nothing comparable.

With twenty-twenty hindsight, it is easy to see the secularists never had a chance. As members of the westernized elite they had little in common with a typical working class city dweller let alone the rural peasantry. True, many of them had what we would now call "street cred." They had actively opposed the shah and done time in prison for it. Under different circumstances, perhaps a few years earlier when the shah was not so thoroughly discredited and the economy stronger, the religious opposition may have been less confident of its ability to topple the shah singlehandedly. The National Front might have been seen as a useful coalition partner and so better placed to guide Iran toward a parliamentary democracy in which the shah would gradually cede power to an elected government.

But in the Iran of early 1979 the Ayatollah Khomeini held unrivalled power. He began to activate the network of oppositionists his agents had created while he was in exile and kept energized with his taped sermons mailed from Paris and distributed secretly throughout the country. Bakhtiar was not one of the shah's men, but had been appointed by him and was theoretically serving at the shah's pleasure. The Iranian military, while beginning to disintegrate, presumably remained loyal to Bakhtiar and indirectly the shah. The US still hoped to maintain a moderate, secular government and sent US Air Force General Robert Huyser, deputy commander of US military forces in Europe, to persuade the generals to support Bakhtiar by using their troops to maintain order in the streets and break the strikes paralyzing the country.[3]

It was too late. When Huyser left Iran on February 2, desertion was widespread and the military did not, perhaps could not, mount

---

3. McManus, Free at Last, 25

any effective opposition to the revolutionaries. The final offensive began on February 9 with an attack on the Doshan Tappeh airbase in east Tehran. Entire units defected and attacked those which remained loyal.[4] At 2:00 p.m. on February 11, General Abbas Gharehbaghi, Chief of Staff of the armed forces, declared the armed forces "neutral in the current political disputes… in order to prevent further disorder and bloodshed." The revolution had toppled the Pahlavi dynasty.[5]

Khomeini removed Bakhtiar and put Mehdi Bazargan in his place. Bazargan was also a member of the National Front, an engineer by profession, who had been acting as Khomeini's political adviser during his time in France. The evolving point of disagreement between the embassy and the desk was here. How much power did Bazargan actually have? There was no question he was subservient to Khomeini; after all, he owed his position to the ayatollah. But would the secular government he now headed actually be allowed to run the country? And if so, to what degree?

These were vital questions because Khomeini also created a largely secret shadow government with its own officials, known as the revolutionary council, and a combined military/police establishment in the form of the revolutionary guards. Initially, the primary para-militaries that fought the shah's army were the fedayeen-e khalq and the mujahidin-e khalq. The former were secular Marxists and the latter Islamic Marxists, but Khomeini gradually replaced them with Islamic militants drawn from the revolutionary committees (komitehs, usually local militias that had coalesced around a particular mosque or mullah, a common name for Shia clerics) with a more strictly religious foundation. These became the revolutionary guards, in Farsi pasdaran e engholabi. Once in Iran, we usually just called them pasdars. We got to know them quite well, certainly better than we would have liked. Although less formally integrated into Khomeini's para-military forces, the komitehs staked claim

4. Ibid, 26

5. Muhammad Sahimi. "The Hostage Crisis, 30 Years On." Frontline, Public Broadcasting Service, November 3, 2009 <http:www.pbs.org/wgbh/pages/frontline/tehranbureau/2009/11/30> February 23, 2012

to particular neighborhoods, like neighborhood watch on steroids. Sometimes they infiltrated institutions such as the airport. Either way, they were a serious, sometimes dangerous presence because they were heavily armed but not trained or well-disciplined.

The shadow government was conducting trials of those considered shah loyalists, many under the auspices of "Judge Blood," the infamous Ayatollah Khalkali, who served also as jury and chief of the executioners. It is hard to argue a government that can execute people is not a real government, while one needing outside permission is, but that was in effect Henry's position.

I am oversimplifying, but Henry had much more faith in the official provisional government than our people on the ground in Iran. Furthermore, the embassy realized we had no meaningful contact with the revolutionary council. They were virulently anti-American and had absolutely no interest in talking with any of us. A few embassy staffers with long experience in Iran, such as Michael Metrinko (our consul general in Azerbaijan who was transferred to the embassy after that post was closed, also a former Peace Corps volunteer in Iran), were able to open minimal communication channels with some elements of the shadow government. This was only because of the personal contacts they had developed over many years. But the people who were willing to talk with official Americans were running significant risks (Khalkali's noose, potentially). The only real result of these meetings was to reinforce the conviction on the embassy's part that our contacts in the formal bureaucracy didn't mean much.

The Department and officials like Henry who opposed the shah and fought bureaucratic battles on behalf of the theory the secular opposition constituted a realistic alternative to the shah refused to believe they might have created a Frankenstein. Sure, Khomeini had a lot of power, but he was a religious leader and not interested in being Iran's chief executive. Bazargan was a trusted aide and Khomeini's appointment of this proponent of secular democracy was a clear sign of the direction Iran would follow.

The St. Valentine's Day occupation took place during this period of chaos and widespread violence. On February 14, 1979, the embassy was attacked by members of the Marxist fedayeen-e khalq.

The Marine detachment, then numbering nineteen, opposed the attackers with non-lethal birdshot in order to buy time for document destruction, but was eventually ordered by the ambassador to surrender. One local employee was killed, and several Americans were wounded.[6] One of the wounded was a Marine, and his story garnered considerable publicity because he disappeared for several days before surfacing in a Tehran hospital. Cora remembers that aspect of the incident very well, noting it made daily headlines in the *Washington Post.* Somehow I do not. But the important point is not the accuracy of the details we ourselves remember, but rather the impact of the attack and, more particularly, its resolution, on the thinking of the Iran specialists. That the takeover lasted only a few hours was interpreted by the desk staff, and ultimately by Department officialdom, as proof of the provisional government's ability to control events. Prime Minister Bazargan himself was involved in gaining authorization for the action, and his deputy, Ibrahim Yazdi, also the foreign minister, personally oversaw the surrender of the compound back to US control. While that could be interpreted as proof of the provisional government's authority, it could also have been a sign of its weakness. When no one below the deputy prime minister can persuade a para-military gang to leave a foreign embassy compound, it says a lot about the lack of real authority of those further down the chain who would normally have dealt with such an issue. The counter-argument was the situation was far from normal, and it would have been unrealistic to expect either the military or the police, two institutions seriously weakened by the revolution, to act effectively on their own. As a very junior officer, I had only a vague knowledge of these arguments flying back and forth. But no one on either side anticipated a future takeover would last 444 days.

As I noted earlier, I personally was not well informed about the details of the incident. I recollect the official emphasis was on the positive, the provisional government's quick and effective response, rather than on the details of what actually happened in the compound. I recall no telegrams in the reading file about it. There was no

---

6. Ibid. 2

after-action report, analyzing what happened, why and whether our responses and those of the host government were appropriate. These documents may have existed, but if so, they were being closely held. The decision to put a positive spin on this incident had an unintended consequence. When the second attack came nine months later we were predisposed to believe it would follow the same pattern as the first. The personal and official decisions we made were premised on the expectation Iranian authorities would remove the attackers within a matter of hours.

In Henry's defense he did give us the opportunity to change our minds about going to Iran. During this period much of the western community left Iran. Many embassies sent their family members home and reduced their staffing levels. The Valentine's Day attack triggered an evacuation of all private Americans who wanted to leave. US embassy dependents were sent home. Many had already left in December when the Department authorized voluntary departure in response to the growing chaos. This paid many of the expenses of going back to the US. What had been one of our largest embassies was temporarily reduced from 300 to thirty-five official Americans. The consulates were all closed as was the tourist visa operation in Tehran. Richard Queen's assignment was changed from Isfahan to visa officer in Tehran. With all these developments, we should have given serious consideration to backing out. We never did. Chalk it up to the foolishness of youth, the desire for adventure and perhaps the practical difficulties of finding a new job that would get me off language probation. We were almost half way through Farsi training. Besides, as a junior diplomat I would be too unimportant to be a terrorist target yet still able to enjoy the benefits of diplomatic status. Could anything that bad happen to me?

So despite everything my biggest concern was the plan to bring Cora and Kathy to Tehran. With dependents banned from the embassy they were in limbo. Cora and Kathy continued with language training because Henry's optimism left open the possibility family members might return before too long. Then Henry raised the prospect of a waiver from the policy if Cora and Kathy agreed to work the visa line. The Bazargan government was keenly interested in seeing us resume issuing tourist visas and our side wanted very much to oblige. But everyone understood there had to be some balance between supply and demand. Rich, Joe and Don could not by themselves even begin to deal with the rush of applicants we could reasonably expect. Additional bodies were mandatory.

The Department had already tried one mechanism for finding Farsi speakers willing to accept assignment to Tehran. Unimaginatively titled a volunteer cable, it was sent to every embassy and consulate in the world. It described the available positions and the alleged benefits (hardship pay, separate maintenance allowance for family members and the possibility of a one year tour). The hope was somewhere could be found several officers who were either pining away for Tehran but had not totally lost their sanity, or, much more likely, whose current work or personal situation was sufficiently miserable they would want to go anywhere to escape it. Volunteers would have their present assignment canceled immediately, no questions asked and no protests from the losing post considered. There were no responses. Personnel also had a process for compelling assignments known as identification, but it was cumbersome and rarely used. So Henry told us once things calmed down he was pretty sure he could get permission for Cora and Kathy to go. In the meantime they would continue with language training and then take the consular course.

Consular training also took place at the Foreign Service Institute in Rosslyn. Known as ConGen (for Consulate General) Rosslyn because much of it consisted of role plays rather than traditional study, it was good preparation for all of us. The instructors, most of whom were Foreign Service officers with extensive experience, would pretend to be, for example, an imprisoned American and a local police officer. The prisoner would push me to help her while the policeman rated my performance on the basis whether I did all I could for the prisoner while avoiding anything that could be interpreted as legal representation or demanding special consideration. The basic rule is we are able to ask only that Americans receive the same treatment as host country nationals. In much of the world that is not so good. The training was effective, certainly more so than just reading a book. Fortunately I never had to do a prison visit in Iran. From what the hostages said after their release it would not have been pleasant.

During those five weeks we continued our regular brown-bag lunches with Henry or Mark Johnson and obtained our weekly heaping helping of optimism. That optimism, combined with his efforts to make sure my wife was able to travel to Tehran, qualifies Henry as the second nominee for the Stan Laurel "Nice Mess" award. Still, our formal training ended with a small acknowledgment Iran might be a tough post. We had a two day security seminar which included a film on what to do if you are taken hostage. I enjoyed the parts of the seminar that focused on espionage, particularly Soviet tricks in the cold war such as planting microphones in official gifts or even the heel of an ambassador's shoe. The movie about hostages included some riveting interviews with people who had survived the experience and discussed the techniques they had used to cope. The narrator talked about basic survival strategies. I don't claim to remember the details. Bad as things were becoming in Iran I didn't think it was something to worry about. Besides, this was standard; everyone heading overseas took the course, so why worry? Well, there was one reason I could not quite erase from my mind. The chaos of constant anti-shah street demonstrations had ended, but there was undeniably confusion about who was in charge. Khomeini had the authority to rule Iran as a dictator every bit as much as the shah did at the apex of his power. The question was whether he would choose to exercise it, and if so, when and how? And more to the point, how would he treat representatives of the Great Satan?

## Part II

Into the Belly of the Beast

or

Life, Love and Lunacy in

Khomeini's Tehran

# 3. Goodbye Washington, Hello Tehran

Unlike most of the people in my A100 orientation class, I was a resident of the DC area so to me the break with home was still in the future. We lived on the 20th floor of Skyline Towers, a collection of high rise condominiums in Fairfax, Virginia. Most of our friends were from our college days, those who had remained in the area following graduation. So as language training came to an end and we were entering the final months prior to departure, we had to come to grips with both the practical and emotional aspects of saying goodbye to our home.

On the practical side, we decided early on to rent the condo rather than sell it. We had lived there for three years and it would probably be difficult to get our investment back in that short a time. So we looked for a property manager. We signed up with a man named Jim Hill, who worked for a real estate company a couple of miles down the road in Seven Corners. Being a landlord was a new experience for me and I concluded Jim would minimize the burden.

The Department pays for ten days only of temporary housing so we set our move for the end of June. Packing was unusually complicated because we did not know how things would work out, particularly for Cora. Normally, an officer going on an unaccompanied assignment can request a separate maintenance allowance. This would have permitted Cora to stay in the condo and my pay would be increased to cover part of the cost of supporting two households. But we had bought into Henry Precht's optimism that Cora would be able to go to Iran within a couple of months after me so the plan was she and Kathy Stafford would get an apartment together. The assumption was both would get permission to travel to Iran at the same time. A further complication was freight shipments into Iran were temporarily suspended. Normally, at posts where the government provides furnished housing the employee is allowed a small shipment by air with a larger surface shipment to accommodate cooking utensils, books, entertainment items, clothing and so forth; all the things the government does not provide.

Because of the mess in Iran we were advised to take as little as possible. Furthermore, even air freight was not being processed through Iranian customs. I was told I would be authorized seven pieces of accompanied baggage plus several boxes I could mail to myself through the diplomatic pouch. I did not even own seven suitcases. The first thing I had to do was buy some cheap ones. Then I had to figure out what to put in them. Simultaneously, Cora was trying to decide what to hold on to both for the months in Washington after my departure, and ultimately, to ship to Iran, as we were advised air freight would almost certainly be available by the time she left.

Meantime, we began our goodbyes. My A100 classmates had been leaving for a while, as some did not require language training so were ready to head to post as early as February. Some were just see-you-laters. Rich Queen invited us to his apartment in a complex commonly called Roach Towers (he told Cora he could hear the roaches scurrying under the cabinets in the kitchen whenever he entered it). It was popular with Foreign Service Institute students because it was relatively cheap and close to the class sites. Richard was due to arrive in Tehran a week after me, and since he was from out of the area he had dealt with packing some time ago. This farewell was more in the nature of a party to finish off the opened liquor bottles, but it happened his mother was visiting from New York so she took us all out to dinner. She was an interesting woman and our paths would cross again in future years. Her choice was a landmark Rosslyn restaurant, the Orleans House. Even then its two-story southern architecture was beginning to look lost amid all the high rises. It has since been replaced by one.

I remember best the last and hardest goodbyes. We had started a bridge group among the old Georgetown crowd some years back; two of the players had asked me to teach them the game. Originally there were five of us with one person taking turns sitting out. One member was also in the Foreign Service and had departed six months earlier for Turkey. So when Cora and I left the game would end. The final meeting took place near the end of June, hosted by our friend Sandy.

Of course the hardest goodbye was still to come. But with everything else going on, it was easy to keep pushing the separation from Cora out of mind. When it came time for us to vacate the condo we moved into a furnished efficiency at Riverside Towers, a short walk from Main State. I still wasn't sure how I was going to travel with seven suitcases, but at least I knew what was going to be in them. Cora had found somewhere to stash her stuff temporarily. We didn't need the cooking equipment as the apartment provided it.

It was normal for officers with consular assignments to get two days of consultation with the Immigration and Naturalization Service (INS - now part of the Department of Homeland Security) office with jurisdiction over the relevant country. For me that worked out well as the office was in New York where we had friends and family. Cora and I and our combined eight suitcases left on July 1st. As the July 4 holiday fell on Friday I did my two days of consultations on the second and third. My days spent with INS, one of which was with the immigration inspectors at JFK airport, were worthwhile. They served to underline the point that it was really up to the visa officers, and I was occasionally to be one, to screen out the people ineligible under law to come to the US. INS did not have the resources and often even the legal authority to do much about them once they touched American soil. I must admit I left at the end of the second day with a much more negative view of Iranian visa applicants. I resented the fact they abused their status as visitors to engage in political activities often directed against US interests. I also felt, and still do, that it was not in the long run best interest of Iran for us to provide refuge to the more educated people who knew what their country needed. Rather than stay in Iran and fight for a better future for their country, they bailed and came to the US. I realize I am over-generalizing and some people really did need to get out of Iran as their lives were under immediate threat, but that was not the case with the vast majority of those who came here.

Cora's best friend Debbie lived in northern New Jersey, as did one of our college friends, so we invited them to come up on the Friday holiday. We all had dinner at Mama Leone's, a kitschy restaurant with a good menu, and then went to see the film *Bloodline*. I remember because it was the last film I expected to see for a while.

It was okay, not as good as billed, but I had this desire to see a movie because I was going to a country where movies were banned. It was a tiny way to protest. The holiday was a small gift. Normally, once you start a trip the government expects you to continue regardless of weekends or holidays. But Tehran had rules about arrival, daylight hours only and no weekends, so I had to layover somewhere.

Cora and I had most of Saturday to ourselves. We visited the Museum of Modern Art where I bought some strange stationery with a pattern of crumpled paper printed on it. I remember it well because I used the entire pad writing letters, mostly to Cora, during the months of bachelorhood in Tehran. My flight left that evening, a red eye arriving in Frankfurt early Sunday afternoon. Cora and I took a taxi to the airport; we had to order a special one to insure it had room for my seven suitcases as well as Cora's single one. We went to what was then called the Pan Am Worldport. There we met Cora's parents as well as Joe and Kathy Stafford. Joe was going on a temporary assignment to Rome. Since tourist visas for Iranians were not available in Iran certain posts in Europe had been authorized to deal with Iranians. Normally the US expects people to obtain tourist visas in their home country. Rome and Athens were the two primary posts handling Iranians and Joe was perfect for Rome because he spoke Italian as well as Farsi. His flight departed shortly after mine.

We found a filthy snack bar and had a terrible meal. Cora's dad, who liked to collect coins, gave me a Susan B. Anthony dollar. They were brand new at the time, so I figured I would take it with me as a good luck charm because it would probably be the first one in Iran. I guess you could say it worked, although for obvious reasons I was not able to bring it home with me.

The good thing about saying goodbyes at airports is the time limit. The plane leaves; you have to be on it. Having a crowd around was also helpful, because it is hard to get too maudlin and sappy when your in-laws are right there. Besides, I was pretty sure my separation from Cora would not be long. She and her folks were going to stay until Joe's flight left, then they would take Kathy back to their place in Oceanport, NJ.

After the plane took off and I was alone, I started to feel depressed. This was the culmination of many years effort when as a high school junior I decided I wanted to join the Foreign Service. That said, heading off solo to a country in the middle of a revolution is not exactly what I had planned. Earlier I had been looking forward to my twenty-four hour layover in Frankfurt as a chance to see a bit of Germany. And I did, mostly from the air as it was a clear day when we landed at Frankfurt airport. I was exhausted by the time I had wrestled my seven suitcases to the airport baggage storage facility on the ground floor. Frankfurt is and was a very modern airport and there are baggage carts everywhere; porters, on the other hand, do not exist. The carts are even capable of riding up and down the escalators. But they are not designed to carry seven reasonably large suitcases so it was a definite trick to keep the stack stable as I worked my way over to storage.

I grabbed a taxi to the hotel which was near the airport. I did not know Frankfurt then so did not realize the airport was in the middle of nowhere, at least to the extent any place in a crowded country like Germany can be. There were no restaurants nearby and as I was tired I had an early dinner in the hotel and went to my room. There I was able to watch a *Star Trek* rerun on American Forces Network television. There were so many US military personnel stationed in the Frankfurt area they broadcast the channel unscrambled. It was fun to catch a bit of Americana before heading off.

The next morning things were worse. First I grabbed a cart and retrieved my six pieces of luggage (one had gone with me to the hotel). Then I stacked them scientifically on the cart so as to minimize the chances the suitcase tower would fall while I took the escalator up to the departure level. I suppose there was an elevator somewhere but in those days elevators in airports were rare and I didn't want to go exploring with my overloaded cart. I did make it to the departure hall without incident but found myself in a two hour check-in line. I was a great fan of Pan American World Airways and much saddened when they went bankrupt but no doubt episodes like this contributed to their demise.

I was booked on Pan Am 2. While like most airlines Pan Am had a great number of flights, 1 and 2 were the classics. 1 went around the world from east to west and 2 hit the same destinations but in the other direction. My flight stopped in Istanbul then Tehran.

It would go on to Karachi, New Delhi, Bangkok, I think Tokyo but maybe with a stop in between, Los Angeles and on in a never-ending circle. One of the items on my to-do list was to take this flight in one direction or the other and stop at every destination. Pan Am went out of business before I could do it but I had rather different thoughts about the airline as I waited in the two hour check-in line. I reached the counter and disgorged my cart's contents about five minutes prior to scheduled departure, then ran all the way to the gate only to learn the flight was delayed a couple of hours. Posting that information at the check-in counter would have been helpful. At the time I was grateful for the delay because an on-time departure would almost certainly have disconnected me from my seven suitcases. Given the importance of their contents for the next two years of my life, I was relieved the delay meant they were probably traveling with me.

On the other hand, we were supposed to arrive in Tehran during daylight hours only because of roadblocks and other potential hazards of travel at night. I arrived around 10:00pm and was met by Steve Lauterbach, one of the general services officers. I had known Steve briefly in Washington as he was in the orientation class before mine. He was about my age, very shy and quiet even by my standards. He had been in Tehran long enough to be familiar with airport procedures and got my bags cleared with no problems. Steve said we were lucky because there were no komiteh thugs around at customs when my stuff came through. Exploring the seven suitcases would have been like a shopping excursion to Macy's for them.

It turned out our new administrative counselor, Bert Moore, was also on the flight. Gary Lee, who as supervisory general services officer was Steve's boss and Bert's subordinate, had come to meet his new chief. I had not met Moore in Washington but you'd think someone would have told us we were both on the airplane. I also noticed he was not traveling with seven suitcases, at which point either Gary or Steve said they had informed the Department a couple of weeks earlier the air freight clearance problem was solved. I guess one advantage of being the administrative counselor rather than a junior consular officer is the information that reaches you. When I explained about the delay in Frankfurt and expressed concern about the roadblocks, they said that issue as well was no longer as serious and the Department had been informed.

They loaded us both aboard a full-size Chevrolet van and we headed for the embassy. It was too dark to see much, but I noticed immediately the driver did not stop for red lights or proceed through green ones. Regardless of signal color he slowed down enough to make sure there was no cross traffic, honked a couple of times and then kept going. Bert, who had spent a lot of time in third world countries took no notice, but I had to ask. Gary told me Iranians did not pay attention to lights so the safest strategy, especially when traffic was relatively light, was to be prepared to yield at all times. As we drove, I dozed but caught pieces of the conversation between Bert and Gary. I was surprised how well informed Bert was, but then he was the administrative counselor and, as I was to learn later, it was part of his job to learn the situation he would face at post and talk to all the relevant Department actors before heading out. One thing was clear: he had gotten much of his information from sources other than the Iran desk.

They dropped me first at the Ardalan apartments, not surprisingly located on Ardalan street, the second east-west street north of the embassy wall (it ran along our wall at the far east end, but I learned that only later). We rented the entire building and it was a combination of temporary and permanent housing. Given the unsettled circumstances since the revolution, there wasn't much practical difference between the two since even permanent people like me needed, not just furniture, but linens, towels, cookware, the kind of stuff that normally would be provided only in temporary quarters. Bert's house, I later learned, was on the next street to the south, Bijan, which ran along another section of the north side embassy compound wall.

The drive from the airport took about an hour and with time spent waiting for luggage it was midnight when I got in. I was tired but the first impressions were indelible. It was hot, despite the lateness. There was an outer gate then a large tiled courtyard which smelled like garbage, not surprising as there was a pile of it inside the gate. The elevator was an oversized vertical coffin, suitable for perhaps three people, and slow. Despite these shortcomings, I came to appreciate it because it was often broken. Even a slow ride in a hot box was better than hiking up the equally hot stairs. Steve helped me carry my suitcases to the lobby. It took two trips for us to get them to the fourth floor apartment.

The apartment itself was a shock. The walls were dirty. The carpeting looked as if the place had been used as a kennel. The only wall decorations were cheaply framed Department of Agriculture photos of farm scenes in the US. The furniture was massive old style, mahogany finish, typically American. There was too much of it and it was too large. I had a table for ten in a 6' X 10' space. The kitchen had a beautiful tile floor. I found later that by Iranian standards it was nothing special, but it was attractive compared to what I had encountered in the States. But then Iran was famous for its tile work. The bathroom was small and lacked a tub. Instead there was a stand-up shower in one corner. The shower base and sink were a pale blue, contrasting with the deep blue tiled walls. There was no shower stall, just a rod bent 90 degrees supporting a shower curtain in a cubicle shape. There was a small window to the left of the mirror which opened onto a ventilation shaft. I later discovered I could often hear what people were saying in their bathrooms as the sound echoed in that shaft. I don't remember the color of the floor tile, but I do recall there was a deep blue, ratty, old carpet in the center of the floor. It was one of those rubber-backed non-slip kinds, and I noticed early on it effectively plugged the drain in the floor. I didn't know if that should concern me, because where I came from bathrooms did not normally have floor drains anyway.

The apartment had two bedrooms, one small and one tiny. The tiny one had been converted into a den, though it still had a single bed. The larger one was, like most of the apartment, overfull of furniture. It had a double bed, a dresser, two night stands and a chest of drawers, all packed into a 10' X 12' space. I later learned there was some logic to the drastic oversupply of furniture. With the embassy staff much reduced, many leased houses were returned to their owners and the government-owned furniture removed. While the oldest items were sold, the remainder was put in the warehouse in anticipation of the day when staffing would return to more normal levels. But even the warehouse could not accommodate everything the post wanted to keep so some of the overflow ended up at Ardalan. Still, my major complaint was the drapes or technically, vertical blinds. Unlike ones I had seen before these had connecting strings on the bottom as well as the top, and one of the bottom ones was broken. This made it impossible to close them completely.

There was no central air conditioning in the building. Each apartment was equipped with window units. Since some rooms did not have windows, the cooling was uneven. For me, the most important room was the bedroom. As long as I was comfortable at night, I could put up with heat in other rooms. Fortunately, the bedroom had an effective air conditioner. Besides, I had lived with worse as a student in DC.

I spent over three months in this apartment. Over time I learned to avoid bumping into the excess furniture. All in all, it was not a bad place. Although the refrigerator was empty when I checked it someone must have been awake because they gave me a beer. It was probably Steve. I was so tired I couldn't remember who the next day, but the beer was welcome and helped me fall asleep. Before saying goodnight, Steve told me it was okay to drink the tap water and gave me a note from Cy Richardson, the acting head of the consular section, asking to call him. I did. I think I woke him up given how late it was but he was gracious and said I did not need to worry about getting in to work on time in the morning. He gave me instructions on how to get to the embassy. I did not realize as we talked I was probably a hundred yards away from the back gate, as the crow flies, although the actual walk was a bit longer.

I awoke hungry. There was nothing to eat in the apartment. Although I wanted to unpack a bit before leaving and take advantage of Cy's offer to come in late, I decided food was the higher priority.

I distinctly recall my first walk to the embassy. Ardalan Street was about 500 yards long, with the east end hitting Roosevelt Avenue, a major arterial, and the west another little street called Kuche Dahmetri. Kuche means a small street or alley and it was one of those Farsi words that had been incorporated into our English speech. Our building was near the center of Ardalan. On the map it appears the apartments face the embassy north wall, but in fact they are across the street from a hotel/restaurant and the embassy wall is further east. My first impression of Dahmetri in daylight was that it was dirty and squalid. Ardalan at least had a sidewalk and while there were some cars parked half on it there was adequate room to walk. When I turned left onto Dahmetri that little luxury disappeared. The shoulder of the road on the east side was dirt and there were many cars blocking it. The shoulder was wide enough for only half a car width so I often had to step into the road itself in order to get by. There was a tall wall along the entire west side of the street and no parked cars or place to walk on that side. Walking was not a problem the first morning as it was well past rush hour, but I later found going to or from work during peak traffic required caution. Even little Ardalan Street was hard to get across sometimes.

A further obstacle was the jube; for some reason I tended to spell the word that way rather than joob because it sounded like tube. Jubes were a combination of an open sewer and a storm drain. They were ubiquitous in residential neighborhoods, less common along major streets. They smelled bad and when they overflowed it was sometimes difficult to get by without traipsing through the you-know-what. I didn't know the word jube at first. Our language teachers had decided not to tell us about them, perhaps because they did not want to acknowledge Tehran still had open sewers in some areas. But it too was one of those Farsi words that entered common English usage. In any case there was a jube along the east side of Dahmetri, running immediately adjacent to the street. Every time a car parked on the shoulder forced me onto the street I had to hop the jube. It was narrow, a foot wide, but a problem on the days it overflowed.

Tehran is in the foothills of the Alborz Mountains at an average elevation of almost 4,000 feet. The wealthier people lived in the north. I assumed it was a bit cooler higher up, but there may also be another reason. The jubes flow downhill.

A day later I noticed the guard tower. I am not sure how I missed it the first day; probably I was overwhelmed by all the new impressions at street level. It looked like what you would see in a prison movie. The frame was made of poles like an oil derrick and there was a vertical ladder leading up to a trap door in the floor. The upper deck was probably 20' from the ground, which meant about 8' above the wall, with wooden sides extending about three-quarters of the way to the peaked roof. It stood just inside the perimeter of the wall I had vaguely noticed the previous day and which I now concluded must be some sort of military compound. It was large as its southern wall paralleled part of the embassy compound, including the building that would soon become the new consulate. I never had reason to find the north side.

The tower was usually manned by someone in what looked like a military uniform. The guard did not bother us most of the time. Once in a while, though, he would chamber a round and take aim at one of us as we walked past. There did not seem to be a pattern to it. Maybe it was one particular individual but it was impossible to know, both because of the distance and because it seemed unwise to try to make eye contact. There was nothing for it except to pretend not to notice and keep walking, but it was disconcerting. While I did not think there was any danger the guard would shoot me, except perhaps by accident, this was an example of the kind of harassment foreigners in general and official Americans in particular had to put up with. Unfortunately, our own government expected us to tolerate these things. I am not sure we could have done anything about it. These incidents were widely known including to senior officers at the embassy. Yet I doubt we ever bothered to lodge a protest.

My instructions from Cy were to go right out the Ardalan gate, turn left when the street ended, then turn into Bijan on my left. The embassy pedestrian gate would be on my right after 100'. As I walked I realized how hot it was; afternoon temperatures this time of year often reached 100° with 105° not uncommon. I was wearing a coat and tie as I did not realize hardly anyone bothered with suits, especially at the old building in which the consular section was temporarily located.

Since I did not yet have an embassy ID badge I called Richardson from the gate and he sent one of the local employees over to escort me back to the consular section. My introduction to life and work at embassy Tehran was now to begin.

# 4. Check Your Guns at the Door

I had arrived in Tehran late on Sunday the seventh of July; added to the actual travel time were the overnight in Frankfurt and the time change. I remember thinking as I waited for the employee Cy Richardson had sent, it was good this was Monday, just the second day of the work week. I would have plenty of time to get oriented before the Iranian weekend, Friday and Saturday.

Other than the walk from Ardalan, the first thing I remember of the day was an early lunch with Cy at the embassy restaurant known as the Caravanserai. Caravanserais were the traditional roadside inns along middle-eastern trade routes so the name was appropriate. The restaurant was located next to the co-op or commissary, a five minute walk from the consular section. Before the revolution when Tehran was home to thousands of Americans many were authorized to shop at the co-op and use the Caravanserai. In order to minimize security hassles the two facilities were side by side in a corner of the compound with its own entrance to the outside. Cy explained all of this in the course of telling me the restaurant was soon to become the new consulate building. As we came to the glass doors, I stopped in my tracks and stared at the hand-made sign taped to the inside of one door. It read: "Weapons not allowed in the Restaurant."

*"Just like an old west saloon. Why is it here?"*

Lunch was good, just a hamburger and fries. I would have plenty of time to sample Iranian cuisine. We had a few opportunities during language and area studies. One of the drill instructors (the teaching assistants who made us repeat words and phrases over and over again until we wanted to strangle them), a young Iranian woman married to an American, had taken us under her wing and had us to her home a few times to cook and eat Iranian food. I wasn't all that impressed, not being particularly fond of a dish that featured what tasted like half-burned rice and which unfortunately seemed to be a staple. During lunch I asked Cy about the sign. He said it was meant for the embassy komiteh, another Farsi term that crept into

English usage. As I mentioned earlier, it literally means committee but in practice it referred to an armed gang in charge of an area or an institution. I was soon to learn more about komitehs but at the time my reaction was shock. As it is not usual for embassies to have their own komiteh (our embassies are at least theoretically American soil), I asked for an explanation. I learned after the Valentine's Day takeover, a small group of young men under the leadership of a brute named Mashallah had stayed behind allegedly to protect us. In exchange for protection, they occasionally helped themselves to cigarettes and liquor from the co-op and they would bring their "friends" over to the consulate for visas. These friends undoubtedly paid well for the service. Cy said he generally took care of their requests personally, but once I got my feet on the ground I might be dealing with them also.

The lunch was the beginning of my introduction to the real situation of our embassy in Tehran, as well as another hint perhaps Henry and the Department didn't understand things as well as they thought they did. Not one word had been said to me about the existence of the komiteh. They had to know, so the only conclusion I could reach was the presence of an armed gang within the embassy walls had been rationalized away as unimportant, a temporary problem to be resolved as we solidified relations with the new government.

After lunch Cy took me to the co-op. I bought some basic food items, American canned goods for the most part as well as some beer and the last bottle of Johnnie Walker Black. Although I usually went for cheaper stuff, at duty free prices it was only $5 for the liter and it was my favorite. The place was huge and messy and I looked forward to exploring it at length later. There were other things I needed to do first. At the co-op I was introduced to the first of the three really good things about Iran: the plastic bags. They were indestructible and would not tear no matter how much you put into them. The "three good things" was a bit of gallows humor shared among we four A100 classmates, our wives and a few others. It is quintessentially American to look for the positive. As we tried to do this, we found three things that were uniquely good about Iran. I will mention the others as I discovered them.

Cy offered to take my purchases back to the consular section and I found my way to the commercial library. The commercial library is where Iranians could come to learn about doing business with American firms. In these pre-Internet days they had Thomas registers, thick volumes containing information about producers of virtually anything made in the USA. There were other resources as well, but I went there because part of the security office shared the space. They had a Polaroid ID camera and in a couple of minutes I was an official member of the embassy staff. They gave me a handful of extra photos I would need for other purposes, such as a driving license and residence permit. Armed with an ID I was now able to get into the chancery where the budget and fiscal and personnel offices were located.

The chancery itself was a typical massive government building; it could have been a library or museum. It had two floors and a full basement. The basement was only partially underground. There were windows allowing natural light and it was necessary to walk up steps in order to enter the first floor. I noticed immediately many of the windows on the upper floors had small balconies, more for aesthetics than practical use. Each balcony had a concrete box in front of the windows. I later learned the boxes were filled with sand and their purpose was to help block small arms fire into the windows. Until recently Iran was friendly territory so the chancery lacked the latest security upgrades, but the Department was trying to make some quick improvements.

The stairs to the first floor were wide, and surrounded on both sides by stone grill work in a generic middle-eastern style. As I entered the lobby, I saw there was a Marine security guard inside a bullet-proof enclosure, which I soon learned was called Post One. He controlled the doors to his right and left. The door on the right led to the second floor. This was the classified floor, restricted generally to American personnel with security clearances. It contained the ambassador and deputy chief of mission offices, the political and economic sections, the CIA station, the defense attaché and the communications vaults. The door on the left led to another controlled area, but less sensitive as some local employees worked there. Here one found the administrative counselor's office, part of the defense attaché's staff and the main part of the security office including the two American security officers.

Tehran had been a huge embassy and there were remnants of many other agencies and offices. I can't pretend to remember them all. For example, the Military Assistance Advisory Group, or MAAG, had been a key player in our relationship with the shah's government (I had occasional contact with the MAAG liaison officer while I worked at the Army Materiel Command). Although it was still headed by an Army major general, its functions these days were more focused on closing out old weapons sales programs and figuring out who owed whom and how much, although there was always hope over time the relationship might improve.

That day my focus was on the basement, the one area that could be accessed without permission from the Marine during normal business hours. There I was able to cash a check and obtain both dollars and Iranian rials and begin in-processing with personnel. I filled out some forms and grabbed some others to work on later. I also went to the mail room and filled out a card so my mail would go to the consular section. I was surprised to find the four large boxes I had mailed through the diplomatic pouch already there. I could not carry them but said I would come back later when I had a car.

By this time it was 2:30pm. Office hours were 7:30am to 4:00pm so I needed to get back to the consular section in order to have time to meet at least some of my co-workers. On the way I stopped by the motor pool. Steve Lauterbach was in charge and his office was located there. He agreed to let me have a car and driver to get my boxes and purchases home.

The temporary consular section was at the far north end of the compound, the motor pool in the southwest corner. As it was close to 100° and I had been doing a lot of walking (I did mention earlier that the compound was twenty-six acres), the tie was gone and the jacket was slung over my shoulder. Fortunately there was little humidity so all in all I preferred Tehran weather to what I would have been experiencing in Washington in mid-July. Still, all the walking left me looking forward to a shower.

By the time I reached the consular offices, there really wasn't time for more than a quick introduction. The most important people

I met were Bob Sorenson and Tom Farrell. I would eventually replace Tom as chief of American citizen services while Bob was the sole visa officer. They lived in Ardalan so I was counting on them for both company and education over the coming weeks. I also met Bob Anders. He was in his early fifties, handsome, with graying hair and a ready smile. I liked him immediately. Bob was leaving in a week on family visitation travel, special leave provided when an employee was assigned to an unaccompanied post. My first job was covering for Bob, but as he was one of the few not living in the immediate vicinity of the compound, I didn't expect to see him until work resumed the next morning. Tom and Bob Sorenson seemed to be good friends and they offered to feed me that evening.

By this time I had to trudge back to the motor pool, again making the trek to the far opposite corner of the compound. The driver took me to the back of the mail room which even though it was in the basement had a direct entrance onto a small street so mail could be trucked in and out. We loaded the boxes and exited out the motor pool gate onto Taleqani Avenue. Although it was not a long drive I could not follow the route because of all the one-way streets. It was also rush hour, so while I appreciated sitting in the white, (all our vehicles were white, except the ambassador's limo, probably a good idea in that climate) air conditioned Chevrolet Malibu, it took almost forty minutes to get home.

I spent the remainder of the afternoon sorting my possessions. The seven suitcases were mostly clothes. While that may sound like a lot I was operating on the assumption this would be my wardrobe for the next two years. Given its altitude of 4,000 feet, Tehran has a high desert climate. The winters are cold and it snows occasionally. So I had brought winter as well as summer clothes: an overcoat, different types of shoes, suits for work, etc. The four boxes were mostly books and cassette tapes but no player as I'd been told the co-op had tons of electronics. I had recorded my favorite record albums onto cassette for ease of shipment and also to protect the original record albums in case I could not get my stuff out of Iran. We were advised to protect against the possibility of a rush evacuation; no one anticipated the reality. All of my music would have fit easily on today's smallest capacity iPod but at the time cassettes were the best option.

To finish my settling in process I would need something to play the tapes. The co-op had a special section open only on Wednesday afternoons where they kept all the valuable stuff. I made sure to find some time the first Wednesday as later Bob Anders would be gone and I would be too busy. The co-op was a pack-rat's dream and Bert Moore's nightmare, as management of the operation fell under the administrative section. The inventory predated the revolution. We had tons of diapers and piles of dried Japanese food, not to mention what looked like 100 cases of Gallo Thunderbird wine. Everything was covered in the fine dust that filled the Tehran air. Much of the merchandise was in bad condition. The only beer we had was Asahi. The co-op manager had been Japanese. Though the beer was generally okay, Bert told me before reaching us it sat in the blazing heat on a customs dock at a port in the south. One can in a dozen might be filled with a putrid white liquid. I learned never to pop the top and take a sip without careful inspection. I also bought a small Panasonic cassette player for my music collection as well as a fancy Dunhill cigarette lighter and a few other goodies such as a silver Cross pen and pencil set at markdown prices. Bert routinely put me in stitches with his half-serious complaining about all the unsellable junk he had in there.

I had accomplished some organizing when it was time to head to Bob Sorenson's apartment on the floor below. Bob was tall and thin, a fastidious dresser who preferred a suit and tie even though our section didn't require it in our makeshift quarters. He wore horn rimmed glasses and smoked a pipe. Tom Farrell, who was already there enjoying a beer, was more casual, choosing khakis and an open collar shirt with the sleeves rolled up. He had the build of a natural athlete and he struck me as good looking. I don't usually judge other guys that way but Tom could probably have been an actor or model. He wife had a doctorate in French and was working at a university in France; I wasn't sure whether this arrangement predated the evacuation or not. Bob wasn't married.

The steaks were a little burned but otherwise it was an enjoyable and interesting evening. Bob and Tom began my education about Tehran and the embassy community. The two of them were among the few remaining alumni of the February takeover. As I have mentioned previously the Department was making efforts to replace everyone who had suffered through that experience, which in hindsight should have struck me as odd. After all, if nothing much happened, then why go through all the effort? Unfortunately, neither Bob nor Tom could tell me much, probably because the consular section was not located on the main compound. That section, with the exception of the student visa annex, was then located on Iranshahr Street, a couple of blocks to the west of the compound. As I understood it the consular annex had not been attacked. Still, Bob and Tom would have known the basic details of the takeover and the fact they didn't think it was a big deal tended to support what Henry had told us.

We talked about work. Office gossip is useful when it is important to get a quick sense of new co-workers. I would in time develop my own opinions but it was interesting to hear their views. We also talked about life in Tehran after the revolution. Both men found things tolerable. They were managing to maintain a reasonable social life mostly within the foreign community but not surprisingly they were ready to go home.

They also told me about the second really good thing about Iran: a type of bread called nan-e barbary. From the name I thought at first some barbarian invaders must have brought it to Iran, but later learned the Barbars were a tribe in Eastern Iran. It is an oval-shaped flat bread cooked in a wood-fired brick oven. The dough is slapped up against the wall of the oven and when it falls off it is ready. The bread was not sold in stores; the ovens were usually outdoors on street corners. The closest to us was at the corner of Taleqani and Roosevelt avenues, at the south east corner of the embassy compound. I went there Friday morning. A loaf, if that is the right term, cost ten rials. At the time the official exchange rate was seventy rials to the dollar, and the market rate, which was also legal, about 100. The bread cost a dime.

It was amazingly good. I was told to eat it with feta cheese, but since I hate feta, I just put butter on it. I ate over half the loaf; it was a more than sufficient breakfast. Nothing is perfect, however, and by lunch time it was getting hard. By dinner it could have knocked someone unconscious. I have spent the rest of my life looking for this bread, trying all kinds of nan (eastern and middle eastern breads) but with no success. The closest I came was in Kuwait, where they make something similar but not as good.

While Monday was devoted largely to settling in paperwork, on Tuesday I began to spend time with Bob Anders and figure out how I was going to do his job for the next three weeks. As in my first Army job, I was blessed with a great sergeant-major, this time in the person of Farideh Navab-Safavi. Had it not been for her and the rest of the staff, I would have floundered despite my Washington training and Bob's tutoring. Farideh was sharp and maintained her tart sense of humor despite the high workload. She almost never asked a question; usually it was the other way around. Only rarely would we find ourselves researching the Foreign Affairs Manual looking for some obscure regulation.

Overall, the employees were a blessing. Rima Vartanian was young and eager, a pretty, dark-haired girl who was always cheerful and made the days much easier. She was engaged to someone who was going to the States to study. Ali Hashemi-Far was a stocky, good-natured guy who never looked comfortable behind a typewriter. I kept expecting his large fingers and hands to crush the machine as he hunched over it. He had been in the Iranian Air Force and was sent to the US to study, so he understood Americans well and had excellent English. Despite getting to know him better over the months, I never did figure out how he came to be a clerk in the immigrant visa unit, but I was glad to have him.

We became friends after I left the unit and was no longer his boss. We visited his home a few times. He had a wife and three children and lived in an apartment near mid-town. Ali was probably forty, his wife some years younger. She did not speak much English but made up for it with her culinary skills. Unlike some of the dishes I had tried earlier the food she prepared was excellent. The children had studied English in school (I presume this has changed but do not know for certain) and seemed to enjoy using it with us. Like many middle class Iranians, Ali was no supporter of the shah and celebrated his departure. His hope for Iran was real democracy and he was troubled by the emerging theocracy. As a moderate Muslim, he enjoyed an occasional alcoholic beverage or a visit to the cinema.

His wife wore western clothing, at least at home. He acknowledged the course the revolution appeared to be taking was not what he had wanted or expected. In this he was not alone. The tourist visa section when it reopened would see hundreds of people like him every day. I later learned he'd been killed in a cross-fire between rival militias a few years after the takeover.

There was Hasmik, like Rima an Armenian. Once in a while I heard disparaging references to the Armenian mafia that allegedly ran the embassy; there was no doubt Armenians were over-represented in our workforce. That had more to do with education levels and cultural compatibility than anything else. Hasmik had red hair so clearly was not ethnically Iranian. Then there was Gila, who came to the office later. She had a reputation as something of a misfit and troublemaker. This job was her last chance to show she could perform satisfactorily. I didn't notice any real problem with her and don't think Bob did either, though she impressed me as a fundamentally sad person. There was one other guy with a big handle-bar mustache. I can't remember his name, but then he never did seem to do much work either. His specialty was maintaining a low profile. Since I was only temporarily in charge I was not going to stick my nose into personnel matters.

As I mentioned earlier, prior to the revolution most consular operations were centered in an annex building located on Iranshahr. After the St. Valentine's Day takeover, we ceased issuing tourist visas and the Department terminated the lease on the annex. The now much smaller consular section was operating from ramshackle quarters that had served as the student visa annex prior to the revolution. At one time it had been the old Marine House, for which purpose it had presumably been constructed. The immigrant visa unit operated out of three rooms. Bob's office was right up against Bijan alley. We joked that the pile of bricks outside his window was conveniently placed for use by unsuccessful applicants. There were often large crowds in the alley. One of his windows was in fact broken and held together with tape.

There was a window air conditioner behind his desk and it tended to shoot a mixture of sand and cool air into the office. He had an older IBM typewriter, the kind without the ball, which I learned needed to have a piece of cardboard sitting on it whenever it wasn't in use to keep the sand from wreaking too much havoc on its guts. Bob had many boxes of files in his office and they were routinely covered with sand. These files were the correspondence backlog, piles of letters, some dating from before the revolution. They were everything from attorney petitions from persons seeking investor visas to congressional inquiries to applications from persons claiming refugee status.

The problem was a huge jump in workload combined with the disruptions caused by the revolution. Many of the visas we were issuing were to former employees. The Department had a policy stating employees with fifteen years of exemplary service could request to immigrate to the US. In normal circumstances meeting the standard required the employee's boss and possibly several previous bosses to persuade the ambassador to make the request. But the situation in Iran was not normal and we were being liberal in the interpretation of exemplary service. Mere association with the US government was dangerous and many of these people were Christians to boot. Other people also wanted to leave Iran. Some had or hoped they might have a claim on an immigrant visa. Others came because with the tourist visa section closed, temporary visitor visas were limited to students and medical emergencies. Real tourists had to travel first to Rome or Athens and take a chance there.

Bob's office did not have a door, just a rounded archway into an outer area divided into two sections. The one closest to Bob's was seating for the immigrant visa clients. Further away was a bullpen where the office staff was located. Most days the waiting area was full of people in the morning, thinning out as we approached noon and then filling up again after lunch. Mornings were devoted to interviews and actual issuance of visas, and in the afternoons we accepted petitions (basically a request to consider issuing an immigration visa on one of the grounds allowed by law), dealt with re-entry permits (documents that allowed immigrants who had entered the US and then left without completing their processing to have a second shot) and handled various other unusual situations.

Bob was a great boss. He provided just the right amount of guidance and approached everything with a sense of humor, clearly necessary given the working conditions. During the three days I shadowed him, I felt I picked up most of what I needed to know. Oddly enough, what gave me the most trouble after he left was administration of the oath that takes place before an immigrant signs the papers, testifying everything in it is true.

*"Do you solemnly swear that the statements you have made in this application are true, so help you God?"*

Not complicated, but I continued to stumble over it. The time I wasn't spending with Bob was used to finish in-processing and to meet people. Someone took me around the chancery, probably Cy. With no families at post and limited social outlets outside the embassy, we were a close-knit community. I didn't feel like a newcomer for very long.

During my first week I did receive a formal security orientation, although not in time to prevent making a big mistake in the first days after I arrived. After Cy told me about the embassy komiteh at lunch the first day I started looking around for them. I saw these men dressed in tan uniforms. They were clean-shaven, disciplined, polite and generally spoke decent English. So I figured someone must have persuaded Mashallah's men to clean up their act. It took a couple of days before I realized the men in tan were the embassy's own guard force (no one had ever told me embassies employed local guards). I figured it out when I was passing through the motor pool area and got my first glimpse of a real komiteh member. He was 17 or 18, with a scraggly beard and unkempt hair, wearing camouflage pants and jacket, and sitting backward on a small Honda motorcycle. He was playing with his AK-47, aiming it at various targets around the area, not people as far as I could tell. Fortunately, they kept a low profile and we didn't see them often. Usually it was at the motor pool or the back gate, where they would sometimes try to inspect what we were carrying in and out. This happened to me only one time, when I was carrying a six pack of beer home. I just ignored the guy and he let me pass.

We had two security officers, Al Golacinski and his assistant, Mike Howland. Their technical title was Regional Security Officer because in those safer days there were still many embassies without a resident professional security officer. We, on the other hand, had two because of the unique threat situation. I don't recall whether Al or Mike met with me, but a lot of the substance was what I would now call boilerplate, focused on taking proper care of classified information (meaning documents classified as confidential, secret or higher). In a normal post this would be a key part of the security program. In Tehran at that time, classified documents were restricted to the chancery. We were expected to go over a couple of times a week and review the reading file, as we had done at the Iran desk while in DC. The Marines still patrolled the offices at night and issued violations to those who forgot to lock their safes or left documents on their desks. Although I referred to it as boilerplate because it was information that applied to every embassy in the world, it was new to me at the time.

I knew my particular job did not involve much classified so I was far more interested in the broader security situation. I learned there were thirteen Marines, charged primarily with access control and the security of classified information. As everywhere in the world, we relied on the host government to provide overall security for the embassy compound. I was told to avoid demonstrations, but also that in the months after the St. Valentine's Day takeover there had been no attacks against individual Americans. I was advised not to go anywhere far alone, and that it was a good idea to make sure that someone knew where I was going and when I planned to return if I strayed far off compound, even with a buddy. The in-house komiteh was mentioned in passing; ignore them if possible, but if a situation became confrontational, back down and report it. Golacinski had a working relationship with their boss, Mashallah, and he would take steps to keep the peace. We were told travel at night could be dangerous because of roadblocks. If we encountered one, we were supposed to show our diplomatic Identity cards and ask to be allowed to proceed, but also to avoid arguments with men with guns. Sounded reasonable to me.

I didn't always follow the advice about avoiding travel at night but I did try to stay away from demonstrations. There were occasional protests in front of the embassy on Taleqani avenue. This was a wide boulevard large enough for a crowd to form, although given the bumper-to-bumper traffic I always wondered how they managed to stop it. For the most part I was not aware of these demonstrations because my office was at the far opposite end of the compound, too far away to hear the chanting. If I had reason to walk to the chancery or especially the motor pool, where the vehicle gate opened directly onto Taleqani, then I might hear something but as it was on the other side of the wall it was easy to ignore.

In August I learned how people stop cars. I borrowed an embassy Malibu to run some errands and was driving back to the embassy. I was heading east, planning to turn onto Roosevelt and then Taleqani so I could scoot back into the motor pool. I was on a two lane street with wide sidewalks and the traffic wasn't moving. This was not unusual because it was mid-afternoon, nearing rush hour. What was unusual was the sound I heard, like a pounding or drum beat. At first I thought there was something going on at the sports stadium located a little north-east of the embassy. But the noise kept getting louder and soon it was clear it was a crowd chanting. I could not understand what they were saying, but it did not sound like "marg bar Amrika" (death to America) which was the standard tune played in front of the embassy. This was reassuring but before long my vehicle was engulfed by the marchers. I could not make out most of the signs, but they were kind enough to have a few in English and I realized they were protesting cuts in education. Although it was now obvious the demonstration had nothing to do with the US, and logic told me Americans should not be targets, it was immensely uncomfortable being trapped in an obviously American car with US embassy plates. I sat, with my head down, avoiding eye contact with the marchers, and waited for them to pass me by. The crowd was funneled into the street so people were on both sides of the car, often brushing against it. The scary element was not the subject of the demonstration, although clearly something anti-American would have been far worse, so much as the feeling of complete powerlessness; probably a thousand of them and only one of me. Finally they passed and traffic started to move again. I knew I had been lucky. Given the intense anti-Americanism everywhere on display, it was almost laughable to get caught up in a demonstration about education. But I wasn't laughing. Fortunately, despite the frequency of demonstrations during those days, this was my only encounter until the takeover itself.

Rich Queen arrived four days after I did, having taken a few days off in London en route. I went to the airport with Steve Lauterbach to meet Rich as we were going from there directly to a wedding. The niece of the Farsi drill instructor I mentioned earlier was getting married and she had invited us to attend. As usual the plane was late, so it was a rush getting to the Hotel Miami on Mossadeq Avenue. Mossadeq had been Pahlavi Avenue until the revolution and I couldn't help but wonder how long the Miami Hotel could keep its western name. We were so late everyone had already eaten, but the hotel managed to rustle up some meals for the three of us. This was already the Islamic republic, so everyone drank Coca Cola rather than cocktails. This family was clearly well-off financially and I suspected there would be a more private reception later with black market booze. Still, seeing trays with hundreds of Coke bottles flashed the thought through my mind, *"maybe Coke is the real sponsor of the revolution."*

I assumed we must have missed the wedding but it turned out in Iranian tradition the meal comes first and then the ceremony. The wedding was a mixture of east and west. The music and dancing were Persian but the band played on electronic instruments closely resembling those of an American rock band. The clothes were western, down to the groom's black tuxedo and the bride's white gown. We three were the only Americans and I recall feeling a little out of place. Everyone was very nice to us, but as we didn't fully understand what was going on and didn't know anyone except our teacher, we were basically spectators. It should have been a chance to practice Farsi but most people switched to English after a few words.

The wedding took place on Friday, July 11. As Friday and Saturday were our weekend I had spent the earlier part of the day exploring. I started in the immediate neighborhood and found the local grocery store then headed to the area of Taleqani Avenue to the west of the embassy. I was stared at once in a while but for the most part no one paid particular attention. Tehran had hosted tens of thousands of foreigners before the revolution. There were far fewer now but not to the point most locals thought much about it. Also on Taleqani I found a great bookstore. It was huge and totally disorganized. There were books in many languages but not separated on that basis. After Farsi, English was the dominant language so browsing was fun. Rich Queen was a book lover also and I made plans to bring him over on Saturday.

Several days later, Don Cooke arrived. Although we had finished Farsi together the system could not accommodate all of us in consular training at the same time. Don got a later slot. I didn't go to the airport to meet him. It wasn't a fun trip and there wasn't a wedding this time. My first memory of him in Iran is when he arrived at the Ardalan apartments with three small trunks. Somehow he'd managed to persuade Pan Am they were suitcases, but then Don was a charmer when he needed to be. In addition, by then air freight was flowing so he was able to ship 450 pounds as well. As a young bachelor Don didn't have much stuff. I recall he even shipped the thick and heavy Washington DC telephone directory. At the time I was irritated I had been forced to travel with so little. But considering what happened to it in the end I came out okay.

Don, Rich and I were all stashed in the Ardalan apartments. Don was immediately above me, and Rich immediately below. The building was all male, except for a brief time when a secretary on temporary assignment lived there for a few weeks. It reminded me of a college dormitory. We used to take turns cooking two or three times a week and people didn't mind if you just dropped in to chat or have a drink.

Gary Lee was the unofficial chairman and founder of the Ardalan Key Club which played an important role in our daily lives. Gary had come to Tehran after a brief stay in Washington, before which he had been in Sana'a, Yemen. I gathered something that happened in Sana'a had gotten him into trouble and volunteering for Tehran was a way to make good. That made him similar to many people staffing the embassy. Some were there for the extra pay, others to get away from something or someone. As far as the key club and our morale went, however, the most important thing was that Gary had a real zest for living in the hard-drinking, two-fisted sense. He was no angel, though it didn't surprise me he was the son of a missionary. I had met others with that background who turned out to be as wild as Gary could be.

I can't judge him from any angle other than as the social director of our building. He managed to lessen the loneliness and boredom. His penthouse apartment, occupying the entire seventh floor, had a huge deck about one-third the size of the apartment itself. The interior had been painted blue for one of the embassy secretaries, who ultimately chose to move because we were too far (seriously?) from the compound. Gary grabbed it, knowing the apartment had been designed for the owner of the building and had state of the art German appliances and matching cabinets as well as the huge patio. I can't remember exactly how or when the key club got started, but I think it was in late July or early August. At first it was just a joke, but later a well-defined social program emerged. Several times a week, those who wanted would bring some food and drink up and Gary would take charge of the cooking. Aside from the fancy kitchen, he had a huge barbecue made from a fifty-five gallon drum on the deck.

The club had a good membership. In addition to Don, Rich and myself there was Don Sharer. Don was a Navy commander and F-14 pilot. He was in Tehran to straighten out the problems surrounding the F-14s we had sold to the shah. I didn't know him as well as some of the others, but I liked him a lot. He had a great sense of humor that could alternate between charming and vicious and sometimes meld just the right combination of the two. It was a bit eerie because his facial expression – a cross between a smile and a smirk – could catch the same attitude. He used the expression often. When we were back in the Department watching the Christmas propaganda tapes released by the terrorists, I was reassured when I saw Don make that expression. It meant he was still coping.

Another member was Al Fine. Al was an Army officer who roomed with Sharer for a while. He too was in Tehran to assure an orderly shutdown of military assistance to the Iranians. Fortunately for him, he left about the time Cora came, well before the takeover. Bruce German was our new Budget and Fiscal officer. He arrived in early August. I can't say I knew him well, but he seemed like a solid guy to me, a little too solid perhaps to be in Tehran given so many of the people there were taking unaccompanied assignments to evade family issues or escape uncomfortable working environments elsewhere. Bruce had a great collection of oldies music tapes which we often played on Gary's stereo. There were many occasional visitors, among them Tom Ahern, the CIA station chief, Bill Daugherty, one of his lieutenants, our new consul general Dick Morefield, and on one special occasion Liz Montagne, the chargé's secretary. Liz had brought a friend, Birgit Jank from the Austrian Embassy. Don Cooke kept trying to put the moves on Birgit the entire evening, but Liz managed to put a humorous light on the whole thing, so Don didn't feel bad and the rest of us didn't have to feel awkward. I think Cora had arrived by then as I remember it was chilly on the deck. And although once Cora came she was invited to the parties, we were already talking to the housing office about finding an apartment on our own. Ardalan in general and the key club in particular were a great morale boost because they functioned like a fraternity, and keeping married couples out seemed important to me although no one ever suggested we were no longer welcome.

Another flashback to college was playing war games with Rich Queen. These were incredibly complex games with hundreds or thousands of pieces each representing a military unit of some kind. Most were from Avalon-Hill or Simulations Publications, the same companies my room-mates and I used in college. Each game generally represented a particular battle in historical detail and the point was to see whether you could do better than the historical commander.

It did not take long to get a handle on Bob's job so I started trying to get control of the correspondence backlog while he was still in town. I didn't get too far but at least managed to fish out the congressionals. The Department generally insisted those be answered immediately, but we were a special case. Whenever someone said a particular task needed to be done right away because the Department or Congressman X would be annoyed, we had a standard response:

"What are they gonna do? Send me to Tehran?"

Once Bob left I had much less time for correspondence but still managed to move a little. Much of the job was routine. I had a few interesting cases. There was an Iranian naval officer married to an American woman. She wanted a tourist visa for him which was improper but made sense in our situation because it would get him out of harm's way much more quickly. Cy wouldn't break the rules. Another interesting one was a man who had played on the Iranian Olympic soccer team and was now a coach at a university in Louisiana. He was hoping for a tryout with the Dallas Cowboys as a placekicker. He already had a green card, but had been back in Iran too long and so invalidated his re-entry permit. The US considers that if you immigrate, it means you actually want to live in the States. It was reasonable to have limits on how much time you can be away. This man had a valid excuse so we gave him a new re-entry permit. A week or two later a big can of pistachios arrived at my parents' home. I must have mentioned they lived in California and with a name like Lijek they were not difficult to find.

There were hard cases too. A Kurdish man with a brother in the States wanted to immigrate. The brother wasn't a citizen and so couldn't use the provision in the law allowing preferential status for relatives. The man claimed he and his family were in danger because he had cooperated with US and Israeli intelligence personnel who were aiding Kurdish rebels. I had no way to judge whether the story was true, although Kurds in general were not popular with the revolutionary government. But even though the man was convincing, that made him a refugee and we had no authority to process refugees. I explained he would have to take his family to Athens, the nearest refugee processing center, and take his chances there. I really wanted to help him, but given Cy's hard line attitude, didn't see there was any hope of getting an okay to bend the rules. I was beginning to understand why, during the first dinner with Bob Sorenson and Tom Farrell, there was some complaining about Cy. Tehran was an exceptional situation. We did break rules. Cy did issue visas to Mashallah's clients. Granted a rifle was present during these transactions, but that did not mean we could not use flexibility when it was consistent with the intent of the law.

Other than the special cases the only real complication I faced with any regularity was people who would wander in from another section, particularly the failed student visa applicants. Sorenson held court on the floor above and too often one of his rejects would come wandering into my office, pleading in the usual Iranian fashion that he was a special case and if only he was given a chance to explain fully then of course he would get the visa. Convincing an Iranian he really doesn't qualify is very hard. Yet another problem was our backlog. Valid applicants hoping to travel within weeks would be unhappy to learn our minimum processing time was three months.

Bob returned from his leave in early August. I continued working for him focusing on the correspondence backlog. Before long I figured out who were the sleaze ball attorneys, mostly in LA but some in New York, that were charging their clients a lot of money for basically nothing. Some of the cases were automatic approvals not requiring attorney intervention. Others would never be approved regardless of how many expensive letters the attorney wrote. Of course not all were cut and dried and that provided some level of interest to the work.

Farrell and Sorenson were set to leave around the end of the month and I needed a week or so with Tom to get a handle on his job. Meantime, I wanted to help Bob get to a point where he could keep up with the incoming workload. I was partially thwarted in my goal because Cy decided I should help with the student visas at least one day a week. I didn't understand the decision since the unit had gone from Bob Sorenson as a one man operation to having Rich and Don with him. But I assumed the demand for student visas was infinite at least relative to our resources and there was pressure from the American colleges these kids attended. I won't name names in order to protect the guilty, but there were about ten schools, some community colleges and others allegedly "universities," issuing the bulk of the invitations for Iranian students. To them it was money. For the kids it was an opportunity to enjoy life in the land of the great Satan.

Shortly after I arrived, construction started on conversion of the Caravanserai into a proper, high-security consulate. The new Caravanserai was already being built when I came and opened shortly thereafter. It was between my office and the back gate, right next to the pool. Sometimes, when Cora and I had dinner at a poolside table under a large umbrella, it was possible to forget we were in Tehran. By the second week of July construction of the new consulate was underway and moving rapidly. This was a high priority for the Department since there was no way in the world we could issue tourist visas on any significant scale while housed where we were. I developed tremendous respect for the people, Cy included, who worked under these conditions for many months. Aside from the decrepitude of the physical surroundings there was no security. Sorenson interviewed his students sitting across from them at his desk. I think we had a metal detector operated by a local guard, but it would not prevent a punch in the nose or worse. And the clients, especially the unhappy rejects, were wandering around the building and able to go most anywhere. Strict access controls and bullet-proof glass were becoming standard in consular sections around the world. Instead, we had the embassy komiteh and, unlike the Caravanserai, not even a sign prohibiting weapons in our building. When a thug brought someone to see Cy for a visa, he brought his AK-47 as well.

My main activities, especially before Cora's arrival were work (often overtime for lack of anything better to do) and reading and writing letters, usually to Cora. As the weeks progressed I began to develop a social life. Tom Farrell hosted a party to which he invited a mix of embassy and outside people. I met Richard Sewell from the New Zealand embassy for the first time, as well as Cecilia Lithander from the Swedish Embassy. Both would play important roles after the takeover. I also became friendly with Joe Subic, a non-commissioned officer in the defense attaché office. Joe was widely referred to as the embassy social director since he frequently organized events. He took me hiking north of the city. We got lost and ended up driving backward through a remote village on a road barely wide enough for his Chevy Blazer. We did eventually do some hiking but nowhere near the area we were trying to find.

The second trip with Joe was to a ski resort in the Alborz Mountains at a place called Dizin. Bert Moore and Jim Wiley, the temporary chief communications officer, went with us. We did have fun hiking and then we took the chairlift to the top of the hill and had a good meal at the restaurant. There were not many people around and the views were spectacular. It was great to get out of town, but I vowed after I got back home I would never go on a road trip with Joe again. Driving in Iran was scary under the best circumstances. Joe, who was in his early twenties, drove like a teen-ager. We continued to be friends and I enjoyed his social events, but I always looked for excuses to avoid the road trips.

Rich Queen and I sometimes went out together. I guess I was his wing man, in the current parlance, if a wing man can be married. He became friendly with two young women from the Austrian embassy, Marieta and Eva. They invited us to their place in Niavaran, a ritzy part of town also home to the shah's palace, for drinks and what eventually ended up being dinner as we stayed until 1:00am. We were sampling schnapps, white wine, beer and probably some other things as well. I stupidly managed to get totally blasted. I don't remember how we got up to Niavaran, but we got a ride back from a Dutch helicopter pilot named Heinz. I was feeling terrible in the back seat of his Paykan, a British vehicle of some sort made under license in Iran, when we came to a roadblock. There were other people in the car and one of them started yelling to leave us alone because we were Russians. Apparently it worked because we made it through the roadblock without stopping. This almost certainly saved me some serious problems as diplomat or not being intoxicated was an invitation to trouble. I learned my lesson: drink moderately if you are planning to go back out on the street afterward.

Several weeks later Heinz invited us to a party at his house, also somewhere in North Tehran. This was in early August and my first experience driving at night. Since employees generally did not have personal cars we were allowed to use motor pool vehicles. I borrowed one of the standard white Malibus. With Rich Queen navigating we got to the party without incident. We had a map but maps were decreasingly useful as the revolutionary government changed street names to honor revolutionary heroes.

Heinz barbecued chicken, steak and sausage. The food was great, and the party overall was not terrible but there were a lot of people and we knew only a few of them. I restricted myself to one beer since I had to drive back, and being on the shy side I usually counted on a few more to help lubricate social situations. Also, no one made an effort to introduce newcomers. I did meet Bob Conkey from the Australians and a few other people including an Austrian guy who was apparently dating Eva. Meanwhile, she spent a good part of the evening doing marginally indecent things with another man, an Australian, I think. Around 1:00am Rich and I decided to pull the plug and Eva's date asked us for a ride home. We felt sorry for him and agreed but he had been drinking a lot and, I am not kidding, forgot where he lived. It took an hour of what seemed like random driving before he finally recognized something and could guide us to his home. Once we dropped him off we were able to find our way back to a major arterial that actually appeared on our map. But as we were congratulating ourselves on our navigational good fortune we ran into a roadblock. During the security orientation we had been told roadblocks were frequent at night but it was not clear to me what purpose they served. They were usually manned by men from the local komiteh, so I guessed it was a combination of neighborhood watch and minor extortion racket. I doubted most of the komiteh men had real jobs so a small fee for safe passage through a roadblock would help bankroll the operation. The security officers didn't really want us out late at night but if stopped we were supposed to show our diplomatic identification and demand to be let through.

We had no choice but to stop behind the line of cars. There was someone ahead with a flashlight with an orange beacon and he waived on the vehicles in front of us. When it was our turn he motioned us over to the side of the road. With the diplomatic plates and the big American car I thought we might as well have had one of those taxi-type signs on the roof:

*"Stop Me -- US Embassy."*

The man who came to my window was not what I expected. Besides being older than a typical komiteh thug he knew how to wear a uniform properly. His pants were starched and creased and his boots were polished, the pants properly bloused into them. He had his rifle slung over his shoulder in correct army fashion and wore a pistol on his web belt. Compared to the usual teen-ager with camouflage pants and a dirty t-shirt he was a sure fire winner as soldier of the month.

He asked what we were doing and who we were. We immediately produced our passports and foreign ministry ID cards while explaining we were diplomats returning home from a party and they had no right to detain us. Although I had said all the right stuff he asked me to get out of the car and open up the trunk. Remembering the security briefing guidance about not getting into arguments with armed men (I probably could have figured that out on my own), I did not think it was wise to say no. In any case the trunk was empty except for the spare tire and a metal box bolted to the floor, which with its wires and cooling fins should have been recognizable as a radio. It seemed to interest him very much. He told me to get back in the car and follow him. For a fleeting moment I thought about letting him get a bit ahead and then gunning (no pun intended) down the road, but even though the Chevy was lightly armored and undoubtedly much faster than the Paykan parked nearby and presumably his, it did not seem like much of an idea. I did not want to get into a chase in unfamiliar territory. There were probably other armed komitehs nearby and the man had not seemed particularly threatening. He hadn't waved a gun at us and spoke reasonable English in response to my Farsi.

When we reached the komiteh headquarters several blocks away things started badly. It was dark and I parked too close to the jube without realizing it. Richard could not see it either and stepped into it as he exited the car; he lost his balance for a moment and was immediately suspected of being drunk. Rich never drank much and it was soon obvious he had simply tripped. We were escorted to a drab brick building; there were several stories but I didn't pay much attention to the exterior as we quickly entered a well-lit room on the ground floor, perhaps 20' X 20'. There were bare fluorescent tubes on the ceiling and the floor was a dirty beige tile. The far wall had a counter like you might see at the DMV for filling out forms and some stools close by.

Inside the headquarters were ten or so youths, more typical komiteh types in terms of their age and ragged appearance. Several carried rifles and others wore pistols in holsters. They gathered around us as the older man began to ask us questions. Few were relevant to anything connected to the stop. Were we married? Did I have children? Where in the embassy did we work? They seemed interested when we both replied we were in the consular section. Several remarked they would come see us for visas. We of course encouraged the idea. A number of comments made by members of the group were anti-American but no one pointed a weapon at us. While the experience was nerve-wracking there was only one really tense moment. The worst then, and funniest now, occurred when one of the komiteh men asked Rich why he had been called a camel jockey during his school days in the US. It was obvious he himself knew the answer, but Richard feigned puzzlement and steadfastly denied any knowledge of what the term meant. Despite the potential danger I could tell it was hard for him to keep from laughing, as it was for me.

Everything remained under control. Surprisingly to me the older man seemed not to be the boss, as he apparently consulted with one of the others briefly even as he took steps to keep us under his control. Picking up several official Americans, visa officers no less, must have been worth a few points to him. Finally he was able to get us away from the others and into a side office with a desk and several chairs. He sat behind the desk and Richard and I were offered seats in front. He then proceeded to give us a lecture, the essence of which was Islamic morality required everyone to be in bed by midnight and as guests in the country we should behave by its norms. We, or at least I, should have children and Richard was too old not to have a wife. I didn't comment. Richard was truthfully able to respond he agreed it was time to get married. We shook hands and for some reason, perhaps relief it seemed we were going to be alright, I gave the man my card. We were then allowed to go and even guided back to the main road. Unfortunately, that did not help and we ended up getting lost. The map was almost useless thanks to all the street name-changes and we were reluctant to stop and ask for directions. Finally, we stopped to help some kids who had run out of gas. We dropped one of them at a gas station and he gave us good directions back to the embassy, happily less than a mile away.

We learned important lessons from this. One was to leave parties before 11:00pm or after 6:00am. Apparently bringing a sleeping bag and a toothbrush to social events was common practice but we hadn't known. I also began to consider a lesson of a different sort, one that troubles me to this day. It is a fundamental tenet of diplomacy and of other programs designed to promote international understanding that we can do this by spending time in other countries and learning about their cultures. Yet we had huge numbers of Iranian students in the US. The guy who was razzing Rich about being called a camel jockey may have had a bad experience, but I encountered many other Iranians who had studied in the States and yet seemed to have no understanding or appreciation of our values and culture. Some of these contacts were job-related; men who had married American women and brought them back to Iran with the apparent expectation they would then behave exactly as Iranian village girls. Others, including high-ranking participants in the revolution such as one-time Khomeini advisor and later foreign minister Sadeq Gotbtzadeh seemed to have learned a little but ultimately were unable to bridge the divide. And still others returned to Iran with a deep hatred of America; apparently some were active participants in the attack on the embassy. At the same time, many Americans, perhaps too many for the health of good relations, lived for a time in Iran and experienced the culture first-hand. Yet in the end all of this cross-cultural bridging produced almost nothing positive.

We were obligated to report the incident to the security officer, Al Golacinski. He criticized us for revealing where we worked in the embassy and for not standing more strongly on our diplomatic immunity. While this code of conduct had been touched on at our newcomer's security briefing, it was never made clear how we were supposed to square it with the more compelling suggestion we not argue with armed men. In the actual case I don't think even a more enthusiastic defense of our diplomatic status would have accomplished anything except to prolong our detention. And while I didn't mention it to him, I wondered why, if it was so easy to insist on diplomatic status, we couldn't get rid of our in-house komiteh or have something done about the gun-happy guard in the tower.

The older man who stopped us turned up in my office several months later. It seems he had a brother in Southern California whom he wanted to visit and requested tourist visas for himself and his family. He presented a reasonable application with a claim of a day job other than his komiteh activities and produced the usual bank statements, deed on a house, etc. Although I suspected he was an "intending immigrant," the term we used for people who applied for tourist visas but really planned to remain in the US, I thought he was a better shot than most, figuratively speaking. For one thing, he had obviously made his peace with the revolution, which was not true for many applicants. Also, if he did come back there was a chance he might turn into an interesting and valuable contact. I decided to give him the visas.

I certainly don't intend to document every party we went to, but there is one more that gives a flavor of how things were in Iran for the expatriate community. Our social director, Sergeant Joe Subic, decided to have a big party at his apartment. He lived in the Bijan apartments which also contained the Marine House and were directly across from the embassy north gate. This was toward the end of Ramadan, a month long period of religious observance during which Muslims are not supposed to eat, drink or smoke from sunrise to sundown. Joe recognized it was a sensitive time and said he had made arrangements with Mashallah to have his men provide extra security for us. I think he bribed him with several cases of beer. There were probably a hundred people at the party. For the second time I met some Canadians, security people (military police) I had first encountered at a German Embassy mixer. Bob Anders, who spoke a little German and wanted to improve it, and I had several times gone to the German Embassy parties, but their security chief was married to an Iranian and it always seemed the conversation turned to visas. So after a while we quit going. Joe's British girlfriend, Alice, and the Austrian girls were there also.

Several hours after the party began a Jeep pulled up at the Bijan apartments and three goons with German G-3 machine guns got out. They stayed at the gate while two others came to the apartment door. I believe Joe had already called Mashallah by this time because he arrived soon after the two komiteh types. Joe went to the door and talked with the (now) three men while those of us inside tensed up and wondered what was happening.

Finally the word came back that they – whoever they were was never made clear – were looking for Iranian women who had been corrupted by us and would not leave until they had a chance to search the apartment. One of the thugs entered the apartment at this point with his .45 pistol drawn but considerately pointed at the floor. He seemed rather nervous and conversation hushed as he moved around the room. The search was not very thorough as there was at least one Iranian woman present. Don Cooke had brought (our former language teacher) Mehri's niece. She was very afraid and probably hiding in the bathroom or under a bed by then. Another Iranian woman was married to a Belgian diplomat and when approached she responded in perfect English and bluffed the gunman. Shortly thereafter he left, proclaiming himself satisfied no Iranian women were being corrupted.

As I watched the slow procession of the man with the gun around the room I could not help but notice some of our Marines as well as the Canadian military police and a few others were doing their best to restrain themselves. I have little doubt they could have jumped the gunman easily and broken his neck before he knew what happened. Given there were other Iranians with guns around it was wise to do nothing. I respected the discipline these men demonstrated.

After this episode, chargé Bruce Laingen issued a decree that embassy personnel would not sponsor any more big social events off compound. If someone wanted to have a large party they could do it at the ambassador's residence. That was good enough for Joe, who then started planning a formal ball for Thanksgiving.

The chargé held a daily staff meeting as well as a weekly country team meeting. The difference was the staff meeting was smaller with mostly State Department section heads and a few others like the public affairs officer, whereas country team meant every agency was expected to send a representative. The consular chief, first Cy and later Dick, would attend, and one of us junior officers would also go as part of our training. The meetings were extremely interesting, especially listening to what the political people had to say as well as the overall assessments from Bruce and his deputy Vic Tomseth. These meetings served to confirm further my belief Henry and the Department in general were seriously confused. The constant theme of our meetings was the relationship between Bazargan's provisional government on the one side and the Ayatollah and his revolutionary council on the other. There was a clear consensus Khomeini had near total power should he choose to exercise it, while the secretive revolutionary council was increasingly taking control of the day-to-day administration of government.

Near the middle of August we learned at one of the meetings that Al Golacinski had a plan in the works to get rid of Mashallah and his gang. After much pleading on our part, the foreign ministry had finally agreed to approach the central komiteh and ask for their removal. We had only the vaguest sense of the relationships between the various komitehs around town, but apparently there was some kind of structure. It worked. Mashallah and his men were rounded up and removed and presumably either bribed or intimidated into not coming back. Laingen had decided to close the embassy for the day. In case there was a confrontation, he didn't want any employees caught in a cross-fire. Somehow I didn't get the word and was nearing the back gate when Vic Tomseth, who lived on Bijan, saw me and sent me home.

About a week later came an RPG attack that blew out the window in the new consulate lobby. There was limited shrapnel damage inside, but the building was not yet finished so there was no furniture and concrete walls are sturdy. Although no one knew for sure, it was widely suspected Mashallah, who apparently had been released by this time, was saying his goodbye. It was a Saturday afternoon and Bob Anders and I were returning from one of our increasingly infrequent trips to the Germans. We picked up some chatter on the car radio about an explosion on the compound. There were no details but we decided not to return the car to the motor pool and instead parked at Ardalan. We went to Gary's penthouse. He was away, but there was a bunch of people hanging around waiting for news.

After an hour Mike Howland showed up to brief us. He was wearing a flak jacket and carrying a short-handled sawed-off shotgun. He said someone had fired an RPG into the new consulate building and the extent of the damage was not known. I was secretly hoping the place had been blown to pieces as I did not want us to open (no new consulate, no need for Cora to come), but of course didn't say anything. While walking back to the compound, Mike was ordered to stop by the man in the watchtower who pointed a gun at him. Several other men came out of the compound and were getting ready to take Mike away when Golacinski and one of the colonels from the defense attaché office drove up in the armored van the security office had for situations like this. Al managed to calm everyone down, get Mike into the van and drive back to the compound.

The RPG attack had little impact on the construction schedule and the remodeled building was still going to be ready at the end of August. Cora told me later it did have an effect in Washington. For a time at least Henry Precht was concerned enough to tell Cora and Kathy they might not be able to go. When this turned out be an isolated incident, the plans to open the new consulate were again on track. Meanwhile, I continued to assume Cora and Kathy, as well as Joe, would arrive in time for its opening. We all knew there were tens of thousands, perhaps hundreds of thousands of visa applicants waiting for it. Bob Sorenson and Tom Farrell were leaving and had turned down offers to return in temporary duty status, although their departure dates had been put back a little. I understood Dick Morefield, who himself had arrived a couple of weeks prior, had told Washington he needed Cora and Kathy or two more officers on-site before he would open.

I had very mixed feelings about Cora coming. My almost two months in Iran led me to conclude this was a dangerous place. There were lots of ways to get in trouble: roadblocks, kids with guns and the general dislike for Americans. On the other hand, though, the political situation seemed to be stabilizing and we finally had control of our compound. I would have preferred to continue unaccompanied and try to leave after twelve months, but felt I didn't have enough specific reasons to make the case to Cora she shouldn't come.

Regardless of my feelings I knew I was powerless to do anything. The decision was not mine to make, at least not then. My coming to Iran at all was premised on Cora being able to join me. Although we realized it was theoretically possible the separation might last the entire eighteen months of my original tour if a request to curtail to twelve months failed, there was never any discussion of Cora voluntarily foregoing an opportunity to come. And though my own view of the wisdom of her coming did change once I arrived, I never seriously considered trying to talk her out of it. For one thing it would have been virtually impossible for me to describe my reasons in a letter or short phone call (international calls were unreliable and expensive in those days, often several dollars per minute), just as it was impossible back in July to predict how I would feel after two months there. Also, it would have been unfair to Cora, knowing she would prefer taking her chances with me In Iran rather than worrying constantly from a safe distance. At times my own attitude struck me as vaguely sexist. If I could chance the risks in this unstable place had I any business arguing she could not do the same? And lastly, of course, I would be trying to substitute my judgment for that of the Iran desk, which undoubtedly was seeing and continuing to sell the positive side and probably remained blissfully unaware of goings on at street level. How could my analysis compete with all the good news coming from Henry and company?

The one thing I (we) overlooked was the possibility of what actually happened. Being a hostage is terrible. Having a spouse held as a hostage is terrible. But neither compares to the possibility of both you and your spouse being held hostage by the same people at the same time. I believe we can be excused, however, since the discussion of the possibility of embassy staff being taken hostage was at the time restricted to the highest levels of our government.

# 5. Cora Comes to Tehran

Tuesday, September 4, was the day. I had hoped she would make it a little earlier because the day before had been the Labor Day holiday and, combined with the Iranian weekend, we had three of four days off (one of the benefits of serving abroad is embassies take both American and local holidays). We would have had some free time over the long weekend. Once the consular section reopened in its new location time would be pretty scarce. But at least the uncertainty was over. No more worrying about whether it was the right thing to do. I took an embassy car and went to the airport to meet her. By this time I had made the run often enough I wasn't concerned about doing it myself. I didn't have any trouble getting into the baggage claim area. Technically, a diplomatic ID was supposed to be enough to permit entry, but these days it was always a question whether you could get past the normal public waiting area.

I had come early. I remember I felt a little uncomfortable hanging around for over an hour; I probably smoked half a pack of cigarettes watching people come through the immigration point. For whatever reason I remember that visit to the airport very clearly. I noticed the floor was the exact same type and color as at the shopping center near our condo at Skyline, some kind of dark gray vinyl with one inch diameter dots extruding from the large rectangular tiles. There were a few revolutionary posters on the walls and I practiced talking to them in Farsi as I waited. I also noticed someone had finally thought to remove the sign on the baggage carousel reminding how much duty free liquor could be brought into the country. It had been covered over with masking tape so it was still possible to read it.

When Cora finally arrived we kissed very lightly or perhaps just hugged. No reason to risk violating Islamic sensibilities. Then we went to the baggage claim area. Cora's luggage did not show up. I learned her flight was five hours late out of Washington and she had almost missed her connection in Frankfurt so I was not surprised.

We found a man at the opposite end of the room who was handling the lost luggage. He told us it would probably come on the next Pan Am flight from Frankfurt which was several days away. This was not a happy note on which to begin her stay, particularly since Cora had not followed her usual practice of putting some basics into her carry-on.

After we finished filling out the claim forms we exited baggage claim into a narrower section of the building where the customs inspectors were. I showed them Cora's diplomatic passport and had no trouble getting through, but after the regular customs there was a line of scruffy komiteh men who had decided to make themselves responsible for checking everyone again. In fairness they seemed to be having a lot of success since the wall behind them was lined with liquor bottles, many broken with their contents leaking onto the floor. For some reason I became determined not to let the barbarian search the Hartmann and I waived the black passport at him, repeating "siyasi", meaning diplomatic. After a moment he let us through, telling me he did not like America.

The next morning, Wednesday, Joe and Kathy arrived from Rome. Kathy had gone to spend a little time with Joe and renew her acquaintance with the Eternal City. The Iran Air flight was five hours late, landing at 6:00am. Initially we heard they were unable to get a seat on any flight but Morefield intervened. He said he would not open the tourist visa section without them and the word went down the line to government-owned Iran Air. Somehow they managed to find space.

Thursday was a normal workday in the sense we had to get up at the usual time and go to the consulate. Although we had not yet opened to the public our files and equipment had been moved to the new building. This was our last day of preparation before the tourist visa operation opened to the public. I had not yet taken over American citizen services; Bob was in Athens helping his family as they had just moved there from the States. That meant I was again in charge of the immigrant visa section. Since Cora didn't yet have her luggage she stayed behind at Ardalan to do some laundry.

The new building was a great improvement over our previous digs: fresh paint, central air conditioning, new carpets and no broken windows. In fact, there were hardly any windows at all and those we had were made mostly from bullet-proof Lexan. The large window over the main stairwell, through which the RPG had been fired, was bricked up. We'd had a couple of days to set up shop, a bare minimum. I focused on getting the immigrant visa unit organized and Bob returned shortly before we reopened. That was the basis on which Morefield agreed to the leave so soon after his family visitation travel. Since Tom was still around I moved to the tourist visa section temporarily and on Sunday morning the great onslaught began.

Within a few days of our opening there were thousands of people signed up for interviews. People were enrolled into groups of fifty, the groups were given numbers and each day we would post the groups to be interviewed the next day. By November 4 we had an estimated one year backlog. This system was a joint venture between us, the police and some independent entrepreneurs who were charging a small fee to get onto the list. This wasn't exactly proper but under the circumstances it was the best we could do. There were other entrepreneurs who sold drawings of the visa officers with a profile of each. Some were considered tougher than others. An applicant armed with a drawing could try to maneuver his or her place in line to get one of the allegedly easier ones. These drawings were to raise some concerns later since they served to add to the risk Cora or the Staffords would be identified as we tried to leave. If there was a portrait of me I never saw it. I presumed my relatively few hours on the line meant I didn't rate.

The tourist visa operation was on the first floor. Probably 60% of the floor space was a waiting area with cattle rails like one might find at Disneyland. There were eleven interview windows arranged in a line on one side of the room with bulletproof glass and a pass-through slot for documents, although for some reason the area below the slot was just plywood and provided no security at all. I guess the theory was an applicant who managed to smuggle a weapon to that point would aim for the head. It was not the most welcoming atmosphere in which to conduct the visa interviews, but the emphasis was on security and efficiency. There was a working area on the secure side of the interview booths along with a huge mass of filing cabinets. Upstairs were the immigrant visa section and American citizen services as well as the consul general's office and the personal offices of the Americans who worked the visa line.

For me, the best thing about working the interview line was it was temporary. We were caught between the desire to be fair to each applicant and the need to protect US interests by keeping out ineligibles. We had to work fast while overcoming language problems, hard to read and potentially forged documents, and the depressing knowledge that, no matter how quickly we worked, the long lines in the cattle rails would remain. Even with the air space around the sides of the interview booth windows the noise from the waiting area made comprehension difficult. Applicants would often talk into the document slot hoping to be understood. The one great advantage over the old office was we could definitively end the interview. After turning down someone and explaining the reasons, as often as not the applicant would continue arguing. All we had to do was walk away and turn on a light that signaled a local guard to remove the person.

Aside from document fraud perpetrated by desperate applicants the consulate as an institution had to deal with the potential of internal fraud. Among the scammers who obtained money from rejected applicants with promises of influence it turned out there was at least one who could actually deliver. While we tried to maintain as much American control over the process as possible, a critical area was the filing system, especially the records of rejected applicants. We had to rely on our local staff to maintain these files and in particular not to remove rejected applications. These were critical for determining whether someone had applied before and changed his or her information. Although our employees were paid reasonably well the potential profit in removing rejections was far beyond anything we could offer. Shortly after we opened Rich Queen was approached by a man who said he had been offered the removal of his nephew's rejected application for $1,000. He told Rich he would prove this to us if his nephew was granted the visa. Morefield gave the okay and Rich told the man to proceed. A couple of days later he gave Rich the actual rejected application. The nephew got his visa and Al Golacinski took over the investigation. One of our local staff was fired. Neither Cora nor I can remember his name, but we both agreed he had a sneaky look and we were not surprised when he turned out to be the culprit. While it was good to be rid of him, we remained vulnerable to the problem simply because there was the temptation of so much money.[1] We liked most of our Iranian co-workers and wanted to trust them, but it was impossible to ignore the pressure they were under.

Despite the vastly improved work environment the fundamental problem of tourist visa issuance in a revolutionary environment remained. There were some people who were clearly eligible, others clearly not, and the remainder, probably half were a gray area. Mike Metrinko, whom I mentioned earlier as one of the political officers with extensive Iran experience, was a great font of wisdom. He volunteered to do interviews once a week if his schedule allowed. He considered it a good way to keep his finger on the pulse of the country. Depending on what an applicant had to say, he might slip in a question or two that would help him better understand how ordinary people saw things. Another political officer with excellent Farsi, John Limbert, also came from time to time for the same reason. They both told us virtually any document could be forged. So while we studied intricate property deeds even the locals had trouble deciphering we wondered whether they were real. All we had left was instinct. Sometimes I felt like I was flipping a mental coin. The reactions to denial were sometimes hard to take. The ones who argued or yelled were easy. The quiet ones were the hardest, particularly when there was any question of the individual's safety.

Many of the people we were interviewing, including some of the students, were more properly refugees than temporary visitors. To deal with these cases the Department developed the Beirut formula, named for the city where it was first applied. This meant we were to look at the applicant and try to decide if this individual would return to Iran should the political situation stabilize. If we concluded they would then we could issue the visa. The Beirut formula met with considerable resistance among the line officers. There were two assumptions implicit in the formula: stability would return to

---

1. Richard Queen with Patricia Haas, Inside and Out (New York, Putnam, 1981), 25-6

Iran before these people put down roots in America, and it would come in a form acceptable to them. Most were from middle class Western educated backgrounds and would probably not want to live in an Islamic theocracy, no matter how stable. How one viewed the Beirut formula depended on a vision of Iran's future. Most of us had a negative view, so using the rule to the extent Washington wanted required us, at least as I saw it, to ignore the law we were sworn to uphold.

Separate from the Beirut formula was another Washington policy that Jewish applicants were to be approved. Under the shah, the Jewish community in Iran had thrived. No more. We were sympathetic to their plight. But there were other religious minorities, Baha'is and Zoroastrians, who were at greater risk but lacked influence in the US. Should we give them less consideration? This rule too was widely ignored. Several weeks after I moved to American services Morefield lectured everyone on both of these issues, but I sensed he understood and shared the concerns. Still, as the boss he had to pass along the orders and make a reasonable effort to obtain compliance. On the other hand, the law says the visa officer has sole discretion whether to grant a visa so most of us treated these as suggestions and nothing more. They provided useful flexibility, something I desperately wanted during July and August when Cy was insisting everything be by-the-book.

On September 23rd, Tom Farrell was finally allowed to leave and I moved upstairs to take over American citizen services. My new office was on the north side of the building with the only window facing to the outside of the compound. It was 12" X 30" high, little more than a slit, and it must have been at least a foot thick. It was designed to withstand an RPG of the type that had blown out the now bricked-up window in the waiting area. Outside was a bullpen area where the staff work stations were located. Our area was up against the north wall. To our immediate south was the immigrant visa unit where Bob Anders worked. He too had a private office and a bullpen area for his employees. We shared a waiting room divided from the work space by a counter. It extended all the way from the north wall to the interior wall that separated us from the employees-only space at the south end of the building. Here the consul general and his deputy had their offices, each of the American visa officers had a small work space where they could handle their paperwork and the employee rest rooms were there also.

As chief of American citizen services, I was responsible for providing a range of assistance to Americans and on a more limited basis, to Iranians. I considered my job to be a combination of attorney, social worker and bureaucrat. I also had the sometimes bothersome task of answering letters sent to the embassy that no one else wanted to deal with, such as kids asking for Iranian postage stamps or for help with an essay on the Ayatollah Khomeini. For the most part, though, and despite the unglamorous nature of the work it was the area where Americans, the people who were paying our salaries, were most likely to come for help. Whether it was finding a relative who came to Iran and disappeared or helping an American who was having difficulties with the local authorities and wanted us to intervene, my office was ground zero. Sometimes I was just an initial contact for an American unsure where in the embassy he might find help. This was the case with Jerry Plotkin, a businessman who was interested in meeting with someone in the commercial section. I arranged the appointment, unfortunately for the morning of the takeover. Plotkin became one of just two hostages who were not employed by the US government.

American services work was a great improvement over visas. I had an excellent local staff. Mrs. Afshartous handled passports and other citizenship related work and Mrs. Mohseni did notarials (certification and occasional translation of documents pertaining to legal matters in the two countries) and was the cashier for the entire consulate. Both were long-time employees, one married to an admiral, the other to a wealthy businessman. They worked for us because they thought the US presence in Iran was beneficial to their country. Unfortunately, as we were soon to learn, others felt differently. My chief local employee, Massoud, was a combination investigator and fixer. In Iranian terms he was an expert practitioner of partibazi, the art of developing, maintaining and manipulating a network of contacts in order to maneuver through what otherwise could be an impenetrable bureaucracy. This was a word with no exact English counterpart and therefore another Iranian term that was used routinely in our conversation. Lastly, there was Pouja, the consul general's driver who worked with us when he wasn't otherwise needed. I thought he was a bit of a flake, but some of the local staff told me he was a decent poet and worked on improving his English in his spare time, so I decided maybe I wasn't being fair. In any case, his main job for us was to run errands, taking documents to the foreign ministry or other offices, and to handle minor clerical work.

While I did have my share of routine stuff like answering correspondence, signing the passports that Mrs. Afshartous would prepare or reviewing and signing the notarials coming from Mrs. Mohseni, most of my time was spent on assistance work and status inquiries. These last categories were the most interesting, although many assistance cases were depressing because there was little I could do.

As an example, my first case concerned an American woman who showed up at the embassy with her suitcase. Tom was still around but it was the weekend and the duty Marine couldn't find him so called me. She had lived in Iran for some years and had a five year old daughter with her Iranian husband, whom she had met while he was a student in the States. Her marriage was falling apart, largely because the Mohammad who seemed westernized when she'd known him in Florida had been replaced by a traditional Muslim male. Furthermore, she was living with his family in a small town with no one to whom she could turn even for elemental companionship. She didn't have much money so I put her into the cheap hotel across the street from the Ardalan apartments. When I came back in the morning to check on her, she was gone. The desk clerk told me she'd left with some Iranians. My guess is her family found her, which means she very likely called them. In the end she couldn't leave her daughter.

This pattern repeated itself more than once during my brief tenure. Sometimes assistance cases grew out of "welfare and whereabouts" inquiries, the term we used to describe a request to determine the status of an American citizen allegedly present in Iran. Usually it would start with a letter from the family or even their congressman, saying they had not heard from the relative for a long time and asking us to locate the person. This is where Massoud came in, putting on his Sherlock Holmes hat. He would generally be able to locate the individual and sometimes all would be well. They just hadn't been writing. Rarely, the person did not want contact with their family in which case all we could do is report the information back to the Department since privacy considerations did not allow us to do anything else. More often than not, unfortunately, the circumstances were more like the first case. Because most of the Iranians who studied in the States were male, most of the spouses we had to deal with were female. There was little we could do. Under Iranian law children belonged to the father and a wife needed her husband's permission to travel outside the country.

Perhaps the most unusual case concerned a woman who claimed she had been raped by her Iranian boyfriend and later decided to marry him anyway. The girl was born before the marriage and had never been legitimated. The husband eventually left her and took the child back to Iran. She argued he had violated Iranian law because an illegitimate child was not entitled to the Iranian passport he had obtained for her. Even though this was a case where the law might be on our side, we had little cooperation from the Iranians and the woman did not know where the girl was being kept. The husband's extended family was involved in hiding her. Unfortunately, we were still working this case when the takeover occurred.

Welfare and whereabouts also applied to the dead, so I had responsibility for a dead body in Mashad, a city in north-eastern Iran. Local authorities said the cause of death was a drug overdose. The addresses he had provided for next of kin in his passport and on some other papers were false. Morefield suspected he was traveling under an alias. In any case, we were at a dead-end, so to speak, as far as finding someone to notify who might tell us what to do with the remains and personal property. In addition, although the body was kept refrigerated in a morgue they told us normal deterioration had made taking fingerprints impossible. I wondered why the local authorities, including presumably someone who functioned as the equivalent of a coroner, hadn't anticipated the problem and taken prints while it was still possible. Perhaps they were waiting for a request from us, but this was before CSI made us all expert forensic investigators and neither Tom nor I knew fingerprints disappear over time. I was planning a trip out there to talk to the locals and bring back his possessions, hoping I might learn something, but again the takeover intervened.

Another job of mine was dealing with the personal effects of deceased Americans. I had some luggage sitting in the store room that had been brought from the consulate in Isfahan when it closed. My recollection is this person had relatives back in the US we'd been able to find, but they didn't want to pay for his stuff to be returned. So, had time permitted, it would have been turned over to the general services section for sale at the next auction of surplus property and the proceeds remitted to the family. I know some of this work sounds depressing, but believe me, it was wonderful compared to facing the visa line on a daily basis.

Of course there is more to life than work and Cora's arrival changed many things. First, we had to leave Ardalan and that meant getting a car. Originally I assumed I could survive without one, but the apartment we settled on was beyond walking distance. General services had its own used car lot. The vehicles were purchased by the government from evacuated employees because there was no way to get them back to the US. In late September they had a sale and although I looked closely I was still debating when Massoud told me he could check what was in the Iranian customs yard. Before coming to work for us Massoud had been with the Military Assistance Advisory Group and had been able to help Americans buy cars from customs limbo. I agreed it would be reasonable to look and he eventually learned of a virtually new US-specification 1978 BMW 320i that was being held because the German/Iranian owner could not afford to pay the "javaz" or customs duty. We contacted the owner and agreed to a price of $7000, with me being responsible for any taxes owed.

So I was now potentially the owner of a champagne green metallic BMW that was a year old but had only 1,200 miles. All I needed to do was get the registration papers, but that turned out to be more of a challenge than I thought. I started out by the book, submitting the paperwork through our customs office to the foreign ministry. Nothing happened. I went to Steve Lauterbach, who was in charge of the office, and found out the Iranian foreign ministry and customs were feuding about the interpretation of the law. The rule said every diplomat was entitled to import one car free of duty, and in the past purchasing a car from customs impound was considered equivalent to importation. Apparently this was now open to question, at least for the minions of the Great Satan.

The next time I had other business at the foreign ministry I mentioned my problem and was assured we were right and the matter would be addressed. Again, nothing happened. So Massoud obtained a letter from a senior customs official stating the car should be released. He then took me to the customs yard, where we spent over three hours filling out forms and pacing around waiting in a building that looked like a pre-fabricated trailer. Another man with a similar problem struck up a conversation with me, until he found out I was an American rather than, as he had for some reason guessed, a German. He then told me he didn't like Americans and left to sit in a corner of the room.

In the end, a minor bureaucrat who apparently also did not like Americans refused to accept the letter. Massoud told me this was not a surprise. He claimed to know of a case where a low-ranking official had shot his boss and gotten away with it. In addition, in the current environment anything directed against an American would be viewed sympathetically around the bureaucracy. We were then invited into the boss's office. He said even though he agreed with us, he couldn't order his subordinate to change his mind because his interpretation was defensible. The unsaid message: it was just too risky to appear pro-American.

We returned to the consulate disappointed. I was regretting I had allowed my love of nice cars and the opportunity to get this seeming bargain cloud my judgment. We were spending too much time and effort. It was tempting to blame Massoud, since his assurances had influenced my decision, but I believed he had given me his best judgment. Like the rest of us, he was finding rules from before the revolution could no longer be relied on.

Still, the next day, Massoud pulled the rabbit out of his hat. We went back to the customs yard and everything was approved, no questions asked. I worried there would be a price to pay later, as I didn't know what favors might have been promised. Massoud insisted he hadn't promised anything, and although he was deliberately vague regarding what had changed since the previous day, I tended to believe him if only because the primary currency of value the US had was visas and he had no access to them except through me. By this time the car had been sitting on the embassy compound without license plates for three weeks and we were two weeks away from the takeover. Hardly worth the effort, but that is hindsight of course.

We were able to take two weekend trips out of Tehran, one before the car and the other after. The first trip was to the Caspian Sea. It was late September but still acceptable swimming weather. We borrowed one of the embassy's Malibus and Joe and Kathy Stafford came with us. Not the greatest cars but they had certain advantages, or maybe just one advantage: size. We arranged rooms at the former Hyatt Regency through the foreign ministry. We needed their permission to travel any distance from Tehran. The hotel had been expropriated from Hyatt, or more probably from Iranian owners connected to the previous regime, and given to the Alavi Foundation, a new organization which was supposed to use its profits for the benefit of those who had suffered under the shah.

We left early on a Friday morning. Although the Caspian is less than 100 air miles from Tehran the road mileage is about double and the drive takes six hours. We started out heading west on the highway to Karaj, at which point we turned north. We passed through Dizin, site of one of my Subic adventures. The scenery on the southern side of the mountains was rugged and barren. Exposed veins of coal and other minerals our in-house geologist Don Cooke had pointed out to me on another trip erupted from the mountain sides.

The road itself was horrendous, generally narrow with many treacherous bends. Iranian drivers made things much worse. Passing on blind curves was common. At the summit we found a two mile tunnel that was one way only, controlled by a stop light. Once our turn came the accumulated traffic squeezed through the tunnel. The single lane tunnel again turned into a two lane road, and we cleared the line of southbound cars waiting to enter the tunnel. Then the traffic degenerated into an incredible, dangerous race as nearly every driver tried to pass every other, even as the road snaked down the mountain and regardless of sight distance. We found a place to pull off the road and wait until the crazies seemed safely ahead of us, something we repeated several times. Once there was a car following close behind and honking its horn and flashing its headlamps. Finally I pulled over and the man behind stopped and handed me one of our wheel covers. It was another of those occasional kind gestures Iranians made and part of the reason it was hard to form an opinion of post-revolutionary Iran in general. Shortly after we got back on the road we passed a small crowd gathered along the side of the road. In the ravine below we could see the burning hulk of a car that had apparently been forced off the road.

We had left without breakfast so we finally decided to stop at a roadside tea-house, or chaikhane. It was a single level wooden building with a peaked roof and an open front. There was no glass in the windows; the place would close as winter approached. There was a display case filled with various kinds of pastries, but we made do with several glasses of tea and nan-e barbary, the wonderful Iranian flatbread. Unfortunately, what I remember best was the horrendously filthy outdoor toilet, situated at the side of a stream that was probably also the sewage disposal system. Just getting to the place was a challenge as there was mud at least half an inch deep everywhere.

Other than having to deal with filthy shoes and carpets in the car the rest of the trip was uneventful. Once we got to Chalus where the road split, we had to make some choices, but we found our way to the town of Kiyakala and eventually to the hotel. Although it was starting to show some wear and tear from lack of maintenance, it still looked like a Hyatt. To the south of the hotel was a large, heavily forested park with horse trails.

We had come primarily to swim in the Caspian, the world's only fresh water sea, which I suppose also makes it the largest fresh water lake. We needed first to find out whether anyone was enforcing a rule against mixed bathing. We actually did find some signs indicating men's beach and women's beach but there didn't seem to be any komiteh types around and the few people swimming were ignoring the rule. The hotel was virtually empty due to the lateness of the season as well as the fact that Iranians who would normally have frequented this class of hotel were maintaining a low profile and wouldn't like the mixed bathing ban any more than we did.

We decided it was too late in the day for the sea so we checked out the hotel. The casino was closed, replaced with pin ball machines. The pool with its semi-submerged bar was closed also. Then we took a walk on the beach, looking for sea shells. There were none to be found. Finally we went hiking in the park. It was green and cool, everything Tehran was not. None of us felt like driving anymore so we had dinner in the hotel and an early evening. Aside from being tired after a long stressful day on the road there was no night life to encourage us to stay up.

After breakfast the next day we took our chances at the beach. Again, there was no one around so we relaxed and enjoyed the water. It was still warm enough we were in no rush to get out. Both the beach and the sea floor were sandy just as one would expect at a normal salt sea, but of course there was no salt and there were no waves. It was fantastic, a unique experience well worth the long drive. Unfortunately, we had another one ahead and needed to check out of the hotel before noon. So we limited ourselves to an hour at the beach.

After checking out, we explored the town of Kiyakala. We walked around the shops; the place looked poor, obviously missing the tourist dollars that no longer flowed from visitors to the former Hyatt. We did find a magnificent old hotel with the white stucco still gleaming. The owners were apparently determined to keep it the centerpiece of the town. We had lunch there: barbecued sturgeon. It was very tasty. I don't know whether eating sturgeon is bad as far as the implications for a sustainable caviar regime are concerned. I do know that caviar, the good kind, is sturgeon eggs, and there had been concerns about over-harvesting in the Caspian. With the revolution in Iran came a collapse of authority and the harvesting limits negotiated with the USSR (which controlled the other half of the sea) were not being observed. After lunch we decided to buy some caviar since it was the equivalent of $10 for a tin that would cost at least a dozen times as much in the US. And so we discovered the third and last really good thing about Iran: cheap high quality caviar.

The trip home was routine. No flaming cars and no backup at the tunnel. When we hit Karaj, however, I started hitting objects. First I hooked a taxi with the rear bumper, my fault. The driver said to forget about it as the damage was hardly visible. Then a motorcycle hit us. His fault, but again no injuries and no serious damage as the handlebar had scraped our door.

As we neared Tehran, we passed a deserted construction site several acres in size. There were skeletons of at least half a dozen tall buildings, each with a yellow construction crane on top. It was a sad reminder of the economic collapse that had contributed to the shah's downfall. Presumably this was to have been decent housing for Iran's burgeoning population. Instead, it was a crumbling ruin. The abandoned yellow construction crane was, unfortunately, very common all around Tehran. We had already named it the national bird of Iran. I dropped Cora at Ardalan and took Joe and Kathy to their temporary accommodations in one of the three decrepit old bungalows across the way from the co-op. I then went to the motor pool and showed the duty driver the damage to the bumper and the door, but he waved it off as normal wear and tear for Iran driving.

Since the Ardalan apartments served as both temporary and permanent accommodations, Cora and I stayed on for about a month. Cora became an honorary member of the key club, although it remained Gary's intent to keep the building all-male. As long as the weather held she adopted the schedule I had been following. Often after work we would take a quick dip in the swimming pool. Evenings were generally spent at home, listening to music, reading, writing letters and occasionally socializing with neighbors. Iranian television was terrible and video recorders were not yet available for home use. Once or twice a week there would be a key club dinner. The Marines showed movies at the Mushroom Inn, a former warehouse partially converted into their social facility while the new Marine House was being built where the ramshackle consular section had been. The windowless and aptly named Mushroom later became notorious as the place where many of the hostages were held and abused for extended periods. In general, parties were fewer. After the raid on Subic's apartment, events tended to be smaller and people stayed close to home.

At this point our most important personal concern was the move to a permanent apartment. We knew Ardalan was temporary and Cora wanted to get settled somewhere. The embassy had, with a few exceptions like Bob's apartment, terminated its leases so we could sample the market. One of Gary Lee's employees arranged for us to see several apartments, all within a mile or two (straight-line distance, not road miles, per the security officer's orders) to the north of the embassy. After looking at three places we selected the smallest and also the furthest away. It was a two bedroom on the second floor of a low rise building about a mile and a half from the compound (again measured in a straight line). We chose it because the other places seemed too large to maintain (a guest room was pointless) and, as I was in the process of buying a car, the five mile commute seemed acceptable.

It took a week for the paperwork and the furniture to be delivered, along with Cora's airfreight which we decided to store until we had the new place. The only serious problem was trying to fit a breakfast table into the kitchen area. It was smaller than we had realized and even the smallest table in the embassy warehouse took up too much room. But with just the two of us we made it work. The big problem turned out to be the landlady. She and her husband were elderly, both Armenians, which gave them a reason to be wary of the revolution. I know they were not particularly happy to have official Americans in the apartment, but the real estate market was depressed and money is money. My problem was by the time we'd moved, I had the BMW, and the landlady would not allow me to park the car in our designated space inside the gate. She was concerned I would drive home with a bomb attached and her building would be collateral damage. I kept trying to explain to her that a car with US embassy plates parked in plain sight in front of her building was probably a greater threat than one hidden inside, but to no avail.

Meantime, the car was vandalized. Someone stole the driver side rear view mirror. I managed to buy a new one for $45, but after I confirmed with Gary's office that the parking space was in the lease, I went for a final meeting. No progress. She insisted emphatically she had told the embassy the parking space was not included. Luckily, the government is a slow payer so I was able to get the check canceled. We quickly found a new place a couple of blocks further north. With the benefit of experience, we made sure the new kitchen would accommodate a small table and there was no paranoia about the parking space. There was even a small outdoor swimming pool. We said nothing to the previous landlady while waiting for the unit to be painted and the paperwork finished. The embassy would have to sort out what we owed for the three weeks we'd actually lived at the Majidi street apartment.

# 6. The Shah Goes to New York

Although I am not a historian and promised at the outset to keep this account personal to the extent possible there is one matter that deserves more than the paragraph or three I have given others. This pertains to the admission of the shah to the US. It was the pivotal decision in the chain of choices that led to the hostage crisis. The situation in Iran was unstable and no one can predict what would have happened if the shah had remained in exile outside the US. Still, there is ample reason to believe admission of the shah created the conditions that made the embassy takeover not only possible but likely and perhaps inevitable, and that the US government fully understood the risks to us.

When the shah left Iran on January 16, 1979, he had a standing invitation to come to the US. The Annenberg family had offered the use of its California estate, Sunnyland. Instead, he chose to go initially to Egypt and then to Morocco.[1] The shah remained in Morocco about six weeks, during which time the US changed its mind. The shah was asked to leave Morocco because King Hassan was preparing to host the Islamic Summit and considered his presence might be awkward. David Rockefeller, the recently retired chairman of Chase Manhattan Bank, was a friend of the shah and one of those supporting his admission to the US. He was contacted by David Newsom, State's Undersecretary for Political Affairs, and told intelligence suggested that, if the shah were admitted, the embassy could be taken and there was a threat to American lives. Newsom also mentioned the shah's assets might be subject to US court action, implying it was in his interest also to remain outside the US. Rockefeller was asked to deliver this message but refused. Instead, he helped arrange for the shah to move to an estate in the Bahamas, and it ultimately fell to a CIA officer who had been friendly with

---

1. Terence Smith, "Why Carter Admitted the Shah," New York Times Magazine, 1981 Special Edition, 37

the shah to inform him the asylum invitation was withdrawn.[2] On June 1, the Bahamian government told the shah his visa would not be renewed when it expired in ten days, triggering another scramble on the part of the shah's friends, who included former Secretary of State Henry Kissinger and John J. McCloy, an influential attorney who had been the US military governor of Germany after World War II as well as president of the World Bank. The result of their efforts was the shah went to Mexico on June 10.[3]

Meantime, these influential friends worked behind the scenes from the time when Newsom called Rockefeller. Rockefeller spoke personally with President Carter on April 9, to no avail. He communicated his disappointment to Kissinger, who that same night gave a speech in which he stated it was "morally wrong to treat the shah like a Flying Dutchman looking for a port of call." That colorful phrase was picked up by the media and served to move the discussion from a private one among some of America's political and economic elite into a more public venue.[4]

The administration itself was divided. While Secretary of State Vance opposed giving the shah asylum, the national security adviser, Zbigniew Brzezinski, strongly favored it. He believed the issue had become controversial only because the US wavered at the outset. Vice President Walter Mondale initially opposed asylum, but was convinced by Kissinger in June to change his mind.[5] Carter himself remained opposed. On August 10, Carter received a personal letter from Princess Ashraf, the shah's twin sister, indicating the shah was sick. The princess stated she was writing for herself, without the shah's knowledge. Vance replied on behalf of the President, stating there would be no change in US policy. In late September an assistant to Rockefeller asked a medical doctor, Benjamin Kean, to evaluate the shah's condition, and it was only at this point the US government became aware the shah had lymphoma. He kept this condition secret from the CIA and apparently even from many in his family, as it

---

2. Ibid, 40
3. Ibid, 42
4. Ibid.
5. Ibid.

might have emboldened his domestic opponents and caused the US to re-evaluate its long term commitment to him.[6]

The record at this stage becomes confusing. Carter claims he was told on October 18 the shah was at the point of death and the medical care necessary to save his life was available only in New York. Vance was directed to verify the medical information. Dr. Kean stated that he told the State Department's medical director, Dr. Jerry Korcak, that while it would be preferable for the shah to be seen at New York Hospital the treatment could be done in Mexico or almost anywhere else.

Vance was also directed to prepare the Iranian government for the news of the shah's admission. Bruce Laingen and Henry Precht, who was visiting Tehran, met with Prime Minister Bazargan and Foreign Minister Yazdi on October 21. The Iranians were not happy with the information although they did promise security for the embassy. Still, Precht remembered a comment by Yazdi: "You're opening a Pandora's Box with this."[7] The shah was admitted to the US and New York Hospital the next day. I do not know how much of this story was known by how many people at the embassy. Clearly Laingen knew the most and undoubtedly his deputy Tomseth and some others had the information as well. We were not told the Department had anticipated the possibility of the shah's admission months earlier and Precht himself had done an analysis of the potential consequences. I saw it only later, courtesy of the Iranian puzzle experts who reconstructed our shredded documents. While it was prepared before the US knew of the shah's medical problems it made a number of points that still applied. I will quote them in full:

*****

"We have the impression that the threat to U. S. Embassy personnel is less now than it was in the spring; presumably the threat will diminish somewhat further by the end of the year. *Nevertheless, the danger of hostages being taken in Iran will persist* (emphasis mine).

---

6. Ibid, 46
7. Ibid.

"We should make no move towards admitting the Shah until we have obtained and tested a new and substantially more effective guard force for the Embassy. Secondly, when the decision is made to admit the shah, we should quietly assign additional American security guards to the Embassy to provide protection for key personnel until the danger period is considered over."[8]

*****

The embassy takeover was not an unanticipated event. Aside from Precht's memo, Carter himself is on record asking his aides, during a discussion of the issues surrounding the admission the shah,

"What are you guys going to advise me to do if they overrun our embassy and take our people hostage?"[9]

The recommendation for an effective guard force was not implemented; it was probably not realistic. I doubt the US government was prepared to use lethal force against the people storming the embassy even if we had enough suitably armed and trained guards to make it feasible to defend a twenty-six acre compound with a mile of wall. Additional security for the chargé and perhaps some others made sense and could have been done. It was not. There was instead another recommendation I believe belonged on this list: severe downsizing of the US presence in Iran. The vast majority of the Americans at the embassy were not directly involved in the fundamental task of diplomacy, maintaining lines of communication between governments. Our continued business-as-normal presence was really based on nothing more than inertia and wishful thinking.

In fairness to Precht, he would probably have argued our staffing level was appropriate to the importance of Iran and our need to build a relationship with the new authorities. He could also have said his policy of encouraging a Western-oriented democracy was never given time to develop. The admission of the shah changed

---

8. McManus, Free at Last, 252, citing "Planning for the Shah to Come to the United States," State Department Memorandum dated August 1, 1979. A copy of the document as reconstructed by the Iranians is also in the author's possession.

9. Hamilton Jordan, Crisis (New York, Putnam, 1982),32

everything. It shattered whatever trust we had been able to build with the new government, both the official Bazargan version and, to the extent we had any success at all, with the revolutionary council. It also demolished the credibility of anyone in the Bazargan government who might have argued in favor of trying to create a new relationship with the US based on mutual respect and our non-interference in their affairs. Certainly it played into the hands of those who insisted the US could not be trusted and would continue to meddle, some going so far as to claim the shah's entry was merely preparation for our returning him to power. I do not know whether Khomeini himself believed this, but four days before the takeover he gave a speech in which he called for actions to neutralize American plots against Iran. It would certainly have been reasonable for some of his followers to conclude taking out the "nest of spies," as the embassy was commonly termed in the media, would be a good first step.

Given this situation it is fair to ask why the staff of the Tehran embassy did not all head to the airport and get on the first available flight. There are several answers. First, despite our reputation in some circles, most Foreign Service officers are dedicated and courageous and do their assigned jobs even in difficult circumstances. Second, we collectively knew only bits and pieces of this information. Of course we knew of the shah's travels, but nothing about the secret documents repeatedly expressing concern about hostages being taken. The majority of the embassy staff, including me, was briefed on October 21st and 22nd. The rumor mill worked much faster so even before the briefings the word had gotten around (my recollection is we knew on the 19th).

The security officer, Al Golacinski, wanted to meet with us in groups of ten to allow ample opportunity for questions. He outlined a range of possible Iranian responses from none to demonstrations to an assassination attempt. He claimed to believe none was the most likely, but he was in a bad place. Aside from reminding us about general security precautions and suggesting we maintain a low profile for a time, all he could realistically do was pass along the assurances Laingen and Precht had received from Bazargan and Yazdi. He never once mentioned a takeover scenario or the holding of hostages. I prefer to believe he was not made privy to that information, although one would think in this one case the St. Valentine's Day attack would have served a positive role as a foretaste of what might happen. Regardless, I am not sure Al would have mentioned it. After all, there was no way to prepare, nothing we as individuals could do. And as this account should have made clear, we had to one degree or another gotten used to living in a hostile environment. It was similar to what had happened with the smells and the jubes and even the heat; after a while we just didn't notice anymore.

I suspect that is why in the end we reacted to the shah's admission by trying to continue living normal lives. Sometimes in an old war movie there is a scene of a grand ball taking place as enemy forces are closing in on the encircled city. Our situation was different primarily because we didn't know what the enemy would do or when. But we did continue to pursue mundane tasks like finding a new apartment, and we tried to maintain a social life. One party I remember particularly well revolved around a dance competition of some kind. Bob Anders and the Eva from the Norwegian Embassy won the polka contest. Cora dragged me out on the floor for the waltz as we had been taking dance lessons before leaving for Iran. But whatever it was we learned at the class bore little resemblance to what the people on the floor were doing and we were almost killed by the whirling and swirling bodies all around us. Cora was a great dancer. I was lucky not to have been born in the days when the diplomatic party circuit meant lots of formal balls. My career would have floundered. I can see the evaluation report: *"Mr. Lijek is a reasonably competent young officer but his inability to dance is an embarrassment to this mission."* I also remember the Japanese declined to attend this event for security reasons, even though it was at the ambassador's residence and therefore as safe as we could make anything. The decision to admit the shah put a bull's eye on our backs. Even if Washington refused to see it, others did.

Also around this time we were invited by an American woman married to an Iranian to a barbecue in a pomegranate orchard outside of town. This was a mixed Iranian and expat event, and as we didn't get many such invitations, we wanted to attend. It was very educational from a cultural standpoint. We were invited for 3:00pm, so we assumed dinner would be around 6 or 7:00pm at the latest. They didn't start cooking until 9:00pm by which time we were freezing. Thankfully our hosts started a big bonfire and we cooked ourselves, rotating our bodies from front to back every few minutes to balance the heat. We had not realized Iranians ate so late.

Near the end of October we were told adult family members were going to be allowed to return to post as of the end of November. This flew in the face of all the warnings we had received after the shah's admission to the US, but it was consistent with the optimistic view of Iranian/American relations prevailing in Washington. It was perhaps the clearest indication the fears expressed in the Precht memo and even by the President himself were somehow not being translated into practical policy for guiding the on-the-ground American presence in Iran. It was fortunate the terrorists did not wait another month because they might have had a substantially greater number of hostages.

Our last free weekend, literally, was given over to a road trip to Isfahan. We had a three day weekend coming up and I wanted to give the BMW a test. A number of people from various embassies were going to meet at a hotel there so we decided to join. Joe and Kathy rode with us; the others flew.

The road to Isfahan was a great improvement over the mountain path to the Caspian. At least there were far fewer blind corners. The BMW gave me a much more confident feeling than the old Chevy. Still, we passed several fiery wrecks smoldering along the road. In addition I made a couple of mistakes. First was my decision to buy gas. I was down to a quarter tank and saw a station with a huge line. I figured it must the last one for quite a while so we wasted an hour waiting to fill up. Of course within the next twenty miles we passed multiple stations with no lines.

The second occurred as we neared Isfahan. We came to an intersection and I guessed wrong. At first it seemed right, a beautiful, new, four-lane freeway. After a few minutes, however, I began to worry because there were literally no other cars. I was traveling rather quickly when all of a sudden I could see ahead there was a twenty foot gap in the road. I slammed on the brakes, barely managing the dip down to the gravel road bed. This happened several more times and finally the paved road ended completely, presumably another casualty of the economic collapse. We continued slowly along the road bed until, fortunately, another lost soul came up behind. We stopped and consulted. The driver said he thought we were actually in the far suburbs of Isfahan and seemed to think he knew the direction. I probably should have followed him so maybe this was mistake number three. But we saw a sign and decided to trust it. It pointed to a dirt track leading off the road bed. That narrowed and deteriorated until it was more a donkey path than a road and I was bottoming out the BMW on rocks. Suddenly a dirt road reappeared, followed shortly by the return of a paved street.

The Shah Abbas hotel, named after a great 17th century emperor, was an incredible place, probably the most ornate commercial building I have ever been in. Virtually every inch of wall was covered in mosaics, scenes from the Arabian Nights. The hotel was built on the site of a 14th century caravanserai of the same name, doubtless a popular place at the time as Isfahan was a stop on the silk route by which goods were exchanged between Europe and Asia. The architect had preserved the traditional design by putting the rooms around the outside of a large foyer which in the old days would have protected the camels and their goods. The lobby area took the place of the gates and in the back was a chaikhane or teahouse complete with old-style hookah water pipes.

My mistakes extended the 275 mile journey from five hours to seven. After we checked in we looked to see who else was around. The others had already gone out so we went to Naqsh-e Jahan square a couple of blocks from the hotel. The square was actually a large rectangle with a grass field in the middle and two mosques situated on adjacent sides and the palace of Shah Abbas facing one of the mosques. The rest of the area was lined with shops, selling the usual wrangle of products, skillfully worked copper and brass, ornate tiles, jewelry and, of course, the Persian carpets for which Iran is justly famous. The square was enormous, too many shops for the time we had. After a couple of hours browsing it was getting dark and time to return to the hotel for dinner. Then we went to Joe Subic's room and had a couple of drinks before turning in.

Friday morning our group went on a guided bus tour. We stopped first at an old palace, back at the Naqsh-e Jahan square. I don't remember the name. It was in bad shape and there was not much to see except for remnants of a few murals and a massive but deteriorated carved wooden front porch. An Italian restoration team was at work there. Recent photos I have seen show they, or their successors, are doing a good job. Unfortunately, despite my best efforts to recall the name or find it on the Internet, I still do not know what it was called. Anyone interested can look up Naqsh-e Jahan square online and look for a building with a rectangular carved wooden front on the square. It may still have scaffolding as it did at the time of this writing. Next we went to an Armenian church in Julfa that had been founded around 1044. The church itself was an incredible piece of history although modest and plain in comparison with the city's more famous mosques. There was also a museum attached containing ancient bibles, works of art and even the front page from a newspaper proclaiming the founding of the Armenian republic following World War I. On our way out of town we stopped to admire some covered bridges from the 16th century. They were built of brick and interesting from an engineering standpoint because of the long brick arch spans that supported them.

The next stop was the shaking minarets. These were part of an old but otherwise nondescript mosque with twin minarets, one of which was said to shake in some strange manner. Unfortunately it was broken, perversely meaning it had stopped shaking, so there was nothing to see. More interesting was the Zoroastrian fire temple, built, as was the custom, at the top of a tall hill. Zoroaster, more commonly known as Zarathustra in the west, was a pre-Christian prophet who lived in the area now known as Iran and founded the religion that bears his name. Some adherents of the religion remained in Iran and would occasionally show up in the tourist visa section. Kathy Stafford was wearing heels and had a hard time making it up and down the steep path. There was not much at the top as the wooden buildings were ancient and had largely disintegrated. Nevertheless, the site was visibly older than anything else we saw in Isfahan. It was one of those places that, for reasons not easy to describe, inspire a feeling of great age, mystery and reverence.

That night we went to a party at the home of Dennis Wilson, the director of the Isfahan chapter of the Iran-America Society. He was an American married to an Iranian and had lived in Iran for many years. Our invitation was courtesy of Kate Koob, an officer of the International Communication Agency (ICA) who served as the country director of the Iran-America Society. She had come on the trip partly for business reasons. ICA -- a terrible acronym -- had been the US Information Service until Carter changed the name. Apparently there had been some trouble between the society and local Islamic hotheads and she wanted to assess the situation personally. For us it was an opportunity to talk to Iranians. Admittedly, these were westernized intellectuals, but in Tehran we rarely interacted socially with Iranians of any stripe. As I expected, there was a lot of discussion about the faults of the US in Iran and very little about the sad state to which Iran had fallen since the revolution.

The only guest I remember by name was Mike, an employee of Fluor Corporation. He was in the process of getting an immigrant visa and asked me to carry his papers back to the embassy. I did, but all that accomplished was to get them lost in the takeover. Nevertheless, Mike managed to make it here and now lives in Houston. We have been in touch on and off over the years.

The next morning we returned to the Naqsh-e Jahan square and visited the Shah mosque. Cora and Kathy were able to borrow chadors from a small stand near the entrance. Although Kathy's left too much leg exposed because of her height, no one said anything. We were well treated and permitted to take the customary tour. The mosque was phenomenal and well deserves its listing as a UNESCO world heritage site. I will readily admit I am no expert on mosques, having visited only a couple, but the range of color and detail of workmanship came close to another of the spectacular places I have had the good fortune to see, the Taj Mahal in India.

We returned to the hotel, picked up Mike's papers, some miniatures Birgit Jank, the Austrian diplomat and friend of Bob Anders, had purchased and asked us to transport for her (also lost in my safe following the takeover) as well as our things, and headed back to Tehran. Again, the trip was to prove an adventure. About an hour north of Isfahan the engine began to misfire and eventually it got so bad I had to pull off the road. After sitting for twenty minutes, I was able to restart the engine and cover an additional thirty miles before the cycle started again. My initial assumption was bad gas clogging the fuel injectors, or perhaps water in the gas, so I hoped topping up the tank would help. It didn't, at least not at first.

Our normal route would have taken us through Qom, hometown of Ayatollah Khomeini and a center of Islamic zealotry. Perhaps it was paranoia but I really did not want to break down there. We decided to take a longer route that took us to the west of the city. The car continued to act up although it seemed less frequently than before. It got dark. The road had a lot of truck traffic. I learned truck drivers the world over have one thing in common: the guy going sixty-two insists on passing the one doing sixty. I remember gripping the steering wheel, staring into the dark looking for trucks in my lane, all the while hoping the engine would not die at a point where we could not get safely off the road. When we finally entered Tehran it was from the south and on a road I did not know. We were able to make it home but the trip took about ten hours.

I never did learn what caused the misfiring. The car was normal on the commute to work the next morning. I presume whichever mullah ended up with it got it repaired, which is only fair considering what he paid for it. I sometimes wonder what would have happened if we had suffered a complete breakdown and been forced to find overnight accommodation somewhere outside Tehran. We would have missed the takeover, but would that have proven to be a blessing or not?

As I mentioned earlier, Henry Precht had come to Tehran, both to seek assurances regarding the protection of the embassy and to assess how things were in general. One day Henry took the four of us, Don Cooke, Rich Queen, Joe and me to the bazaar. It was my only visit. It was quite a place, open air but generally covered by large sections of roof. Some streets were uncovered, but the buildings along them had roofs. There were different sections dedicated to specific wares, everything from the Iranian version of Tupperware to fancy gold jewelry. The bazaris were influential businessmen, respected even by the ayatollah. Don Cooke, future economic officer in training, made it a personal goal to develop relationships with bazaris, and he did succeed to some extent. It is my recollection he brought at least one to a meeting with Henry and this person's views had a significant impact on Precht.

I am sure Henry met with many others, both in and out of the embassy. Regardless of source or cause, prior to leaving Henry indicated he now accepted Bazargan's government really wasn't running the country. How would Henry's new perspective have translated into policy, both in general terms and as regards the safety of embassy employees? Presumably Henry was now more skeptical of the assurances he had received from Bazargan and Yazdi, but he had no opportunity to do anything. He was heading back but had only reached London when the embassy was attacked. It is interesting to speculate whether anything would have changed had Henry made it back to Washington and had time to recommend policy changes. We will never know.

It is finally time to announce the winner of the Stan Laurel award for getting me into this "Nice Mess." Richard Masters, who asked me to volunteer for Tehran was always a long shot. Henry Precht was a serious contender if only because he had the smarts to anticipate the attack but failed to respond to his own intuition. Although I haven't mentioned it previously, I considered myself a candidate. I could have tried harder to convince Cora not to come, and it was her presence that caused me the greater share of worry during our time in hiding. I could name the influence peddlers who lobbied for the shah's admission, but they were not responsible for balancing the safety of the embassy against policy needs. So the winner has to be Jimmy Carter. He decided to admit the shah against his own better judgment. While a politician giving in to pressure is hardly new, like Henry he seems to have understood the rage his decision could trigger in Iran and its possible consequences for the embassy staff. Yet in the end, he did nothing to address the concern except send Henry to talk to Bazargan.

# Part III

How to Lose an Embassy

But

Find True Friends

# 7. Not an Ordinary Day

November 4, 1979 started off as a bad day. First, it was the equivalent of a Monday after a three day weekend and those are never fun. Second, the skies were gray and it actually looked like it might rain for the first time since my arrival four months earlier. Then I had a strange accident with the BMW which at least seemed to be running normally after the engine problems of the day before. Even though it was early, before 7:00am, it took us a good half hour to cover the approximately five miles from our apartment to the embassy. Apparently my driving was not aggressive enough because at the same instant cars to my left and right both swerved into the small space I permitted to appear in front of me. And both hit the sides of my front bumper with their rear fenders at virtually the same moment. Cora, sitting next to me, saw it coming and yelled stop. I did, but not in time. For once I was grateful for the overly large but ugly bumpers BMW put on its US models. We were only a few blocks from the American Embassy main gate and the rest of the trip was an uneventful crawl.

When we drove into the embassy compound I parked on the adjacent street rather than in the large (and largely empty since most Americans walked to work) parking lot a few hundred yards from the consulate office building. Cora gave me a hard time about not using the parking lot as if there was any chance the BMW could survive any time at all in Tehran without door dings or worse. Given what had happened a few minutes earlier her logic was impeccable. Nevertheless, old habits die hard and in honor of the beloved Datsun (now Nissan) 280Z I gave up before coming to Iran, I continued to look for the most protected parking spot. After parking I inspected the bumper; I could see no damage. Someone up there was looking out for me.

This day was pleasantly unusual for Cora and her colleagues in the tourist visa section. Chargé Laingen had closed the unit to protest the lack of security. Over the weekend the embassy outer walls were plastered with graffiti and posters proclaiming "Marg bar Carter" or "Marg bar USA." As I mentioned earlier, "marg bar" means "death to." While it did not take much to incite an anti-American demonstration or poster parade we assumed a specific reason for this one: the continuing anger at the admission of the shah to the US. While I would have a normal work day, Cora would catch up on paperwork rather than conduct her usual two hundred visa interviews. This meant the consulate's outer entrance area was free from the usual large crowds waiting for their opportunity to persuade the visa officer. Again, someone up there was looking out for me although as I walked to work I had no clue how important the lack of applicants would turn out to be.

Because it had been the club the consulate shared a courtyard with the co-op or commissary. As I wrote earlier, in the old days people could access the club and the co-op through another entrance without having to enter the compound officially and deal with the more stringent embassy security. As we walked from our car we came into the courtyard through an iron-grate gate with an electronic lock, the combination to which was known to all employees. This gate and the iron grillwork fence were a remnant from those days. The sidewalk then split with the co-op to the left and our building to the right. The consulate's bulletproof glass and steel door was controlled remotely by the Marine inside, Jim Lopez. He recognized us on camera and the door clicked open even before we reached for the buzzer.

The work day began with a minor crisis. Two employees were scheduled to leave Iran for vacation, our economic counselor, Andy Grossman, and a secretary, Lillian Johnson. The secretary was detained because she had been in country for over ninety days but the Iranians claimed she had not applied to the ministry of foreign affairs for a residence permit. Presumably someone in personnel had messed up, but we didn't know for sure. Massoud did not normally deal with employee-related issues, but as chief embassy fixer had gone to the airport to assist Lillian. The economic counselor had flown out after apparently pissing off the airport staff by trying to force the issue. Perhaps at one time, an American diplomat might have been able to intimidate low-level Iranian officials, but those days were over and this man had apparently made things worse. Still, in fairness to Andy, bluster was worth a try. The Iranian bureaucracy was barely functional so he could not assume our people were to blame. Massoud had taken Pouja with him. Perhaps one of them could deal with the ministry while the other attempted to devise alternate travel arrangements.

I was settling in with a cup of coffee and was not surprised to see one of my problem world travelers or WTs in State shorthand: Americans who roam the globe, usually with no visible means of support. Kim King, a burly twenty-seven year old with curly, light brown hair, had been in Iran for about nine months. He had lost his passport. Issuing him a replacement was not difficult but Iranian authorities were unwilling to grant an exit visa. They believed he had imported some dutiable possessions, a record of which would have been stamped into his original passport. For whatever reasons, the Iranians decided King had imported and then sold a stereo, camera, and perhaps even a car, so they wanted a fine equivalent to the duty and perhaps more, as much as $6,000. Knowing his date of entry would have helped him establish this was not true, but he said he could not remember. Massoud had been working the case with Iranian authorities. He was scheduled to escort King to the customs office in a further effort to resolve the issue. In the meantime we had contacted his family through the Department and asked them to wire money for a plane ticket home and other expenses.

A telegram from the Department had come over the weekend telling us that Kim's family had bought him the ticket, and as I discussed the remaining details with him and awaited Massoud's return, I became aware of a commotion in the outer office. Two employees from tourist visas had gone to a bakery to buy cookies and as they returned they saw there were demonstrators climbing over the main vehicle gate. Soon they were being chased, but luckily someone noticed and Don Cooke ran out to help them get through the outer gate into the courtyard as quickly as possible.

Our building was designed to withstand limited attack from inside or outside the compound. With just twelve Marines plus the gunnery sergeant in charge responsible for defending twenty-six acres and the mile of wall, it was clear we could never prevent a determined group from entering the compound and ultimately our buildings. The hope was to give ourselves time to destroy sensitive information and equipment and await rescue by local authorities. This strategy even had a name: passive defense. The idea was to hide behind layers of heavy locked doors and retreat as necessary, all the while shredding files. Though the Marines were armed they were under orders not to shoot except to prevent an attacker from killing someone. From the earliest days of diplomacy it has been the responsibility of the host government to defend foreign diplomats. As we were soon to learn, the Iranians were about to break precedent, big time. It was 10:30am.

Lopez hit the switch locking the door from the courtyard. He was in touch with the chancery and knew there were demonstrators roaming the compound. Overall, the chancery had more layers of defense than the consulate as our building did not store truly sensitive information and had no secret communications equipment. But the chancery was the primary target of the attackers because of the personnel and equipment located within, starting with the CIA station. If the embassy was a nest of spies, then the station was presumably a key target.

The CIA in Iran was an agency in transition. In many countries with which we have close relations the CIA station serves primarily a liaison role with most of its officers known to the local government and working with their host-country counterparts. That was probably no longer the case in Iran. My guess is the handful of CIA officers were desperately seeking to develop sources within the new power structure. We had gone from a situation where we had, or thought we had, intimate knowledge of what was happening in Iran to one where we had virtually no contacts and little real information about the new authorities. I was not privy to CIA reporting so can only speculate. But as this story makes clear, if the CIA did know more than State, they didn't tell anyone including the President of the United States.

We did not feel any immediate threat. We knew the building was sturdy. The windows in the office of the consul general, Dick Morefield, were floor to ceiling but bulletproof and behind masonry grillwork. And so far, the attackers seemed uninterested in us. Two questions dominated my thinking as we awaited developments: who were the attackers, and when would the rescuers arrive? I had little information so could only guess and hope. Others, both at the embassy and in Washington, had more information, but still not enough. I would soon have to make decisions based on what little I knew, and choices that seemed minor now would prove vexing later. In order to provide context for the path we collectively chose, I will give quick answers to both these questions, which necessarily include information we did not have at the time.

We had only the vaguest idea of the identity of the attackers. Initially we thought this was just another dial-a-demo that had gotten out of hand. As the protesters took over more of the compound and announced themselves to our security personnel they claimed to be students whose intent was to stage a high-profile sit-in to publicize their unhappiness with US hospitality to the shah. That fiction continued for many months as they later gave themselves the formal title of "students following the line of the Imam" (i.e. the instructions of Ayatollah Khomeini; imam was another Shia clerical title, but when someone said *the* imam, they meant Khomeini). All we knew that morning, and obviously of greatest importance at the time, was their stated intent to depart the compound once they attracted media attention and made their point.

Some, probably most, actually were students or former students, but their group had been infiltrated by a number of revolutionary guards. Revolutionary guards, pasdars, were a security force loyal to Khomeini. I described their origins earlier. Their purpose once in the compound was to take and hold the embassy and its personnel. But again, all we knew in those first hours was the demonstrators claimed to be students intent upon a short term occupation. A complete description of who the attackers were requires me to address the question of how to refer to them. The majority may actually have been students planning a sit-in. But whatever their motivation or previous occupation the one undeniable fact is that, as the takeover dragged on, the occupiers as a group used tactics such as beatings, isolation, sleep deprivation and threats of execution against their hostages. Those real students either took an active part in these actions or at a minimum cooperated passively with persons who were using such tactics. The captors deliberately terrorized their hostages even when doing so did not in any meaningful way further their broader goals. For this reason, I use the term terrorists when referring to the embassy occupiers. It makes more sense than students or militants, terms often used at the time. What is a militant? I never did understand why this word was so commonly used. We all know what a student is but the term has little to do with the needless suffering inflicted on the hostages, the full extent of which became known only after their release. I offer this explanation now so it will be clear why I use this emotion-laden word. I may occasionally use a different descriptor when context requires, but I do think in general terrorist is not too strong.

As for when rescuers might arrive, I think most of us assumed it would take some time, but measured in hours rather than days or months. Iran was still in a state of chaos. We understood decisions were not made quickly and usually took much longer to implement. On the other hand, when the embassy had been taken over before on St. Valentine's Day, the occupation was over within hours. Iranian authorities did come to our rescue. Although it required the intervention of Prime Minister Bazargan and a visit to the compound by Ibrahim Yazdi who was both deputy prime minister and foreign minister, the attackers were removed. Still, much had changed in Tehran since February. My belief now is the Department did not fully understand the differences between the situation in February and in November. Yazdi had lost much of his influence. The group that attacked us then was Marxist. They were tolerated by the Islamists under the old rule, the enemy of my enemy is my friend, but after the shah fled, their success would not have been well received within Khomeini's circle. Could we expect the same response to this group of attackers? What I can say with certainty is, rightly or wrongly, we in Tehran, and many in Washington, considered this attack would follow the same pattern as St. Valentine's Day.

While we fully expected to be rescued, a third question lurked in the back of my mind and certainly that of others. How we would be treated by the attackers if they got to us before help came? Many of the local employees had been through the February takeover and did not look forward to a repeat. As the morning progressed some of them whispered they were afraid because people had been killed and wounded during the February occupation.

I had earlier mentioned the different versions of the St. Valentine's events that were circulating in Washington. This was the first time I heard our local employees discuss their recollections. It was not the time for us to hear information contradicting the idea the first takeover was peaceful. Even now I have no explanation for why I was so wrong about the February attack. Perhaps I had been persuaded by the positive spin some in the Department were selling, focusing on the speed of the rescue rather than the brutality and violence of the attack. I know Bob Anders likewise believed the earlier attack was peaceful even though he recalls the chancery still smelled of teargas when he arrived on April 2, 1979.[1] In the end, I am not sure it matters because of the initially unappreciated but ultimately decisive differences between the St. Valentine's Day takeover and what we experienced on the morning of November 4. Even in hindsight, it is not clear a better sense of the changed realities would have enabled us to respond in a way that would have made a significant difference in the final outcome. Decisions made over the months since the departure of the shah created the situation we faced that morning. But the precedent of the St. Valentine's Day occupation and its rapid resolution certainly did color how my colleagues and I viewed those first hours and days and did affect our decisions.

The design of the building limited our information sources to the Marine's radio and the telephone. Despite their large size, Morefield's windows did not give us much of a view beyond the courtyard we shared with the co-op. We saw the terrorists bash in its door with some steel bars. After that they occasionally entered or left the co-op, presumably impressed they had found so much valuable stuff. They seemed uninterested in our building. Lopez instructed all personnel to move upstairs and most gathered in our waiting area or in the back room where the American tourist visa officers had their work space. Kim King and I walked to the waiting area and joined the group sitting in the poorly lit waiting room my office shared with

---

1. Robert Anders, interview with the author, March 9, 2012.

immigrant visas next door. This was the room hit by the RPG so perhaps no one had thought to add extra light fixtures to make up for the loss of natural light from the now bricked-up window.

Chargé Laingen, in addition to closing the tourist visa unit, had gone to see the chief of protocol at the foreign ministry, taking along his deputy, Victor Tomseth, and the assistant security officer, Michael Howland. We knew from Lopez word had been passed to Laingen, and the chief of protocol was the Iranian official most immediately responsible for the security of foreign missions. So what better place for Laingen to be? The only question, or so we thought, was how quickly could the protocol head find someone with the authority to make a decision and mobilize a force to send to our rescue.

Around 11:00am my office received a telephone call from the Tehran police asking if we needed any help. This is not as odd as it sounds because my office number was widely known as it was routinely used by police officials when an American citizen was in trouble or causing trouble. I got on the line. The caller did not identify himself but spoke in English and indicated there were some reports of a demonstration at the embassy. I then passed the phone to Gary Lee, the embassy's general services officer responsible among many other things for the renovation of the consular building. He was there that morning inspecting the work of the painters he had assigned to refresh the paint on the cattle rails, something that could not normally be done on a workday. Gary was considerably senior to me (who wasn't?) and happened to be close by so I didn't have to ask the caller to wait. I figured he would know better what to say. Gary told the man in clear language we were under attack by what appeared to be a large number of unknown persons and, yes, we needed help immediately. Although we did not know which office the caller represented we doubted he was in a position to send help. Still, temporarily at least, the call fueled hope we might be able to hang on long enough to be rescued.

During this time Lopez was receiving information from the Marines at the chancery and from Howland at the foreign ministry. We were not told much about goings on at either location. At around 11:15, Lopez informed us, when directed, we were going to leave our building and march in-line to the chancery. Because of who and what it housed, the chancery was theoretically better fortified than the consulate. Presumably this was the logic behind the proposal to move us. We did not know the senior security officer, Al Golacinski, had already been in and out of the chancery trying to calm the attackers. In fairness to Al he had on several previous occasions dealt with demonstrators in various situations. To this point he had moved freely around the compound and assumed he would be able to escort us over. I am pretty sure he had talked with some of the self-described students, been presented with the "sit in" scenario and therefore concluded it would be safe to move us.

Based on grumbling and mumbled comments, I suspect most shared my view it was the dumbest idea we'd ever heard. I am not sure we would have liked it better had we known about Al's walk-abouts. So far we had been left alone. Our building was new and theoretically designed for the possibility of just the kind of incident we were experiencing. We were told to expect harassment and allow our briefcases and purses to be searched if a demand was made. But exposing ourselves needlessly to a hostile crowd seemed pointless. Nor did I understand how we were supposed to enter the chancery without bringing the terrorists along with us, compromising those layers of locked doors at the core of the passive defense strategy I mentioned earlier. Maybe our bosses figured there was some benefit to all of us in one place, peas in a pod. I concluded this was an example of the St. Valentine's Day paradigm at work.

Just then our confidence in the building's security was shaken. I will be the first to admit bulletproof glass is generally not a top priority in bathroom design, but in this case it would have helped. There were men's and women's restrooms on the second floor; the windows in them were large enough for someone to climb through but they were not protected. The terrorists realized the vulnerability. We heard a loud crash and the sound of glass breaking in one of the toilets. Lopez ran up the stairs from the first floor. Gary Lee was behind him carrying a shotgun. Lopez went into the room and saw someone climbing a ladder placed against the wall near the broken pane. The intruder nearly reached the top, but when he saw Lopez holding a tear gas canister, he backed down the ladder. Lopez pushed the ladder away and as he had already pulled the pin on the grenade, he dropped it out the window.[2] Richard Queen and I collected coat hangers and looped them over the door handles between the men's and women's restrooms. Fortunately the doors opened in and were hinged on opposite sides. There was a strong pillar between them. Still, the hanger wire would not stop a determined assault. As we could see from Morefield's office, however, the grenade seemed to have an effect. The terrorists went away and we experienced no further attacks.

Unfortunately, according to a State after-action analysis, this incident may have been indirectly responsible for the takeover of the chancery. After Lopez reported there was a group of people in the courtyard, Golacinski decided to head over to see if he could help us. By the time he arrived at the outer courtyard the gas grenade had done its job and the crowd had dispersed. While he walked back to the chancery, Al was grabbed by one of the pasdars mixed in among the students. Apparently he knew the man from previous encounters so realized he wasn't one of the students with whom he had been talking up to that point. The man took a pistol from an Iranian police officer who offered no resistance. I would guess the policeman had been part of our Iranian security force, which would have been too small to stop the attack even if they had wanted to. For whatever reason rather than run off he entered the compound, perhaps even out of a sense of duty and with the hope he could help. We will never know, but it would appear by this time he saw how things were going and chose to surrender his weapon. The pasdar then used it to compel Al to return to the chancery. He then began to threaten to shoot Golacinski unless the Marines opened the door to the chancery second floor.[3]

Aside from the question whether Al made a mistake, there were a number of other Americans whose offices were not in the chancery and who were probably prisoners of the terrorists. They were being held with a much larger group of local employees, perhaps in the custody of the real students who were still not prepared to threaten their lives. It makes sense to believe, however, that sooner or later

2. James Lopez cited in Tim Wells, 444 Days (New York, Harcourt, Brace, Jovanovich, 1985), 51-2

3. "Seizure of US Embassy, Tehran," Case study prepared by the Office of Security Hostage Debriefing Team, in possession of the author (undated)

the pasdars in the group would learn about these other Americans and use them as they had Al.

Shortly thereafter the power was cut off. Because Tehran city power was unreliable, the compound had its own generating station which ran around the clock. The action was probably not directed at us. Nevertheless, the lack of natural light within our building gave it an immediate impact. Other than Morefield's the only window upstairs was the slit in my office. It did provide a little light and a few people had flashlights or candles, but for the most part we huddled in the area where some trace of natural light escaped from Morefield's office. The level of tension increased rapidly. Bob and I, as well as others, heard footsteps on the roof and some said they smelled smoke. I could not testify to the smoke, but about this time we were once again told to prepare to march to the chancery.

My view of this plan had not changed since its first mention. Shortly after the second announcement I suspect Lopez received bad news over the radio. Golacinski was a hostage and the chancery had been penetrated. There was no more talk of moving us there.

I am not sure how much Morefield knew of these developments, but he decided, presumably with Laingen's advice and concurrence that it was time to abandon the consulate. We were told to secure our files and lock our safes. Then we had to destroy the visa plates. In the days before computer generated visas State used intricately designed dies and special inks which stamped a difficult to forge design into successful tourist visa applicants' passports. These dies were custom made for Tehran. Destroying them meant no tourist visas would be issued for a few months. Again, with St. Valentine's in mind Morefield did this reluctantly. On the other hand, Rich Queen and Don Cooke, who brought the plates up from downstairs, watched as Lopez smashed the plates with an iron bar and enjoyed every minute of it. If tourist visas were the only currency of interest to the Iranian government their failure to protect us had just resulted in a big loss on their investment.

I had earlier asked Morefield's permission to destroy some of my files. Although nothing particularly sensitive was allowed in our building, I did have files with names of Iranians who had helped us deal with consular problems. My concern was the terrorists might ignorantly consider anyone whose name appeared favorably as an informer or worse. Dick's response was snappy; my life was more important than some files. I certainly agreed, but at the earlier point it was not an either/or proposition. We could have destroyed the relatively few sensitive files in the time we were sitting around.

I now believe this was another case of the St. Valentine's under-reaction. The fact I did not disobey this particular order remains one of my few regrets from those days. I should note in Morefield's defense the safe in my office was a 900 pound Mosler. It would take one of our security specialists several hours to drill it open. The only people who knew the combination were in the building, although a paper record was kept somewhere by the security office. So we really did not think the attackers would have the opportunity to get into the safe. There was also the undeniable fact if we did destroy files, we would lose irreplaceable information. When it came time to get the office running again we could find ourselves missing important data.

I was no more immune from the St. Valentine's Day paradigm than Dick, and it influenced my actions as we prepared to leave. I took some personal items from my safe including Cora's and my passports. I needed money and was planning to visit the cashier at the chancery later that day, so already had my checkbook in my briefcase. If I'd realized this was a final departure, I would have cleaned out the official cash in the office register. No point in leaving it for the terrorists and it would come in handy if we were going to have to fend for ourselves for any length of time. But as it was, I expected to be back in the office tomorrow and removing the official cash would have left me with a lot of explaining to do. So I left with virtually no money in my wallet and ended up worrying about my penniless condition many times over the coming months.

Now that the decision was made to leave, we were told to break up into small groups and head to the British embassy on Ferdosi Avenue. The local employees were given the option of simply going home. We had a standing mutual assistance agreement with the British; presumably Laingen telephoned them and explained our situation. Each group was to be a mix of Americans and Iranians and include someone who knew the route. In normal times it would probably take twenty minutes to reach the British, but we knew the most direct route, south across Taleqani Avenue and then west, was not an option because we would have to cross the area from which the attack had originated.

Lopez tore the red striping off his blue uniform trousers and borrowed an old jacket from Ismail the janitor. He hoped this would make him less obviously a US Marine. He grabbed a ladder that stood in the corner and popped up a ceiling tile, then stashed his weapons and equipment in the false ceiling. We each gathered our belongings. It had started to rain. I had no raincoat or umbrella.

The far more important problem was we had no way to learn what, or more exactly, who, might be waiting for us on Kuche Bismetri. Bismetri ran west to east starting from our compound's western wall. The section of the kuche immediately adjacent to the consulate was wide; hundreds of visa applicants gathered there daily. Although my office window overlooked it, the thickness of the glass and its narrow width created extreme distortion. We needed to be able to see sharply right and down in the direction of the door, and it just wasn't possible.

The embassy compound was shaped like a backward "L", with the top of the letter facing north. Our building was situated in the crook with the applicant entrance door also facing north. Opposite the door was the large military compound. Its high walls extended north and west for several blocks. The motor pool, where the terrorists climbed and then opened the gate was due south at the bottom of the backward "L" or, put otherwise, the very southwest corner of the compound. We had no clue how big the demonstration that spawned the attack was or how far north along Kuche Amrika, the street to our immediate west, it extended. To the extent I could see through my window, I was able to confirm only that there was no mass of people on the side of the street near the military compound wall. We simply did not know what awaited us.

As we moved into position in the tourist visa waiting area we had to be careful to avoid the fresh paint on the cattle railings. Lee and Lopez unlocked the roll shutter and cranked it up. Lopez opened the electric inner door which on normal days he would use to control the pace at which visa applicants were allowed to enter.

Queen went outside. Rich was not the best Farsi speaker, but he had no fear of trying and made a practice of chatting up police officers in particular. He got to know a bit about their families and made sure to ask how they were doing. This habit came in handy because he recognized the senior of the policemen outside the door. Queen was not sure whether they were real police or pasdars wearing police uniforms, but Rich told him we were going to leave the building and he voiced no objection.[4] Rich reported back to Morefield and the exodus began.

Although we were supposed to go in groups with gaps of a few minutes in between, we looked much more like a continuous stream. Most of the Iranians went first, especially those who were not employees. Whether these policemen were real cops or revolutionary guards they were apparently ignorant of the plan to seize the embassy, not surprising I suppose as it would have been closely held among a relatively small group of conspirators. They glanced at ID cards but as far as I could tell were not making a record of names. Some people were lightly searched. When it came our turn, they looked in my briefcase and Cora's purse, but otherwise there was no trouble. Still, the process left me annoyed and uncomfortable. While I did not expect several policemen to stop the takeover of the embassy, as supposed representatives of the Iranian government their job was to protect us. They were not doing that. Still, I realized we were extremely lucky these men were not part of the plan to seize embassy staff. That they searched us indicated an uncertainty about what they should do. While their natural sympathies were probably with the attackers they let us go because they didn't yet know fully what was happening in the compound or what the authorities would ultimately do.

We were near the end of the procession, but delayed long enough to create some separation and form a defined group consisting of the Staffords, Kim King, Cora and myself, a couple of local staff from the immigrant visa section and Mariya, one of the tourist visa locals who became our guide. We also had another American with us named Lorraine. She was one of Anders' clients, interested in getting an immigrant visa for her Iranian husband. At the time we

---

4. Queen, Inside and Out, 49

left, Morefield, Queen, Lee, Lopez, Cooke and Anders were still in the consulate. Bob Ode, a retiree who was covering for Cy Richardson during his vacation, was right in front of us escorting an elderly blind Iranian to a car where his driver waited.

We turned left out the door and started to follow Kuche Bismetri. It ran parallel to the major road, Taleqani, which is where the embassy main gate was located and, as I mentioned earlier, the site of the massive demonstration. We were momentarily exposed as we passed Kuche Amrika, but fortunately the block was long enough none of the demonstrators noted our quick passing. Furthermore, there was an unusual volume of vehicle traffic on the kuche probably because the demonstration was making Taleqani impassable. In an act both brave and possibly another instance of St. Valentine's under-reaction, Ode turned left onto Kuche Amrika, toward the old man's car (I assumed he would join the Morefield group after dropping the man at his vehicle). That set him moving straight toward the demonstration while we continued west for three or four blocks, dodging cars as we went. Mariya was leading us by the most direct available route to the British embassy.

Mariya was first, followed by the Staffords with Cora sharing Kathy's umbrella. Since the tourist visa unit was closed to the public, Cora was dressed casually. Loose-fitting pants were still acceptable for women so she wore pants with a blouse and jacket. Kathy was 5'11", Cora only 5'2", so they made an odd couple. I noted Joe had on his favorite silver-gray herringbone blazer so at least I wasn't the only one looking over-dressed for a stroll in the rain. I was at the rear with Lorraine and Kim. Within a block or so Bob Anders caught up and joined us. He indicated the rest of the Americans had left the building.

Bob now says he and Dick Morefield were the last two to leave the consulate, after making sure everyone was out. This makes sense as they were the two most senior people. When they left the building Bob decided to catch up to our group while Dick said he would take the other group by a different route. It was Bob's impression the Morefield group did intend to go to the British embassy, but by a less direct route.[5]

---

5. Robert Anders, interview with the author, November 12, 2011

According to Rich Queen and Gary Lee Morefield may have subsequently decided it made more sense for the group to go to his house.[6] Regardless of their ultimate destination, however, they started out heading north while we went west. Walking north on Kuche Dahmetri would soon bring the group to the intersection with Kuche Bijan, which ran to the east along the north wall of our compound. Not far from the corner was the back pedestrian gate and nearby the Marine House. In hindsight it seems likely the area was already under the control of the terrorists and walking right past it a dangerous thing to do. Having over the years read a number of conflicting interviews with members of the Morefield group, it remains unclear to me who spotted them first, where and when they were detained and by whom, but all accounts agree they did not get far. I knew none of this at the time and expected them to be behind us before long.

We still had the large military compound to our north so at the first opportunity Mariya headed south, probably on Mousavi and then west again. I assumed we were going to follow orders and go to the British Embassy, but Bob suggested he might drop off and head to his apartment, only a few blocks away. I asked him to stick with us. Maybe it was my turn to adopt the peas in a pod mentality, but it seemed to me we didn't want people scattered all over town and at this point I was still under the impression Morefield and the others were close on our heels. In hindsight, my pressuring Bob to stay with us was a key turning point, because if he had peeled off we would shortly have been left with nowhere to go. We came to Iranshahr and turned south as the next north-south road was already Ferdosi. It was a big street and it seemed to make sense to keep to the smaller ones. We did have to cross Taleqani, but we were now three blocks west of the embassy gate and figured we had no choice but to cross sooner or later.

After we had gone south another block, the rain had lessened and Mariya and Cora were walking arm in arm about half a block ahead. Kathy and Joe were walking together under Kathy's umbrella. All of a sudden Mariya wheeled Cora around 180 degrees and they turned

---

6. Gary Lee cited in Wells, 444 Days, 75-6

back in our direction. Cora wasn't sure what had happened, but Mariya found us a spot to talk in an alley off the street. She said they had gone far enough ahead for her to see there was a large demonstration in Ferdosi Square, between us and the British embassy. While we could take a circular route and approach the British compound from the south, there was no way to know whether the entrance to the embassy itself was clear. We agreed going there was too risky. She offered to take us to her mother's home but we declined as we did not want to endanger her. Kim King wanted to leave so I gave him Massoud's home number and we wished each other luck. King was planning to pick up his ticket at Pan Am and take his new passport to customs and push for the exit visa. As Kim took off, Bob Anders once again suggested maybe he would just go home, but this time offered to take the rest of us with him. He made the offer even more tempting by promising some of the chicken curry in his freezer. It was past lunch time. His apartment was only a few blocks away. Trying to reach the British embassy was dangerous and heading to his place sounded wise. We said goodbye to Mariya, thanking her for being our guide as well as for the offer to take us in.

Bob's apartment was several blocks north, so we turned back up Iranshahr. We passed a policeman who appeared to be guarding a bank. He must have been there before as we had walked past this spot a few minutes previously, but I hadn't noticed him or the bank building. I tried not to look at him or his pistol, but he was studying us. I felt his eyes on my back. It was all the more reason to get off the street as soon as possible. Cora also felt people staring at us. Unfortunately, the most direct route to Bob's apartment, west toward Villa Avenue and then north until we reached his street, Kuche Salm, would take us right past a komiteh headquarters. So we took a circuitous route that brought us to Bob's street but just north of the komiteh office. Bob pointed out where it was located and suggested we cross the street one at a time. He peered around the corner to make sure no one was paying attention, to minimize the chance of being seen, and walked rapidly across the street. Bob led so he could open the apartment door. Then one by one we followed. None of us thought we'd been spotted.

After Bob closed and bolted the door, we dried ourselves off as best we could. Bob changed clothes completely. He gave me a bright yellow sweater. I took off my suit jacket and tie as well as my damp shirt and put the sweater on over my t-shirt. It was scratchy but warm. The women were reasonably dry thanks to their umbrellas. All of us had wet shoes. I don't recall whether Bob was able to find anything for Joe who was quite a bit shorter and smaller. Bob then offered drinks to everyone. Although it was a bit early in the day I think we all accepted. Bob busied himself locating and warming the curry and someone else found the radio. Every employee had been issued a "lunchbox" radio, a two-channel Motorola about the size of a construction worker's lunchbox which served as the backbone of our "E and E" network. I could never remember whether this stood for emergency evacuation or escape and evasion, perhaps because the Army taught me the second version but the first sounded more like State. It operated on the same frequencies as the smaller hand-held radios used by the Marines and our security officers. It was intended to insure embassy employees did not have to trust the potentially unreliable telephone system in the event of crisis. We switched it on. Unfortunately, the language was increasingly Farsi. But we were off the street, out of the rain, and to one degree or another, still thinking in terms of the St. Valentine's scenario. If we could just stay free for a day, two at most, everything should be okay. For the third time that day, I had the feeling someone was looking out for me. Over the next weeks and months, it happened many times.

# 8. Telephone Tribulations

After the tasty chicken curry lunch, a couple of drinks and the opportunity to dry off, our attention turned to other matters. Lorraine, the American woman who had come to see Bob about an immigrant visa for her Iranian husband, was worried he would learn about the embassy takeover and knowing she was supposed to be there come looking for her. So she asked to use Bob's phone. She could not reach her husband but did contact several of his relatives and asked them to pass a message. Bob started out calling Birgit Jank, the Austrian diplomat whose miniatures were still locked in my safe. He needed a good inside direct number for the British embassy and she was able to provide it. We were hoping for confirmation our comrades had somehow managed to evade the demonstration, but learned only one person had arrived, a local employee. Later we discovered it was one of Bob's people, the guy with the handle-bar moustache whose specialty I earlier described as maintaining a low profile. Apparently he really was an expert at it.

Bob also tried Dick Morefield's house, which had been discussed as an alternate meeting point. It also seemed a likely place for the rest of our group to have gone, as they too would have encountered the demonstration in front of the British embassy. But there was no answer. He then tried Gary Lee's penthouse at the Ardalan apartments. This time we got an answer, but it turned out to be Lillian Johnson, the secretary who had been scheduled to leave on vacation that morning. She had gone there to wait for her exit visa, but given developments since it was unlikely Massoud could help. Bob gave her a quick update on our situation but she had nothing to tell us about the other group. Although several of them lived at the Ardalan apartments no one had turned up.

Not long after we got a call from Kate Koob at the Iran-America Society. It was housed in a separate building several miles from the embassy. Kate was the director of the society while Bill Royer was both her assistant and head of English language teaching, one of the more popular programs available at the society. They were maintaining an open line to the State Department, normal practice in a crisis. She asked whether we had any messages to pass to DC. I don't think any of us did except to ask our families be informed we were so far okay.

I busied myself with Bob's radios. In addition to the Motorola Bob had a shortwave so I was able to get some news broadcasts. There was not much information. The announcer said there were reports the American embassy had been attacked and the US government was seeking "clarification" of the situation as well as assurances from the Iranian government all necessary assistance would be provided to us. It was about what I would have expected. Washington knew pretty well what had happened, thanks to Kate, but did not know how to respond. To some degree this once again reflected the St. Valentine's mindset. We had to recognize the leadership situation in Iran was chaotic and it would take some hours for the government to come together on a plan to remove the terrorists.

The embassy radio was more and more dominated by Farsi-speaking voices. I did not try very hard to understand what was being said as it really didn't matter. Instead, I focused on being ready to track the occasional American voice. We could hear Mike Howland at the foreign ministry talking to Charlie Jones, one of the communications officers apparently still locked within the communications vault. He was talking to Howland but also it seemed to people back in Washington. We learned later he was simultaneously transmitting on a longer range radio that was being picked up by the embassy in Kuwait and relayed to Washington. Of particular interest was an unidentified American voice using the code name "Palm Tree." Somewhere there was a list of all the radio call names, but I couldn't find it and Bob didn't seem to know where it might be. It was not clear to me to whom Palm Tree was talking. I guessed to Mike Howland, but it seemed more he was just reporting what he was seeing. I concluded he must be somewhere off compound but near enough to observe part of what was happening.

About 4:00pm, Charlie said there was smoke coming in under the vault door and he had completed destruction of all he could. Then he said,

"We're coming out."

After that, there was only Farsi on the radio. Even Palm Tree had gone silent. I tried channel two, but aside from a little Farsi from time to time, it seemed unused. The embassy was gone. The chargé and his two aides were at the foreign ministry. Lillian was still stuck at the Ardalan apartments. Kate Koob and Bill Royer were at the Iran-America Society. And then there was our group. We still did not know about Morefield and those with him, but after five hours without contact we strongly suspected they had been captured. Had they gone to any embassy house, they would have access to a radio and would almost certainly have reported to the chargé. The fact they didn't very likely meant they couldn't.

As the afternoon passed, Lorraine was becoming increasingly concerned by her inability to reach her husband. Apparently he was a bit of a hothead and she was worried he would try to break into the compound looking for her and get himself into trouble with the terrorists. It may also have had to do with his political leanings. We learned in the spring of 1980 he had been executed for counter-revolutionary activity. Lorraine contacted us at that time because she wanted to make sure we did not use her last name in any press statements. She started again calling various relatives. All of a sudden Bob's phone went dead. This happened just after she said she was with a group of Americans. In normal times a telephone going dead would be considered a routine event. But it was widely known the shah's secret police had an extensive system for monitoring telephone conversations and was generally assumed the new regime had retained both the system and the technicians who ran it. While the secret police changed their acronym from SAVAK to SAVAMA, and some of the higher up thugs were executed and replaced by new thugs, other things had not changed. We had no way of knowing whether telephones of American diplomats were routinely tapped by the shah's government. If so, the network was now in the hands of the Khomeini's people. Still, we figured the embassy takeover was probably not coordinated with SAVAMA, so even if they were listening, the risk of these calls leading to us was small, at least in the short term.

Bob mentioned the telephone wiring in the building had recently been replaced, leading to a further discussion of whether that made the failure more or less suspicious. But we needed to communicate so Joe went upstairs and arranged to use a neighbor's phone. Bob from time to time went to the landlady's apartment and used her phone, but it soon became clear this made her very nervous. With a komiteh around the corner we did not want to risk creating a situation where someone would feel obliged to turn us in for self-protection.

The afternoon passed slowly. The embassy radio net was now all Farsi all the time. The shortwave news was the same old stuff over and over: the US government was seeking information and asking the Iranians to live up to their obligations under international law. With Bob's phone inoperative his apartment was clearly less attractive as a hiding place. There were still a few Americans on the loose and we needed to be able to talk to them. Furthermore, it was too close to the embassy and far too close to the local komiteh. Despite these disadvantages Bob wanted to remain there. After some discussion, it was agreed we and the Staffords would accept Kate Koob's invitation to move to the Iran-America Society and help staff the phone line. Around 6:00pm Joe made another trek upstairs and called Kate. She would send her driver over later that evening to pick us up.

Around 7:00pm Lorraine's husband appeared. He had gotten the message, though apparently it took a while to track him down in that pre-cell phone era. For the second time that day an Iranian offered to risk themselves for us, as Lorraine and her husband suggested we should all go with them. We declined, both because we had a plan in place to go to the Iran-America Society and because we did not want to impose. And again, tiring as it is becoming to repeat, we were still operating under the St. Valentine's premise this was a short-term problem. Ten minutes after they left, Lorraine and her husband returned with some chelo kabab, Iranian barbecued lamb with rice, a popular take-out item. Several subtle hints such as "I'm hungry" and "It's time to eat" had triggered no response from Bob so Lorraine may have assumed Bob didn't have anything left to offer. Regardless of the condition of Bob's pantry the chelo kabab was very welcome and we thanked them profusely for their thoughtfulness. We never saw either one again, although, as I mentioned previously, Lorraine did call to ask we protect her identity in the months following our escape.

After we finished eating and cleaned up a bit, we sat around and used up more of Bob's liquor. The four of us heading to the Iran-America Society were careful to go slow because we knew we'd be on the street in a couple of hours. Getting stopped at a roadblock was always possible and smelling of alcohol was a guarantee of serious trouble even aside from the day's events. The conversation was desultory. We were emotionally exhausted more than physically tired, but in the end there was really nothing left to say. We listened to the shortwave and kept the Motorola on in the background, but all the voices continued to be Iranian. Bob and I talked briefly about possible future scenarios. Since his phone was not working there was no guarantee we'd be able to reach him through the landlady or a neighbor. Or, if the outage was due to poor workmanship during the repair he'd mentioned, their phones might also fail. So we agreed he should keep the lunchbox radio set to channel two and we would try to reach him that way if we couldn't call.

Around 11:00pm the driver from the Iran-America Society knocked at the door. We grabbed our things and stepped into the street; immediately we felt naked and exposed. Then I saw the car and had to stifle at laugh. It was a Citroen Deux Chevaux which was locally manufactured in Iran under license and known as the Jian (pronounced zha-yen). As may be clear from the loving description of my former BMW, I am a car enthusiast and this particular vehicle falls into a category all its own. With a 28 horsepower, two-cylinder engine, it was hardly capable of winning races. On the other hand, though, many automotive engineers considered it a brilliantly designed vehicle for its purpose, a French Beetle. For our needs it was ideal because it was ubiquitous on Iranian streets. The one concern was space. Although it had four doors, it was a tight fit for four Americans so it turned out Bob's decision to remain behind was wise. The alternative would have been a second trip, another risk at that hour of the night.

We survived the two mile drive to the Iran-America Society without incident. I assumed the driver was well versed in avoiding roadblocks. We were greeted enthusiastically by Kate Koob and Bill Royer with hugs all around. Kate we knew better as our paths had crossed occasionally during language studies and she had been in Isfahan with us the past weekend. Bill was a relative old timer as I recall, having been in Iran for a year or so. The Iran-America Society was untouched during the St. Valentine's takeover. Perhaps for that reason, the International Communications Agency did not consider it necessary to transfer Bill out.

Kate gave us a quick tour of the building as despite several invitations we had not yet had an opportunity to see it. Kate thought it important to keep her operation as separate as possible from the embassy. Although the majority of the funding came from the US government the focus was on cross-cultural understanding not politics, and Kate had hoped to keep that focus despite the fundamental changes affecting the political situation. Even in the absence of the embassy takeover and its aftermath, I am skeptical the Ayatollah Khomeini would have seen much value in an institution whose purpose included the propagation of western values such as democracy and equal rights for women.

Kate and Bill went to nap on couches in the reception area. The tour had included a small kitchen where I located coffee and a machine to make it. Between that and our gradually fading adrenaline the four of us were able to stay awake until Kate and Bill returned from their naps about 5:00am. During our five hours of telephone time we took turns talking to various people we didn't know. Presumably they were among the staff of the operations center, State's 24/7 nerve center that monitors events all over the world and notifies senior officials when something important happens. While I did not know the names of all the big shots yet, I knew those directly involved with Iranian affairs and they were not among those with whom we spoke. And no one identified himself to me as an assistant secretary or even deputy assistant secretary. That was fine, because we really had no important information to pass on. The radio link via the embassy in Kuwait had permitted State to monitor some aspects of the takeover of the compound as they happened. Furthermore, at this time Bruce Laingen was still allowed to call from the foreign ministry. Clearly, no one was better placed than he to tell Washington what the Iranian government was likely to do. We were asked multiple times to describe all the day's events in as much detail as we could remember, to the point it became annoying. How many times did we have to repeat the same information to an op center staffer? We did talk about the specific events in the consulate building as well as our suspicion the other consulate Americans had somehow been captured, but all in all it began to seem pointless. Still, we knew this was standard operating procedure, to keep an open phone line as long as possible. In part it was based on a belief that when dealing with third world phone systems there was no guarantee a connection, once cut off, could be re-established.

At some point during these hours Joe decided to call the embassy. He asked to speak with any of the Americans and was told they were not available. Using his excellent Farsi he tried to engage the man who answered in conversation, asking how the hostages were being treated and similar questions. The man was willing to talk for a while. He told Joe the hostages had been fed and were now sleeping. So far, okay. But when Joe was asked who he was, he gave his real name. I did not have a big problem with the idea of calling the embassy. After all, the terrorists would not know where the call was coming from; it could potentially have come from outside Iran and for all I know State itself may have called more than once trying to establish a dialog with the captors.

Joe's decision to give his name caught me off guard. At the time I thought it was careless and unnecessary. I still do, but it may be better considered yet another example of the St. Valentine's mindset. At this stage it had not occurred to us the people holding the embassy staff might soon have the means to send search teams out for us. Also, in Joe's defense, he and the other visa officers were minor celebrities in town. Their names were well enough known the terrorists had probably already figured out they didn't have all the visa crew. What Joe did not know was other people in the consulate, Rich Queen and Don Cooke in particular, had been interrogated about our whereabouts. They tried to protect us by insisting we were out of the country on leave. I don't know whether the terrorist made a record of the name or passed it on to anyone, but Joe giving his real name could have been a problem. Joe had no way of knowing about the interrogation and neither Don nor Rich ever said anything to indicate they were punished for attempting to protect us.

So we did our duty continuing to take turns until Kate and Bill awoke. Bill took over the phone and we sat down with Kate to talk about what to do next. During the night those of us not on the phone or dozing had discussed our options. We agreed our best move was to relocate to Joe and Kathy's apartment. It was on a little street called Ziba, near where the street ended. That section of the neighborhood was surrounded by two major arterials forming a "V" and Ziba ended near the bottom of the "V". There was no direct vehicle access to the arterials which made the area quiet and relatively isolated considering it was in the middle of a big city. The apartment itself was better suited than ours because it was on the ground floor and had direct access to the street. Our apartment, besides being on the first floor and at the end of a hallway, had the uncooperative landlady. More people would potentially see us enter and sooner or later we might have to leave, again exposing ourselves to the other tenants, all of whom knew we were with the American embassy.

Kate agreed to have her driver take us. We asked what her plans were. She said she and Bill intended to remain on the phone. We asked them to come with us, but she declined. She said she hoped the people who had taken over the embassy would not consider the Iran-America Society as part of the official US government presence. And keeping it operating normally would underscore the point. I remember thinking that was probably naive as well as brave, but again, as with Joe giving his name, I now also credit the St. Valentine's precedent. Had Kate and Bill realized this situation was far worse than the earlier takeover they would probably have decided differently. But the previous experience indicated the Iran-America Society would be left alone and the whole incident would probably be over by the end of the new day. In any case the car could only take the four of us, and perhaps Kate and Bill would rethink their situation as the day progressed. I am not sure what options they considered and when, but they were hostages by evening. Later, when all the hostages were home and we had a little time to talk about that day and its aftermath, Kate mentioned the terrorists later presented her with a bill for the equivalent of $6,000 for the cost of the open line to Washington. Sometimes, all you can do is laugh.

129

At 5:00am it was still dark, but it was probably the best time to travel because the roadblocks were generally gone and traffic was still light. Nevertheless, I again felt naked and exposed. Unfortunately, this feeling would come over me whenever I was outside. My dirty blonde hair and light complexion made clear I was not Iranian. There were still foreigners around the city, but far fewer than before.

We decided to make a side trip to our apartment to collect clothes and food. The drive was uneventful until we reached Shahid Malekinasab as the street is now known. Perhaps the name was the same, but even in the first months of the revolution changing street names was common. Who knows what has happened since then. In any case, our apartment was on Majidi, a street that still exists under the same name. It is only two blocks long then dead ends into a highway. Unfortunately, there were two komiteh types warming their hands around a fire in an oil drum, on Shahid Malekinasab, literally right before the corner where we had to turn. The fire gave off a very yellow light, painting the men and the surrounding area in a hellish glow. Thankfully, they ignored us completely. Perhaps the pedestrian look of the Jian indicated no one of any interest was inside. Fortunately the society was not required to register its cars through the embassy so we did not have US diplomatic license plates. Our apartment was on the second block not far from the end of the street, so at least we were a little distance from the corner.

During the last few minutes before we arrived, I had been inspecting my keys. There was one for the gate and two more for our apartment door. All three looked virtually the same. They were European style keys, a little smaller than ours and with finer teeth, so telling them apart was not easy. We had not lived there long and in normal times it was not a problem. But I did not want us standing on the sidewalk, particularly because if the two komiteh men by the oil drum decided to venture away from their nice warm barrel they could see us reasonably well from a block and a half away. If they were neighborhood regulars, they might even have been aware an embassy couple lived in the building. The license plates on the BMW certainly made it easy.

The driver pulled up in front of our building. I chose a key and prayed. I heard the reassuring click and we entered the small courtyard area and then took the steps to our right to the first floor. Joe and Kathy cleaned out the kitchen. We had ten pounds of fillet mignon in the freezer (the co-op was having a sale) and Massoud had managed to procure some eggs which were in short supply. Cora and I grabbed our overnight bags, still partially packed from the weekend trip. I dumped out the dirty stuff, grabbed some clean socks and underwear, a pair of slacks and my two favorite Dior cotton shirts, a bargain find at Burlington Coat Factory, plus a pair of Hush Puppies. Cora took an equivalent amount and both our carry-ons were pretty stuffed. If we had realized this was our last visit to the apartment we might have thought to take some other things. There were a few important papers that would have come in handy, but of course there was no way to know. At the time, I thought the four sets of underwear would be more than enough to see me through to the end of the takeover.

With the addition of our luggage and the food we had to inhale in order to close the doors of the Jian. We could have used the trunk, but that would have meant more attention-getting activity and more time in the open with the bad guys too close for comfort. As it was, we drove off without incident and arrived at the Stafford's apartment ten minutes later. Although not an ideal hiding place, it was very private with a tall wall protecting the windows from surveillance.

# 9. Britannia Overruled

The Staffords lived about half a block from Roosevelt Avenue, the major north-south arterial which also happened to run alongside the east wall of the embassy compound (this name too had undoubtedly been changed by then, but everyone still called it Roosevelt so I never learned the new title). There was a white grated gate and then a few steps led to their door. The apartment itself was very spacious with the enormous combined living room and entrance foyer typical of upper middle class Iranian homes. The three bedrooms were on the small side, also typical. As the apartment was on the ground floor it had a small courtyard and garden, then a wall separating it from the property next door.

The chelo kabab was a distant memory now so the first order of business was breakfast. Cora and Kathy went to work in the kitchen. Joe went looking for his old shortwave and I powered up the Motorola. I don't remember what we ate other than it was something with eggs. There was no point in hoarding our scarce supply when we did not know our future from one minute to the next.

The radios provided little consolation. BBC and VOA passed on what by now was becoming the standard Washington line. The US government was seeking additional information regarding the situation in Iran and expected the government of Iran to meet its obligations under international law. Wonderful. Meantime, the Motorola was dominated by Farsi voices. We did hear Palm Tree again, either then or later, but it was still not clear to whom he was talking. By this time the battery of Mike Howland's small hand-held radio had undoubtedly died so unless he had the foresight to bring his charger the group at the foreign ministry was limited to telephone contact. Since we had been up most of the night the breakfast made us sleepy. Kathy showed us a spare bedroom and we dozed off with our clothes on. After a couple of hours, around 10:00am, we awoke and took turns in the shower. Cora and I put on some of the clothing we'd brought with us whereas Joe and Kathy had the choice of their entire wardrobes. Unfortunately, Joe was a bit shorter than me and Kathy much taller than Cora so there was no opportunity for us to hit them up for additional clothing.

Joe called Bruce Laingen at the foreign ministry. Bruce was still permitted unlimited access to the telephone so had talked with the British ambassador about helping us. The details remained to be worked out. We did not know at the time that Laingen had also disclosed our existence to the chief of protocol. Maybe he was hoping the Iranians would do something to aid us, or perhaps he figured they were monitoring his conversations so there was no down side in making a formal request for help on our behalf. At this point it was still unclear what position the foreign ministry would ultimately take, but yet again, the St. Valentine's precedent was still in all our minds. Laingen was being told the truth: the ministry did not have the authority to end the takeover and it was taking longer than expected to organize a rescue. But even had we known, I don't think we would have been too bothered because we presumed our communications with Laingen were being monitored. Perhaps because he was hoping the Iranians would step forward with an offer of assistance, Bruce did not at this point formally request the British take us in.

We did talk to the Brits not long afterward, not yet to request help but to let them know where we were. The downside of our isolated location was it was not the easiest place to find, although that was not yet a concern. I remember the conversation because although Joe was doing the talking at some point I was asked to get on the line. Apparently there were three American businessmen at one of the hotels in a panic about what to do. They had contacted the Brits and the Brits in turn wanted me to help them. True, in normal times that would have been my responsibility, but in the circumstances it seemed a bit odd. I took the number and gave them a call. It turned out they were frightened by the attack on the embassy but did not have any real problem such as a lost passport preventing their departure. I told them, at the risk of sounding melodramatic, they should go to the airport and get on the first available flight to anywhere. At this early stage I thought it was very unlikely airport officials had been ordered to detain Americans. Nor did I think the action against the embassy presaged a general attack on Americans in Iran. I had Massoud's number and was planning to call him shortly but there was nothing he needed to do for these guys. If I was right that unofficial Americans were okay, then they would be able to leave. If I was wrong Massoud's intervention would not be enough to keep them from joining the hostages. In any case, while I don't remember their names, they did not end up at the embassy so I assume they got out without further problems.

Afterward I did call Massoud. He again offered to help us. I said thanks but we were coping so far. It seemed to me we were both better off if we kept him as a last resort. He asked me what he should do about the embassy car he still had. He had taken a motor pool vehicle to the airport the previous morning when he attempted to help Lillian Johnson and obviously there was no way for him to return it. We decided it would be best if he could get it off the street, as big American Chevrolets were not common even aside from the diplomatic license plates. We agreed he should not draw attention to himself as having a connection to the embassy. He said he had a place in mind for the car. I then asked about Kim King. He had not heard from him. I suggested he contact the American priest who ran an assistance program for foreigners; I had given Kim his name and number at some point. The bottom line was Kim had Massoud's home number and if he didn't call, then Massoud should assume Kim was managing on his own. His plane tickets were available at Pan Am and maybe some Iranian official had taken pity on him and given him an exit visa.

Later on, I learned in this case pity ultimately cost about $1500, which Massoud had advanced from his own money after finally hearing from King. It was a poor investment. Massoud was never repaid. I tried to raise the issue several times after we were home, but the bureaucracy was understandably preoccupied with the hostages. Worse from our perspective was King's behavior on arriving stateside. When King reached New York he told the immigration inspector he had information about the embassy takeover. Immigration put him on a plane to Washington and he was taken to the Department and debriefed. He was asked to say nothing to anyone about us, but the temptations of fame were too great. Several days later he showed up on the *CBS Evening News*. He told Walter Cronkite and the Iranians that a group of Americans were on the loose in Tehran. Thankfully, we did not learn about this until we were safely home.

I handed the phone back to Joe who called a friend who was a pasdar. Joe wanted to be (should have been, and ultimately became) a political officer, and from the earliest time in Tehran he missed no opportunity to cultivate contacts which is basically what political officers do. This particular man felt strongly enough about his friendship with Joe he had gone to the embassy the previous night to get Joe out. He did not get far enough to learn Joe wasn't there, but apparently he earned a good beating for his efforts. Joe remained in contact with him over the next few days, but it became clear there was no real reason to continue calling so the conversations ended.

We also kept in touch with Bob. Since his phone remained dead Joe called the apartment upstairs and the occupant got Bob. Both Joe and Bob were getting bad vibes from this neighbor. Again we discussed a switch to the radio, using channel two which still did not have much traffic. Joe called again and told Bob to monitor channel two and we would call him if anything important came up. We also would keep our radio on two so he could reach us if necessary.

After a brief discussion of how bad an idea it was we decided we would each risk a telephone call home. As I wrote earlier we did not know the monitoring capabilities of the new regime, but it seemed unlikely a brief call would bring the police to our door. After all, in theory at least the police were still on our side and we did not think even an intercepted call would be passed on to the terrorists quickly. We did expect our stay in the apartment would not be lengthy. When it came my turn I called my parents in Huntington Beach, CA. It was now Monday, November 5, but with the time difference it was still the middle of Sunday night on the west coast. I figured my folks would pardon the interruption of their sleep to hear from me. We talked for no more than five minutes. I told them we were not hostages and so far we were doing okay, but we would need to find a better place to hide if the embassy takeover continued. I also said they should not automatically believe anything Washington told them. In hindsight this was needlessly melodramatic, but I was still thinking about the policemen at the consulate door and melding that with Henry Precht's conviction the Bazargan government was for real. I was angry about the entire situation and not inclined to be forgiving about the mistakes that had been made. I was afraid our government would bend over backwards to give Bazargan the opportunity to end the takeover, no matter how long it took, even to the point of pretending progress was taking place when it wasn't. Still what I should have said is assurances the US government was doing everything possible needed to be taken with a grain of salt. I was getting frustrated by our inaction.

We allowed twenty minute breaks between calls, hoping if there were surveillance, this might help minimize the chance of us getting caught. While others were on the phone I decided I would risk a radio check with Bob. In the "old" days prior to the takeover we had done radio checks weekly. I had no assurance Bob had participated or now that we really needed to communicate this way, the thing would work. I guess my radio protocol was not what it should have been because everyone laughed when I said.

"Bob, Bob: Come in Bob. Do you read me? Over."

I said it fast, hoping someone who didn't know English well might not understand completely. I thought it was okay, other than not using the call names neither of us could remember, but for whatever reason the other three thought it was hilarious. Fine. We all needed a laugh. Bob replied. I said great to hear from you. Glad the radio is working. He said he could hear me fine. We signed off. The entire conversation took less than thirty seconds, which is exactly what I wanted. At least we knew we could reach Bob when and if there was a need.

After we finished our calls and ate lunch we discussed what our next move should be. We all agreed the apartment was not a suitable long-term hiding place. It was too close to the embassy, probably less than half a mile as the crow flies. Why that should matter I am not sure but at the time we wanted to be further away. There was a host of other reasons. Neighbors knew it was an embassy apartment. The embassy housing office had a record of it. And our rental of it had probably already been registered with the foreign ministry even though it was a new lease taken out just for the Staffords. None of these things meant we were in immediate danger, but, with the takeover now past twenty-four hours and no end in sight, we had to start thinking longer term.

Fortunately the problem was solved for us. Laingen and Tomseth also wanted us in a safer place and about 1:00pm Vic called and said the Brits would take us in. Joe called their deputy head of mission and explained where we were, this time with a lot of detail. A pick-up was set for 5:30pm when the employees who were to get us would normally head home from work. We then contacted Bob on the radio, this time explaining in very general terms what was in the works. He definitely wanted to come with us. I did not give him a specific pick-up time, not wanting to put that information over the radio. I said something like "around rush hour." We spent the remainder of the afternoon listening to the radio and tried to relax. There was not much news. As usual the US government was studying the situation and expected the Iranian government to live up to its obligations under international law. Whoopee. But at least we were temporarily safe. I was still short of sleep from the night before and dozed off a couple of times. Somehow the afternoon passed.

Joe decided to put in another call to the number two around 5:00pm. He figured it would be worthwhile to confirm the people coming to get us had been able to locate Ziba on the map. Although it was one of the seemingly few streets not renamed after a martyr of the revolution, it was, as I described earlier, a confusing place to find. I wasn't paying much attention to the conversation. I heard only one side in any case, but all of a sudden I perked up when Joe abruptly put down the phone. He turned to us, and with the droll tone he sometimes used said,

"The Brit hung up. His last words were: 'The bastards are coming over the walls.'"

I wish I had had an opportunity to meet the British deputy. His words exactly caught the spirit of past two days and are forever engraved in my memory. Although this was a setback and we were concerned for the British as faithful allies, we had to laugh. Furthermore, this was not really a surprise. The demonstration we had seen the previous day was from earlier reports still going on. The British were barely more popular than the Americans. It seemed reasonable the organizers of the demonstration, not wanting to be outdone by their compatriots at the American compound, would decide to take things a step further and actually occupy the premises. What we did not know was whether the two employees coming to pick us up had managed to leave the grounds before the attack and there was no way to find out.

I got on the radio again, to let Bob know there had been a problem. I stuck with my proven radio technique.

"Bob, Bob; Come in Bob. There's been a glitch. Please stand by."

As before, everyone gave me a hard time. Someone even questioned whether glitch was a real word. But Bob had acknowledged so the important thing was he understood. Now there was nothing to do but wait and watch the minute hand of my wristwatch. The half hour passed and no knock at the door. Then another half hour and hope began to fade. We started to consider fallback plans. We would have to spend the night where we were but should probably try to contact Vic and tell him what had happened. Still, we waited. At 6:15 there was a buzz from the outer gate. Joe released the latch and a moment later two men appeared at the open door. We introduced ourselves. They were Mike and Martin. They apologized for being late and said despite the directions and map they still had a hard time finding the place. They knew their embassy had been taken over but said it would have no impact on their plans to take us to their residential compound to the north.

I again called Bob on the radio. This time I just said we were on our way. Bob replied he'd be ready and watching for us. Unfortunately Bob's apartment was a little south of where we were so we would have to backtrack. Mike and Martin decided both vehicles should stick together even though it would have been possible to send three of us northward while one went in the vehicle going for Bob. We didn't quibble. Their cars were parked several blocks away as they had finally given up trying to find the Stafford's apartment while driving. We grabbed our bags and followed them. Even though it was dark already I was not thrilled walking about in Bob's bright yellow sweater. Although I appreciated its warmth, I was kicking myself mentally for not having taken the time to grab a jacket when we were at our apartment. Iranians tended to dress in earth tones so I was very conspicuous. At least the rain had stopped.

Within a few minutes we were in the cars and headed for Bob's. He watched from his window and came out as soon as we pulled up. Then we turned north and merged into Karim Khanezand, a major highway. In fact it was the very same one where the previous morning, while going the opposite direction I had been simultaneously hit by the two cars that both wanted the tiny space in front of me. It was almost impossible to believe barely thirty-six hours had passed. Funny how annoyed I was at something that now seemed pathetically trivial. Undoubtedly one mullah or another had hot-wired the BMW by now. I had the key in my briefcase and while the other was at our apartment I didn't think they would wait to find it.

Although it was nearing 7:00pm, Karim Khanezand was crawling. We continued east, then merged north onto what had been the Shahshahi Expressway. The highway, whose name I believe meant shah of shahs, almost certainly had a new name but not one used in the foreign community. It was one of the main north-south arteries and it too was crowded. It was easy to see into the cars stuck next to us. Unfortunately, it was also easy for them to see into our car and there I was lit up by my electric yellow sweater. Finally the traffic lightened as we moved further north and exited the highway.

We drove through the smaller streets and came to a crowd of fifty or so Iranians. They were milling around and partly blocked the road. They made no effort to stop us although they did stare intently. As usual, I got nervous. Although we were foreigners in cars with diplomatic license plates there was no way to know what might happen in this current atmosphere. Were all foreigners fair game now? After an hour drive from Bob's we reached the Gholhak compound. Although it was dark, I could tell the compound had high walls and quite a bit of open land between the western-style single family houses. We were all taken to Mike's home and invited to stay for dinner. His wife prepared a huge meal of fish and chips for the nine of us (Martin and his wife also joined). I drank Dewar's and water and listened to their Zenith World Band. The news was just breaking: the Bazargan government had resigned en masse and the revolutionary council had assumed direct control of the country. We did not even know who was on the council; its membership was secret. Bazargan had reportedly been trying to persuade the Ayatollah Khomeini he should order the occupiers to return our embassy to us. Of course Bazargan also found his efforts to order the police or military to take action against the terrorists were ignored. He was unwilling to remain as a figurehead so took the only honorable course of action open to him.

This news was not surprising. The embassy had been telling Washington for months Bazargan had no power. It was unfortunate it took the seizure of our embassy to bring the truth home. The news was also not upsetting though that was probably due more to the whisky. After all, if we'd thought about it, we would have realized Bazargan's initiative, even though its failure was probable and predictable, had in fact been the best hope for quick resolution of the crisis. To that point we could hope our analysis was wrong; now we were left hoping for a miracle. The St. Valentine's Day paradigm was finally broken. Unfortunately, it was too late to undo the flawed decisions based on the false precedent.

As we sat down to dinner I felt more relaxed than at any time since the takeover. I assumed we were going to be here for a while: that we had found a refuge from what I considered the almost insurmountable risks of trying to make it on our own in embassy housing. Our hosts, who could have been expected to be upset about the takeover of their own embassy, were taking it in stride. Apparently it had occurred several times over the preceding months and even in the face of what happened to us they were confident the occupiers would leave. We had a wide-ranging conversation, comparing for example, how the British foreign office handled personnel matters or spousal employment as compared to State. Both Mike's and Martin's wives were employed, one at the embassy and the other at the British Council, more or less their equivalent of the Iran-America Society. We even got onto the subject of renting houses while abroad as Mike mentioned he was letting his house sit empty rather than put himself at the mercy of London's landlord/tenant laws.

After dinner we wrote some quick letters which the Brits said they would make sure to get posted for us. Mike's comments about the complexity of renting reminded me I needed to get an escrow payment to my property manager, Jim Hill. I debated whether receiving the check would raise questions in his mind as to where we were, but decided he would almost certainly assume I had mailed it just before the takeover. I had my checkbook with me but had to struggle to recall Hill's address. I must have guessed right because I was eventually able to confirm the check arrived. Maybe this was a silly thing to worry about, but while I couldn't do anything about the hostages at least I had an opportunity to make sure our condo payments would continue on schedule. I also scribbled a quick note to my parents. There was not much to write since the phone call of the morning. The resignation of the Bazargan government allowed, or perhaps the better word is forced, me to acknowledge our situation was now even less clear than when I called. While I hoped we had found a safe-haven it was premature to say so to them.

After dinner we were driven a couple of hundred yards to an empty house. It was a very comfortable two level with three bedrooms and a bath upstairs. A living room, dining room, large kitchen and partial bath made up the ground floor. As Martin explained to us how the appliances and other equipment worked, I was thinking this could be a very comfortable place to hide. It was, however, cold. Apparently there was no central heating; not surprising since the British are famous for not having central heating; a small thing in the circumstances. We were cautioned to keep all of the drapes closed. They did not want any light to be visible outside the compound. Also, we were told one of the gardeners who worked during the day was a member of a local komiteh. They were afraid to get rid of him as to do so might create further problems. So we needed to insure there was no evidence the house was suddenly occupied. We said goodnight to Martin and staked claim to our bedrooms. I unpacked just enough to find my toothbrush. There were towels and linens in the house so we made our beds and went to sleep. Despite the cold it was a big improvement over our sleeping arrangements, or more precisely, the lack thereof, the night before. I slept soundly and long.

The bright sun arose on a cold morning. Getting out of the warm bed took an act of will. We washed up quickly and dressed as

141

warmly as we could; Bob's yellow sweater was looking better. The ladies wrapped themselves in blankets. Normally, the first order of the day would have been breakfast, but we discovered there was no food in the house. This was not a big surprise as our arrival had been short notice, but I felt stupid for not suggesting we bring the food we had at the Stafford's. My only consolation was no one else thought of it either, including Bob who had the luxury of planning his departure from his apartment and presumably could have packed food. Maybe his bachelor lifestyle meant he didn't have much around. Regardless, we were not yet accustomed to our refugee status and were all at fault for not anticipating the need to bring food.

While we waited for someone to come, we looked for a way to heat at least one of the rooms. The living room had a fireplace and there was some wood in a shed by the side of the house so we started a fire. We also found an electric radiant heater in one of the closets and we used that to supplement the fireplace until the room was warm. We realized we had broken the rule about making the house look unoccupied. We stupidly had not thought about it when we lit the fire. Once it was going trying to put it out would have made even more smoke. Martin didn't mention it when he arrived a bit later in the company of a Pakistani member of the compound guard force. Martin said we should come up with a grocery list and the guard would buy the stuff. We threw together a quick list and Bob gave the man money. That once again reminded me I was broke. There was no help for it and we were lucky Bob seemed to have a reasonable bankroll he was willing to share. I figured if this did turn out to be our long term hiding place, the Department would have to work out with the British government how our expenses would be covered. The guard took the list and left. Meantime, Martin brought us a Sony shortwave so we could listen to the news.

The guard returned with our food and we made breakfast. Afterward, we listened to the radio. There was extensive coverage of the Bazargan resignation. It had happened relatively late in the day on Monday so the pundits were just beginning to analyze its meaning. To me it was pretty clear. Although several more days would pass before Ayatollah Khomeini would formally endorse the actions of the "students," his acceptance of the Bazargan government's resignation sent much the same message. In effect the holding of the embassy hostages was now an official act of the government of Iran, although exactly what that was other than the ayatollah himself remained to be determined.

I spent the day lying around smoking cigarettes. We had only found one book in the house, James Michener's <u>Centennial</u>, and as the finder Bob laid claim to it. I didn't mind. <u>Centennial</u> is a very long book, and somehow the idea of starting a long book seemed wrong to me. Maybe it was a premonition. As breakfast was necessarily late and we had been invited to Martin's for an early dinner, we dispensed with lunch. Bob buried himself in his book. I felt on edge and suspected the others, Bob excepted, did also. The news that had not seemed so bad last night was sinking in. It was hard to see a way out.

The US government had still not reacted. Secretary Vance had previously communicated with Foreign Minister Ibrahim Yazdi to remind him the US expected the Bazargan government to make good on its earlier promise to protect the embassy. This was a fool's bargain from the beginning. When we informed Bazargan and Yazdi the shah was to be admitted to the US, we sought assurances our embassy would be protected from the consequences of this provocative act. The assurances were granted, but the Iranians understood their value was questionable and we certainly should have. Yazdi's reference to "Pandora's box" was not ambiguous. Since the government that made the promise was now gone President Carter was left with the option of threatening massive retaliation in the event the hostages were harmed. This was necessary but did nothing to bring them home. Of more immediate concern was the komiteh gardener. We heard noise outside the house and peered from behind the curtain. He was raking leaves outside the glass doors that opened into the living room. We didn't yet connect the fireplace smoke with the thought he might wonder who was in a supposedly empty house, but it turned out not to matter.

The 3:00pm dinner is a blur. Only one detail mattered: the Brits informed us we would have to leave. They told us their Foreign Office and our State Department agreed the attack on the British embassy the previous afternoon made it unsafe for us to remain with them. Arrangements had been made to transport us to the house of the embassy public affairs officer, John Graves, who was one of the hostages. Vic Tomseth had been in touch with his cook who was hiding there. This man had agreed to take care of us. I felt wretched, shocked we were being put back on the street so soon after reaching a place we thought would be a sanctuary. It was painfully obvious Martin and Mike felt responsible. We tried hard to appear unconcerned and said we understood it was not their decision.

Everyone agreed it made sense to delay our departure until nightfall. We went back to the house and packed up our few belongings, cleaned the place up a bit (I seem to recall we even washed our sheets and towels, probably as much to have something to do as out of a sense of obligation). Having learned our lesson this time we packed the food. The early dinner at Martin's was canceled, but Mike and his wife invited us back to their house for supper. This one lacked the merriment of the prior evening. We were all preoccupied. I can't remember what we ate. The conversation was perfunctory and forced. We avoided the topic of our impending departure and what the reasons for it might be. After all, we did understand taking us in was a serious risk for our hosts and their government. While we would have hoped this was a risk they were willing to take, there was no way for us to talk about it without appearing to complain.

We would have to wait a few months to learn the full story. When we did things made a lot more sense. Apparently a crowd had gathered at the compound gates the previous night and demanded entry. The Pakistani guard told them no one was there; all of the staff was being held at the embassy itself. We were clearly lucky that either the guard was very convincing or this particular crowd was not too bright, because what else would they have expected the guard to say? We also learned the US and British governments did consult and mutually agreed having us stay was too dangerous. If the US was the great Satan, the Brits were the senior devil. As it turned out, the move was probably a mistake, at least in the sense our governments overestimated the immediate threat from our continued presence on the British compound. Ayatollah Khomeini soon told the occupiers to leave the British embassy and issued a general proclamation telling his followers to leave foreigners alone. Even he realized Iran stood to lose if foreign nationals from various countries and their embassies were to be randomly attacked. There was no further action against the British. But this is hindsight. All we knew was we had to go.

# 10. Roller Coaster Ride

As soon as it got dark, we loaded our possessions into the same two cars. We had already developed a routine as to who sat with whom. Just as we were getting ready to leave Mike gave me a forest green, nylon, rain jacket. It was the perfect cover for my bright yellow sweater. I must have made some comment about feeling conspicuous the previous evening. It was great: I now had a coat at a time of year when every normal person was wearing one. It also helped lighten the atmosphere surrounding our departure as it provoked a couple of silly jokes. I immediately put it on over the sweater; it fit well, both physically and mentally.

We shook hands all around as there might not be time at the drop point and thanked Mike's wife again for the two great dinners. Within two minutes we were out of the gate; back into the world dominated by people who wore camouflage jackets and generally didn't like us. We drove about fifteen minutes. Graves' house was in the Golestan neighborhood, a couple of miles east and a little south of Gholhak, on a street called Golestan 3. The street was one very long block with a major road at one end. Grave's house was on the end away from the big street, on the south side, and close to where it ended. Technically this was not a cul-de-sac because the road took a hitch to the south and continued east as well as south.

We came up from the south on the main street and turned right onto Golestan. Shortly after we turned we passed an old man wearing a khaki field jacket. He stared intently at us as we drove by and I was afraid he kept watching as we continued down the road and stopped near the end. We were sufficiently concerned we grabbed our luggage and the two boxes of food as quickly as possible. We hustled to the gate. It had been left unlocked. We moved inside as fast as we could. While we hoped the old man wasn't anyone special and he hadn't been able to see exactly which house we entered, I remained concerned about who he was and what he might have seen. I was right to worry.

Sam met us at the door and then went out to secure the gate. After he came back we introduced ourselves. In addition to Sam, we met his wife and an older Thai lady, Graves' housekeeper. She barely looked at us. As best I understood the story, Sam had worked for Tomseth when he was posted to Thailand. Vic had then brought Sam and his wife to Tehran to cook and keep house for them (Vic's wife was also Thai and had been in Tehran earlier, before family members were sent out). But over the coming days as we got to know Sam we learned he had cooked for a number of restaurants and he worked for several embassy people besides Vic. Sam's real name was Somchai Sriweawnetr. Sam was a reasonable Americanized approximation of his first name. Vic had been able to contact Sam from the foreign ministry. Vic spoke fluent Thai and the arrangements for us were made in Thai to minimize the chance anyone eavesdropping on the conversation would be able to understand it. While not foolproof, it was a good idea and an indication Laingen and company also understood the St. Valentine's precedent no longer applied.

The house was surrounded by high walls on all four sides; high enough to prevent the neighbors from seeing what was going on inside. The front of the house faced the street to the north and there were houses behind as well as on the west side. On the east side was a vacant lot at the corner where the street ended. It looked as though someone had started some construction there but like many other projects around Tehran it was halted. Although this was a wealthy area and the houses were large, the individual compounds were barely bigger than the houses so there was not much open space.

Inside, the house was more than comfortable. There were large living and dining rooms on one end and three bedrooms on the other. The partial basement contained servants' quarters and a laundry room. In Department terminology this was termed a representational house, one that would be reserved for a senior officer whose job entailed extensive official entertaining. All in all it was not a bad place to hide. The problems were the usual ones. Nosy neighbors might notice activity and wonder who was there. This concern was lessened as the housekeeper had been at the house the whole time and the presence of Sam and his wife would probably not raise suspicion. The greater concern was it was an embassy lease and the property address was somewhere in the housing files. How soon would the terrorists get around to checking out the houses in those files?

We had more immediate concerns. After putting the food away we worked out sleeping arrangements and began a search for bedding. We found only one set of sheets and a blanket. Kathy and Joe made do with a rug while Cora and I used two tablecloths. As senior man Bob got the only real bedding; besides, sleeping solo, he had no one to keep him warm. Then we spent a little time rummaging around the house and discovered there was almost nothing to rummage for. There was a small refrigerator in the master bedroom containing one bottle of Italian Chianti. Outside of a few cans of beer in the kitchen fridge there was no other alcohol in the house. The only good news was a Sony shortwave radio identical to the one Martin had loaned us earlier in the day.

As I recall we went to bed early that first night. There was no reason to stay up and I at least was suffering from nervous exhaustion. After thinking we had found a safe refuge for the duration once again I found myself back in an embassy house. Having Sam around was a huge plus. We could buy groceries, at least until Bob's money ran out, and Sam could answer the door and the telephone if necessary and we would not have to expose ourselves. But the damned housing files....

The whistling watchman didn't help my nerves either. Sam explained the watchman for the neighborhood also happened to be the local komiteh person. His job was to roam the area at night and whistle every ten minutes. The whistle signaled he was on the job and everything was okay, the Iranian version of "ten o'clock and all's well." From the brief description we were able to give Sam he adduced the old man who watched us drive by with such interest was probably the komiteh watchman. That was good news and bad news. On the one hand it explained why he looked at us so closely. It was his job to know who was moving around the neighborhood after dark. The fact we were foreigners should not have meant much as this was a largely foreign neighborhood. But if he had seen which house we entered then it could mean trouble as he almost certainly knew it was an American embassy property. Odds were we would know by morning. Sam explained there was also another watchman, hired directly by Graves and some of the other westerners. He was a good guy and not komiteh. Sam even brought him in to meet us at one point. Although Sam's English was good, I never did quite understand the relationship between the good watchman and the bad one. Besides, if somehow we were turned in, one friendly guard was unlikely to make much difference.

Despite the whistling and worrying not to mention the lack of normal bedding and the absence of a nightcap, we managed to sleep. The next morning, Wednesday the 7th, we started the day by listening to the shortwave and briefly checking the embassy radio net, something we had been unable to do at the British compound. Neither one was informative. Sam fixed us a good breakfast; having a cook as our caretaker definitely had its advantages. Then he went out to buy us a newspaper. Meantime we resumed rummaging in earnest. First we looked again for bedding. No luck. We found the house was equally bare when it came to books or other sources of entertainment. There were a few books but all in French. Bob regretted being honest and leaving <u>Centennial</u> behind. At least we could have taken turns reading it. We found a video cassette recorder, but only one tape, an episode of the *McNeil/Lehrer News Hour* in which Mehdi Bazargan and Ibrahim Yazdi had been the guests. There was a 16MM movie projector, but the only film was of the shah's coronation of all things. Talk about useless. As far as helping us pass the time the only helpful item we found was an old deck of cards. Four of us played bridge so we started out playing for a few hours. But that left Joe out; we started feeling guilty and switched to poker. There were no chips so we used matches and the contents of a box of nuts and bolts. We also had to teach Cora and Kathy the basics of the game. It was not terribly successful, mostly because poker really only works if the stakes are meaningful. Being Foreign Service professionals, of course the idea of strip poker never entered our minds.

I took to reading the *Tehran Times* in earnest, virtually every word. This was difficult to do as the local English language paper was poorly written and edited. It was radically pro-Khomeini, although whether out of ideological commitment or expediency was not clear. I was told before the revolution it had been just as dedicated to the shah. There were a number of foreigners on the staff, judging from the masthead, so I assumed they were probably just protecting themselves. The paper was pretty thin, but if studied intently the process could kill an hour.

That night Sam made liver and onions for dinner. It turned out only Bob and I liked liver and onions so we were able to pig out while the others gingerly picked through their dinners and worked hard not to offend Sam. We were eating well and Sam had not asked for money for groceries even though he was serving things we had not brought with us. On Thursday I finally had to approach him. I was running out of cigarettes. I had kept a carton at the office and took it with me, but we were now into our fifth day. I tried to stay around a pack and a half a day. I don't think any fair minded person would disagree my stress level had been higher than normal. Not knowing Joe's situation I didn't want to put him on the spot by asking to borrow. I was desperate enough to ask whether Sam had access to some stash of money, perhaps at Vic's place, which he was using to supply us. I told him up front I had left the embassy without any cash (after kicking myself mentally a few more times for leaving the official money behind). I asked whether cigarettes were possible. Sam said yes but did not comment further about money. I let it go because it was not a conversation for me to have one-on-one with Sam as it affected all of us. He produced a carton later in the day. I thanked him profusely. While I stipulate I quit twenty-five years ago, I presume any current or former smoker would understand my relief this crisis at least had been delayed for a few more days.

The other event on Thursday was Bob's decision to contact a couple of friends regarding our situation. We had not reached a consensus on what we should do, but Bob thought it made sense to find out whether we did have options. There was no point in having a discussion about what we might want to do until we knew what we might be able to do. We agreed to let Bob make his calls in private so he could speak openly about the situation. If the offers of assistance were limited to him only we wanted to insure our presence would not pressure him in any way.

Bob called first to another Bob, a representative of an Australian governmental agency. I wasn't sure he was technically a diplomat (as if that mattered), but had met him briefly at a party. I had heard a story of him being shot at when he ignored a road block on his way home late one night. That was a positive: he had guts. He said he would help but acknowledged he lived in a one bedroom apartment. The other call was to John Sheardown. I won't go into detail now as it is well covered later. When Bob came out of the room he said the response to both calls was positive, but he had told his friends our situation was not yet critical and we were not ready to move. Still, he explained to them we might need to move fast if a problem developed and both said they would be ready.

This was very good news. While what Bob said was true, we had no immediate need to move, my concern remained we would probably not have much if any notice should the need arise. If a group of thugs from the former embassy showed up to check the house because they had found the address in the files, it would be too late to make phone calls and arrange transportation. Bob's information brought renewed urgency to a discussion Joe and I had been having since we arrived at Graves' house. Joe's position, as best I understood it, was there were great risks to moving and as long as we stayed quiet we should be fine. As I have noted repeatedly, I believed we were not safe in any house leased by the embassy as it was only a matter of time before the terrorists came to check the addresses in the files. I did not say it to Joe, but I felt like adding, by giving his real name to the man who answered the phone on the night he called the compound from the Iran-America Society, he might have lit a fire under them. With a bit of easy research they would know where he worked and connect him with us as we were all missing from the same building. But there was no point in antagonizing Joe and no way to take back the phone call.

Thursday was the day I lost contact with Massoud. I had called him every day or two to find out what news he might have. Initially I still felt some responsibility for Kim King. While theoretically true it was increasingly clear the chances of my being able to help King had disappeared. But Massoud was providing other information as well. He had telephoned the consulate, pretending to be a visa applicant concerned about getting his passport back (successful applicants had to leave their passports overnight so we could stamp the visa into them). Originally he was told not to worry, the takeover would last no more than twenty-four hours. Then, as the days passed, the duration was extended. First they said two days, then three, then quit answering the phone altogether. This was not a surprise, but it did lend credence to the idea at least some of the organizers really did intend, initially at least, just a temporary occupation. Their good intentions provided little consolation.

I tried calling Massoud three times that day. Each time his wife answered and said he was out. She sounded nervous, and perhaps for that reason I got the distinct impression he had decided keeping in touch with me was too dangerous and he was using his wife to get rid of me without having to tell me himself. That would be very Iranian, avoiding a potential confrontation, which is perhaps why I believed it at the time. Of course it is very possible he was with King that day. But it really didn't matter. I was no longer in a position to help Kim or anyone and I had no intention of imposing on Massoud. Given our fear of possible compromise of the telephones, keeping in touch with him had become an unnecessary risk.

Meantime, Thursday ended with the night from hell. For some reason, Sam was convinced the komiteh men would come that night. Perhaps he had heard something from the good watchman but he wasn't specific about his reasons. As this was now our third night at Graves' house, the rest of us were none too stable either. Aside from my personal paranoia about being in an embassy house, which I presume was shared to some degree by everyone but Joe, the lack of normal bed linens was interfering with our sleep and the lack of much of anything to do during the days was collectively picking away at our judgment. We somehow convinced each other Sam was right and they were coming. Sam developed an escape plan. We would go out the back and around the side of the house and out the front gate. Then by going around the block we could eventually make our way to Kate Koob's house which was a couple of blocks away on the same street.

In retrospect, it is a sad comment on our mental state at the time we even bothered to concern ourselves, as the chances of our being able to go around the side of the house and back out the front without being detected were slim to none. The high walls that gave us privacy also made escape into a neighboring yard impossible. We felt it was necessary to do what we could. In order for the plan to have any chance at all, we had to be prepared to exit out the back of the house at literally a moment's notice. As a result we did not sleep much. We changed room-mate arrangements, putting the ladies in one room while Joe and I were in the other. I think Bob, perhaps with the wisdom of years, was willing to let fate take its course. Like us, he slept with his clothes on, but I think he actually did sleep. Joe and I sat up listening to the shortwave, talking and smoking. During the night hours we could receive broadcasts from all over the world including Australia and South Africa. As usual, there was nothing encouraging in the news. The resignation of the Bazargan government had left us paralyzed. Our official position remained that we expected the "government" of Iran to live up to its obligations under international law. But what if there was no government, at least not in the usual sense of the word?

That night was a terrible experience. We listened to every little sound in case it was the prelude to the komiteh raid. Unlike earlier nights, we waited expectantly for the watchman's whistle, because it meant he was on his usual patrol rather than leading the raiders to our door. If too much time passed between whistles we got even more nervous. In the end nothing happened but psychologically it was devastating. When morning finally came, I was clammy from perspiration and exhausted. I napped during the day; it's not like there was much else to do. But there was one thing we now decided was important. When we initially found the movie of the shah's coronation, we joked about the headlines: *"American Spies Found Hiding, Watching Film of Shah's Coronation."* While this did start out as a joke it didn't seem quite as funny on Friday as it had on Wednesday. We searched the basement and discovered a good place to stash the two film canisters.

On Friday the debate about whether to move or stay broadened. With Bob's news now on the agenda all five of us took part. Joe continued to argue in favor of staying where we were, but I think the rest of us were increasingly leaning toward the Canadian offer. This was partly due to the manner in which Bob's call had been received. According to Bob, John answered without hesitation,

"Why didn't you call sooner?"

When told there were five of us, he responded immediately, "Bring 'em all."

It was hard to imagine a warmer welcome. The other Bob had also been very receptive, but the small size of his apartment made it impractical for more than a few days. We were past the point of anticipating a quick resolution to the crisis. Besides, I think even at this early stage we could not help but give at least passing thought to the obvious fact that, of all the places in Tehran where we could conceivably hide, the Canadian embassy was where we would blend in the best.

Friday night was not as bad as Thursday. I think we all felt a little silly for having worked ourselves into a panic. We didn't sleep in our clothes and Joe and I went back to our wives, but we did have our stuff ready to go. Saturday morning we learned of something else that may have gotten Sam spooked on Thursday. Apparently, the elderly lady, Graves' housekeeper, was becoming increasingly agitated about our presence. Shortly after we washed and dressed we found her arguing vehemently with Sam and his wife. Of course they were speaking Thai so we did not understand, but after a few minutes she stormed downstairs to the servants' quarters. Sam explained she was becoming increasingly concerned about what Mr. Graves would do when he came home and found we had been living in his house and eating his food (and yes, we did drink the bottle of Chianti and the three beers). Sam said he had tried to explain in a roundabout way Mr. Graves was probably not coming back, but had avoided an explicit explanation of the hostage situation because he felt it would just make things worse. Sam said he did not know what she was going to do, but he could not rule out the possibility she would turn us in to the komiteh watchman. This explained why the old lady had hardly said a word to us during the four days we had been in the house and perhaps excuses the fact I don't remember her name. I must admit the thought of tying her up in the basement with a gag in her mouth did briefly cross my mind, but it was not a long term solution. Meantime, Sam was urging us to move to Kate Koob's house. It was on the same street but at the other end near the arterial, perhaps the third house from the end of the street. Sam had the keys. He arranged for a taxi driver friend to come get us.

We left as soon as the taxi arrived. Disconcerted as we were, we did not even wait to finish our laundry. I lost half my underwear and a favorite shirt, one of the two Diors from the outlet store. I don't know why we didn't wait to collect the laundry. Maybe for the same reason we stayed up Thursday night or perhaps because we didn't want the old lady to know we were leaving. We would have had to go to the basement to reclaim the laundry. Getting out of Graves' house felt good, until we saw Kate's place. The kitchen windows were large and only ten feet from the street. There were no blinds and the wall was only half-height. We would not be able to go into the kitchen without being seen by anyone passing in front of the house. There was another glass wall without blinds on the west side meaning we could not use lights after dark without alerting the neighbors someone was in the house, assuming they hadn't seen us arrive. After ten minutes in the house, most of us were ready to pull the emergency cord and throw ourselves at the mercy of the Canadians. Joe was not. He thought we should try it at Kate's for a while. Fortunately, we were not a democracy. After briefly consulting the rest of us, Bob made the decision to call John.

After a brief discussion, they decided John would call the British and ask Mike and Martin to make the pickup. As we had learned when they finally found us at the Stafford's, little streets are hard to find and they had delivered us to a nearby house four long days earlier. The pick-up time was set for 1:00pm. To this point we hadn't said anything to Sam. We agreed it was best for everyone if he didn't know where we were going. Bob informed him we had decided we would be safer in another place. Sam took the news badly. Perhaps he felt he'd let us down or Vic would be disappointed. He even offered to retrieve our laundry from Graves' house and deliver it to us. We thanked him for the offer and for everything he had done, but said it was better he not know where we were going.

While we waited for the Brits, we decided to search Koob's house to see whether there was anything worth taking. We had come to the point we no longer worried about what might come after the takeover ended. We found a couple of decks of cards and a bridge score pad and took them. I crawled into the kitchen on my stomach and located a case of beer. I was tempted, but ultimately decided to leave it because it might complicate the process of getting into the cars quickly and it was a contraband item that could by some unforeseeable chain of events cause trouble. Had I known the Canadians were virtually out of beer I might have decided differently. Martin and Mike showed up on schedule. Bob tried to give Sam some money. He had not let us pay for anything and we doubted he had a source of income any longer. The foreign ministry had stopped putting our calls through to Vic or Bruce so presumably Sam and his wife were on their own as well. But Sam refused. We shook hands, grabbed our things and walked out the door.

A week later we tried to check on Sam and managed to reach him at Kate's house. We learned a mullah and some komiteh men had shown up four days after we left, claiming they heard Americans were hiding there. After searching the house they left, but Sam decided he needed to clear out also. Initially, he went back to Vic's apartment and managed via the Thai underground to collect and store some of Vic's more valuable stuff, eventually getting it out of the country. Sam was gutsy and loyal, but things had reached the point where we needed to sever our ties to the former American community and those linked to it.

# Part IV

Home, Sweet Hideout

or

Hello to Hollywood

# 11. Who Is That Young Man?

We drove for twenty minutes. It felt comforting to have Mike's green raincoat over Bob's yellow sweater. I had been in this part of town before, but recognized things only occasionally. Homes in the wealthier suburbs tended to have high walls so many neighborhoods looked alike. Finally we turned into a small street, arriving at John Sheardown's house in Shemiran without incident. I wondered whether I should have grabbed the beer, and then forced myself to believe this time we were not going to be put back on the street in a day or two, so it didn't matter.

There was a tall, somewhat portly but distinguished-looking gentleman with a gray mustache and beard, his hair thin on top but combed straight back along the sides, watering the sidewalk in front of the house. Given the perpetual dust in Tehran this was not an unusual thing to do and it gave John a good reason to keep one of the garage doors open. The house had two garages, one of which held a late-model Mercedes 300S. We thanked our drivers for once again transporting us safely through Tehran traffic as there would be no time once we stopped. Mike and Martin pulled in front of the open bay and we jumped out quickly. They drove off and John closed the garage door. He said hello to Bob and then the rest of us introduced ourselves. The house was built into the side of a hill so the garage was detached and below the main house. John led us out the back door and to a flight of steps. To our left was the pedestrian entrance gate from the street, to our right and up perhaps twenty steps was the entrance to the house itself, behind a set of smoked glass doors.

As we walked through the doors we entered a parlor. To the right were three steps leading into the living room. Straight ahead was the sitting room with a large wall unit on the left. It contained John's stereo as well as records, tapes and memorabilia, There were photographs and nick-knacks from other postings around the world. In the center of the sitting room was a large smoked glass coffee table surrounded by four armchairs. On the right was a glass wall that exposed an internal courtyard. As we entered the room we introduced ourselves. There were two other people, John's wife Zena and a man named Ken Taylor.

Zena was a very attractive woman with jet black, shoulder length hair, parted in the middle. She was from Guyana and her skin was a golden brown that implied a mixed ancestry. She had British nationality and spoke English with a hint of a British accent. She seemed quite a bit younger than John. We pulled up some side chairs that were lined against a wall, squeezing in around the coffee table. Zena offered drinks, which were gratefully accepted. Although we had yet to have breakfast, it would have been rude to decline since she and Ken had already started. For the first time since we left the British compound I felt completely relaxed. That first Ballantine (we were soon to learn it was John's whisky of choice) with a splash of water tasted really good. We started talking and, thinking back to our experience with the British, I could not help but raise a point of business. I asked John whether their ambassador knew he had invited us into his house. I wanted to reassure myself we were not being set up for a repeat of what happened earlier. John let a little smile flash across his face as he puffed on his pipe and told me Ken Taylor was the ambassador. Bob probably knew already. I don't think I was the only one fooled by the slim build, stylish glasses and clothing plus the overall youthful appearance. I had a mental image of ambassadors as old men with balding heads and three piece suits, so the curly mop of hair combined with everything else fooled me. We all laughed, and Bob thanked Ken for supporting our rescue.

We enjoyed several more drinks while Ken gave us a brief sketch of the immediate plan. We were to stay put as long as necessary for the hostage situation to resolve itself. To top it off, he told us Prime Minister Joe Clark personally approved the offer of refuge. It was an open ended commitment, and it is worth noting our impact on the Canadian embassy was not limited to occupying space in their houses.

Our existence was revealed to individual employees on a need to know basis. At least one employee who was informed indicated he was not comfortable with our presence and was transferred out with no negative consequences for his career. Employees who were not told about us were reassigned out of Iran, presumably because it was decided reducing staffing was a prudent response to the higher level of risk resulting from our being there. Furthermore, given the truly exceptional nature of the task the embassy had now undertaken, it would have been unreasonable to expose them to a higher level of risk without their knowledge.[1] As the months passed, care and feeding of the houseguests and other support rendered to the US government increasingly became the focus of embassy operations. I am no expert, but I believe outside wartime this level of support to an ally is without modern precedent.

Although he was not present that afternoon as he was out of Iran on leave, I should also introduce Roger Lucy, because I am unsure when we first met him and because he was very important to our story. Roger was first secretary and head of chancery. We don't have an equivalent position in American embassies, but I understood it to be a combination in our terms of head political officer and deputy chief of mission. Roger was six feet tall with a thick but trim mustache and brown hair kept short and combed forward in a utilitarian Roman emperor style. He was extremely bright and consumed history books the way others eat Twinkies. He was also a collector of military memorabilia as we learned on the several occasions we visited his apartment.

In order to balance the housekeeping tasks and to insure our presence within the Canadian mission could not be interpreted as anything other than an official act of government policy, two of us were to stay at the ambassadorial residence while the other three remained with John. My recollection is Joe and Kathy volunteered to go with Ken. Given that I was probably on my third drink by the time this issue came up I may be wrong. Since there was no question of breaking up couples Bob was not in the equation. It could have been determined by a coin flip between the Staffords and us. But I have no recollection of any discussion regarding a mechanism for how the decision should be made which is another reason I think Joe and Kathy volunteered.

The Staffords departed with Taylor about 4:00pm and we remaining three were given a brief tour of the house and shown to

---

1. Roger Lucy, interview with the author, November 18, 2011

our rooms. We unpacked what few possessions we had. John and Zena asked whether we needed anything, but we found the bathroom contained the items we required immediately, such as shaving cream and toothpaste. They were thoughtful enough to inquire about our clothing situation, but at the time it seemed we had enough to get by. Within a few days I decided to stretch the shaving cream budget by growing a beard. I had made a few attempts but the thing always looked so awful I would shave it off. Not to say I wanted to stay in Tehran, but I figured perhaps now I would have enough time to really find out whether I was capable of growing a proper beard or not.

Cora and I shared a bedroom at the top of the stairs and opposite the bathroom. The space was not large, but it was roomy enough to accommodate a double bed and a large dresser plus one night table. The room was on the second floor. It faced the street and had a good view of the city. We looked down into a valley and across to another hill along which ran the Shahshahi expressway. I could see the intersection with Jordan Street, part of the route we used to take to the German compound, a time that now seemed ages ago. Since the bedrooms were all on the same side of the hallway we all had the view but also a problem. We could see but also be seen. John and Zena were concerned lights in those rooms at night might attract some notice as they had never been used regularly before. So we generally kept the blinds drawn and stayed out of the rooms except to sleep or hide. I do remember being able to read, so perhaps we found a small light we figured would not be visible through the blinds.

The house was incredible, a perfect place to hide and therefore worth a description. It was basically a square, built around an open courtyard in the center. The living room was on the street side of the courtyard, the kitchen on the side opposite the sitting room where we initially had drinks. The dining room was between the living room and the kitchen. Opposite the living room was the family room or den. All of these rooms had one glass wall along the courtyard. As I already mentioned the bedrooms were upstairs. There was a hallway with three bedrooms and a bathroom over the family room and part of the kitchen. The master bedroom was at the far opposite end of the hall, over the sitting room, and had a loft as well as its own bathroom. There was also a full basement which contained several large storage rooms, servants' quarters and the laundry. The stairway from the basement went first to a lobby between the kitchen and the family room, then to the bedroom hallway, and ultimately exited onto the roof. At the back of the house the roof was level with another street, providing an emergency exit into a different neighborhood. While it was undoubtedly possible to drive from John's garage to the upper neighborhood, there was no easy route. At some point later I counted the rooms. There were nineteen.

The floor plan seemed simple but wasn't. There were small flights of stairs here and there. Aside from one wall bordering the central courtyard, rooms even on the ground floor were not generally linear and someone unfamiliar with the house might have difficulty deciding whether a particular door led to another room or just a closet. There were certainly enough of those scattered around. Sometimes I thought or hoped in a worst case situation where we were trapped in the family room, if we stayed quiet John or Zena could have taken someone around the house and left that room off the tour. The door could easily have led to one of the closets. Of course a hostile with the intent of searching the house probably would have insisted on inspecting each closet as well, but it was a reassuring thought as we would end up spending most of our days there. And the den was probably the most comfortable room in the house. It had natural light coming from the courtyard while at the same time not being visible from the street. There were four arm chairs, a desk, a coffee table and a sofa with an ottoman. The two large wall units were filled with books. Initially we played games on the coffee table but later found a card table and some chairs in the basement which we brought up to use for games.

The house was almost too good to be true. If I had to design a house to hide in, I am not sure I could have done a better job. But there were still issues. First was Lolita, the Filipina housekeeper and cook who worked for Zena and John. When we came, Zena asked her whether she knew who we were. She replied she had already guessed. I think she was a good person and would have wanted to help us anyway, but John eliminated any concern by promising her an immigration visa to Canada (this was not done in front of us, of course, but we were told later Lolita was absolutely trustworthy and would be taken care of when the time came). Lolita was an excellent cook and for the first few weeks she made us breakfast as well as other meals. Over those weeks, however, we each developed our own schedules which made a single breakfast inconvenient and it was not reasonable to expect her to spend the morning preparing multiple meals. This led to the second issue. We all agreed making our own breakfasts was sensible but were concerned about entering the kitchen because John's gardener was a member of the local komiteh. In a rerun of the situation at the British compound, John was reluctant to fire the man because it might lead to greater scrutiny of the house or perhaps even some reprisal. So initially we started using the kitchen only after inquiring whether the gardener was around. However, he had a key to the front gate so could show up anytime without notice. He saw me once, but as he didn't know the Canadian embassy staff presumably he figured I was one of them.

Eventually, Cora had the idea of covering the glass wall between the kitchen and the outside yard with white liquid shoe polish. She meticulously covered every square inch of the interior window surface with the stuff. It was perfect; it dried quickly, let a reasonable amount of light enter, but was opaque enough to provide the needed privacy. I don't know if the gardener ever asked, but I think the official explanation was going to be the cream provided modesty for the ladies of the house should they need to enter the kitchen wearing, say, a bathrobe.

Although the kitchen modification solved most of our problems with the gardener, two remained. One was he had to get into the courtyard occasionally to see to the plants there. As we were usually in the den, this meant we had to pull the blinds and sit quietly until he left. It also put Zena or Lolita in the position of having to delay him at the door while passing the warning to us. The second was he was responsible for hauling the garbage down to the street on pick-up days. Six people generate a lot more trash than two, so John started taking a portion of it to work with him. Some days he would leave exceptionally early and toss it out the window as he drove past the local komiteh headquarters. The empty liquor bottles usually went to the komiteh as well because whenever the actual garbage man found one in the trash he would confront John and demand some booze for himself as hush money. Eventually, we started stashing some of the bottles in a closet at the back of the kitchen. It was actually outside and V-shaped. Because the house was excavated into the hillside there were concrete walls on two sides and a glass wall and door from the kitchen. At the top was a metal grate. Presumably it was intended to allow some natural light into the back corner of the kitchen, but it also did make a good hiding place for the empties.

Lolita made dinner an occasion always. Despite the creeping shortages of basic items, she managed to prepare excellent meals. John's tastes ran to steaks and chops, similar to mine so I could not have asked for better. True, I was surprised that a manly man like John would allow squash to appear two or three times a week, but we all have to make sacrifices in difficult times. Otherwise, the pantry seemed inexhaustible. There was no beer, presumably too heavy to ship in a consumables allowance measured by weight and no longer available now the US embassy's huge stock of Asahi had been taken off the market or perhaps moved to the black market. As I am not much of a beer drinker this was a relatively minor inconvenience. Cigarettes, several different kinds, were available. We did run out, probably about the end of December, but John took advantage of the ample black market sources and there was no interruption of supply. This was actually Bob's fault. Zena and I could probably have stretched their stock intended for several years to last the three months. But when Bob reacquired the habit after a two year break, and then dared blame me for his lapse of discipline, there were now three smokers where there had been one. This caused a problem but not one John would consider letting us worry about.

One other issue with the house came up later, probably a month or so after we arrived. The landlord decided to sell so on two or three occasions we had to vacate the house entirely. In addition, at least once there was a maintenance problem that required a work crew and thus led also to a need to vacate. Roger would drive us in his red Peugeot to his apartment, about twenty minutes away. It was not a great risk, but we had become so used to being indoors the trip made me nervous. We were usually able to avoid rush hour, but I did not like having Iranians look at me as we waited in traffic. I realized it wasn't rational, but neither could I prevent it. The reward for these trips was being able to peruse Roger's library and borrow a history book or two. John's library was extensive but tended toward fiction.

It did not take long for us to fall into our own routines. Perhaps this was a small way to calm ourselves by building a confined and predictable world. Aside from Cora, my fellow houseguests and our hosts, the most important characters in my world were books. John and Zena had an extensive library, mostly paperback fiction, but more than enough to keep us occupied. When we first saw it Bob commented it was as if we were being held prisoner in a public library. Within a day or two I had picked up a horror novel, The Search for Joseph Tully. It was an excellent thriller and it helped me to get back into the reading habit. From that point on I spent perhaps half of the average day absorbed in reading. I started keeping track of the books I had read not by title but simply by number. I think it was my equivalent of the way prisoners etch X's into a wall of their cell, knowing each X is one day closer to freedom. While I had no way to know how many days we would be at the Sheardown's, I did know each book I read was one less from the total I would have on the day we left.

As a result of that confinement, I made the acquaintance of some of the authors who are still among my favorites: Laurence Durrell, John Masters, Paul Scott and the inimitable George MacDonald Fraser's Flashman series. By the time of our departure, I had read fifty-seven books, including some rather lengthy tomes borrowed from Roger. One book, The Monte Cristo Cover-up by Simmel (a German and for some reason he used just the one name), became such a favorite I spent years looking for a copy (in the days before Amazon, of course).

Games, or a game, became an important part of our routine. We had only two, Monopoly and Scrabble. Monopoly did not hold our interest very long, but Scrabble has much more depth so we began to play it regularly. We also had chores. We did our own laundry, which was necessary every three days as we had so little clothing. On Sundays Lolita had the day off so we cooked dinner.

We had a duty roster but it wasn't unusual for it to become a group effort. I particularly remember the first time we tried to use the fancy German wall oven. All the controls were marked with little symbols that meant nothing to us. Zena tried to help. Bob looked for a manual, hoping he could use his German to decipher a few symbols, but could not find one. In the end we managed to make it work, sort of. It kept turning off. When Lolita returned we received a proper briefing.

Ken Taylor brought over a Zenith Trans-Oceanic multi-band radio a day or two after we came. It was placed in the den and became a daily companion. The amount of time we devoted to listening served as a barometer of our attitude and confidence. In the early days we monitored the British Broadcasting Corporation (BBC) newscasts almost hourly, plus the Voice of America (VOA) evening summaries, as well as any other broadcasts we could find by sweeping the dial. I remember becoming quite an expert on the Rhodesia talks, as the BBC gave top billing to Foreign Secretary Lord Carrington and his efforts to end the civil war that ultimately resulted in Rhodesia becoming today's Zimbabwe. The news about the hostage crisis did not get better and we listened less and less. Once in a while something like a UN debate would spike our interest, but over the almost three months we stayed in the house there was a clear downward slope to our radio listening.

Even in the darkest days we never fell below a certain minimum news quota. I had taken to sleeping in late, reducing the number of hours I would have to fill each day. Bob would normally get up several hours earlier and catch the VOA morning summary. When I got up, he would fill me in, normally triggering a minor tirade as the news was either bad or on a good day non-existent. After a while Bob said he would stop telling me the news unless I promised to not blame him for it. Of course I wasn't, but I guess I had a greater need to vent than the others, perhaps related to a stronger sense our government should be doing more for the hostages. We would catch the BBC around lunch time and then perhaps once more before dinner. After John came home from work and we had finished dinner, we would listen to the BBC again and then at 8:30 pm the VOA evening summary. My job during these sessions was to sit in the armchair next to the desk on which the radio sat and retune it as necessary when the signal wandered. As well as bringing home the *Tehran Times*, an occasional *International Herald Tribune* and periodic in-house news summaries from the embassy, John would discuss interesting developments from work that were not otherwise covered.

Television never played a significant role in our daily schedule for several reasons. The greatest was the old TV placed in the house by the Canadian government broke several weeks after we arrived. There was no incentive for John to fix it or for us to ask that it be repaired or replaced. The programming was pathetic and the Iranian news of little interest. We did watch one show purporting to prove our embassy was a nest of spies. Some of it was ridiculous, showing items such as Marine security equipment including a metal detector, or normal office equipment such as a Dictaphone with its micro-cassettes and claiming these were tools for espionage. Unfortunately, they were also able to display multiple passports in several nationalities found in the safe of one of the CIA officers.

Speaking of others, this is as good a time as any to introduce Lee Schatz, the embassy's agricultural attaché and the mysterious Palm Tree whose radio transmissions in the immediate aftermath of the takeover left us puzzled. We had been at the Sheardowns for a week when John brought Lee over on Saturday morning. I had met Lee a few times. He was often at the Caravanserai when Cora and I were having breakfast so once in a while we would share a table. He had arrived in Tehran a couple of weeks before the attack and his office was off-compound. Agricultural attaches work for the Department of Agriculture and their main jobs are to promote the export of American farm products and to monitor the local agricultural scene. They don't have that much connection to core embassy functions so their offices are often separately located. Lee was fortunate this was the case in Tehran.

Lee became aware of the attack when one of his local employees tried to make the two block trip to the compound to pick up mail. Lee was acquainted with some of the Swedish embassy staff. Their offices were in the same building on the sixth floor. He moved upstairs in order to get a better view of what was happening inside the compound. He provided information both to Tomseth at the foreign ministry and, via Kate Koob and the open phone line at the Iran-America Society, to Washington. After it became clear to him the attack was serious he went back to his office, grabbed some things and said goodbye to his employees, thanking them for their help and telling them not to worry about him. He purposely did not tell them where he was going. Then he moved back to the Swedes, where for the next two days he stood watch at the window. The Swedes found him a pair of powerful binoculars so he was able to report in some detail what he was seeing. He'd taken the lunchbox radio along so was, like us, aware of the gradual change to Farsi and also heard Charlie announce he was surrendering the communications vault. Near the end of his surveillance he saw rifles being unloaded from what was ostensibly a bread truck. Shortly thereafter, he and the Swedes jointly decided his presence in their office was becoming an unacceptable risk. Besides, the situation in the compound was no longer evolving; we knew our people had become hostages.

Cecilia Lithander, the Swedish consul whom I had met at a few parties, took Lee to her apartment in north Tehran. She did this with the reluctant approval of her ambassador and the Swedish foreign ministry. At the time the Swedes were conducting what they hoped would be effective diplomatic efforts on behalf of the hostages. They were concerned that Lee's presence at their mission if discovered would both derail those efforts and expose their own staff to danger. Yet they couldn't just put Lee on the street so eventually Ambassador Kaj Sundberg approached Taylor hoping fellow North Americans might be willing to help.[2] Ken astounded Sundberg by informing him they already had five of us so one more should not be a problem.

John wanted to have some fun with Lee so he arranged with a friend who was also acquainted with Lee to accompany him to Cecilia's apartment. The mutual acquaintance vouched for John, but did not explain who he was, only that it was safe to go with him. Lee was not thrilled to leave, but Cecilia had made it clear

---

2. Peter Kadhammer, "'Impartial Mediator' Hid Fleeing American," Expressen, January 22, 1986 (Swedish newspaper article in possession of the author, page not known)

her government was increasingly nervous and his new host would take good care of him. Lee concluded he was meeting a CIA officer. John's cosmopolitan manner could certainly have conveyed that impression, not to mention the fancy Mercedes. It became one of John's favorite stories, how on the ride home John explained to Lee he was not CIA but CEA, Canadian External Affairs. He said nothing about us. Lee knew we were out but thought we were still with the British. So it was fun to watch Lee's confusion when he came up the stairs to the foyer and found the five of us waiting for him. Despite our previously casual relationship this day we treated him like a long lost brother. Kathy and Joe were visiting and we all swapped stories, sharing our perceptions of the past fourteen days.[3]

A decade later, Cecilia was our neighbor in Warsaw, Poland. She told me she was somewhat disappointed with her government's attitude and if there had not been other options for Lee she would have insisted on protecting him. But she realized having him with us was better for him and for us. It is worth noting also she hardly knew Lee at the time, given he was so new to Iran. She really had stuck her neck out for a stranger in trouble.

Lee was a few years older than me and quite a bit taller. He had a full, thick moustache which extended a trifle past the corners of his mouth. His medium brown hair had just a touch of red, but I am not good with colors so won't swear to it. He parted his hair in the middle and swept it back on both sides. Lee's personality definitely added a new element to our mix. He was an extrovert, not surprising since an agricultural attaché is basically a salesman. He was a bit on the loud side, quick to laugh or display his big grin. He and John seemed to hit it off particularly well, but his presence was a plus for all of us with one minor issue. We were disappointed he did not play bridge and did not want to learn. With Kathy, the fourth player in our group able to visit only infrequently, we had hoped to add bridge to our game options. This led to a few jokes about us offering to trade Lee to the Taylors for Kathy, but Joe very quickly nixed the idea.

---

3. Cora Lijek, Lee Schatz, interviews, Escape from Iran: The Inside Story (Toronto: Canadian Broadcasting Corporation Documentary, Canamedia Productions, 1981)

\*\*\*\*\*

On November 20th Ayatollah Khomeini ordered the release of thirteen women and African-American employees. The official announcement said it was designed to demonstrate Islamic compassion and to express solidarity with oppressed minorities around the world. Although our TV had already died before the release we learned enough about the propaganda circus from the print media to be disgusted. The Iranians were starting to feel international isolation as even many third world countries condemned the hostage-taking. This kind of pressure was ineffective where Khomeini was concerned, however, although someone must have convinced him the gesture would be beneficial. From the perspective of today it is not clear it was important one way or another, but at the time we were of course happy for the former hostages and their families.

This group represented most of the women and African-Americans at the embassy. Those judged to have important jobs were kept. Once they were out of Iran we heard more details about their treatment. As I wrote earlier in explaining my decision to use the term terrorist to describe the hostage-takers, the treatment included such things as being bound to a chair for hours at a time, beatings, mock executions, isolation and sleep deprivation. I cannot say for certain to what extent any given individual was subjected to this type of cruelty, but their post-release comments in general worried us because we had to assume the remaining hostages were enduring the same or worse.

Even though this was primarily a public relations gimmick, it did raise hope other releases might follow. If the terrorists really were interrogating the hostages they would probably figure out they were holding a number of people who were not spies and did not have particularly important jobs. Some in the media even speculated about a general release and Ken concluded we should be told there was a plan to make sure we were not overlooked in the event it actually happened. The proposal was for a committee of Western ambassadors to approach the ministry of foreign affairs and inform them of our existence and ask we be included in the release.

By now Ken knew from Laingen he had early on informed the foreign ministry there were some official Americans on the loose. Among his many efforts on behalf of the US, Ken was a regular visitor to the foreign ministry, relaying information to Laingen and providing him and the others with clothing and an occasional treat such as whisky smuggled in aftershave bottles.[4] Taylor recognized the news brought by this delegation would probably not be a surprise. Still, I had doubts about the plan from the beginning. For one, who was to say the foreign ministry would even be a player in a general release? The terrorists and their political masters were calling the shots. Secondly, a general release would need to be justified in some manner to the Iranian people. After all the propaganda about the embassy being a nest of spies there would have to be an explanation for letting them all go. The one that occurred to me was the spies had all been interrogated, their nefarious plots uncovered and neutralized, and therefore as proof of Islamic humanitarianism they would now be sent home. There was no room in the explanation for us. To the contrary, the fact we had escaped meant we were probably CIA. There were no further releases, so the concerns I had about the plan faded along with hope the remaining hostages would be let go anytime soon.

Cora pointed out a potential problem for us stemming from the release of the women. The terrorists freed all of the females except two. They named those two and explained why they had been kept. Of course there was no mention of Cora or Kathy. We did not know whether anyone in the media had a comprehensive list of the embassy staff prior to the takeover. We understood from news coverage the Department was keeping mum regarding names and numbers, but this did not guarantee a hard-working reporter would not be able to assemble a list.

Cora and I decided it would be a good idea to write our friends and tell them we were not hostages. After the release of the women, they must be scratching their heads wondering what happened to Cora. Our main concern was we did not want them to worry un-necessarily. And while it was unlikely they would do anything to

---

4. Robert Wright, 174

compromise us, they might somehow accidentally do so in the process of trying to find out where we were. We later learned one of Cora's friends thought she saw her among the women being let go (she looked a bit like the chargé's secretary) and contacted another college friend who ultimately telephoned Cora's mother. That was harmless, but it was not impossible to envision some scenario involving the media. As I have mentioned several times, we were deliberately kept in the dark regarding who in the press knew what about us. It was a good policy but could not stop us from worrying.

*****

The partial release occurred shortly before the Thanksgiving holiday. John and Zena made an exceptional effort to give us an American Thanksgiving. The Canadian tradition is similar but the date falls in October. For some reason, turkeys were difficult to find, but John was able to obtain a suckling pig from an Armenian butcher friend. John was apologetic about the lack of a turkey, but we all assured him we were extremely appreciative of his even thinking about it under the circumstances and were overwhelmed by the quality of the food. Lolita's meals were generally good, but she too wanted to make this one special.

In early December the Sheardowns hosted a party for us. I know there were eight guests because I wrote my parents a letter shortly afterward and mentioned it. I could not include the names of the guests, but there were not that many people who knew about us so I can be reasonably certain about some of them:

-Chris Beebe, early forties, ambassador from New Zealand. Chris was medium height, ruddy complexion with red hair and beard. He still holds the record as the most unambassadorish ambassador I have ever known. His trademark was a pair of jeans made entirely of belt loops from other jeans. He had wonderful stories whether from his previous job as minister to the Gilbert and Cook Islands or from more recent days as a road warrior: his Chevy Suburban versus Iranian taxicabs.

-Richard Sewell, mid thirties, Chris' right hand man. Party animal. Six feet tall, brown hair, handsome with slightly angular features. Knew everyone and how to use his contacts to get things done. Friendly, funny and fearless.

-Trolls Monk, ambassador from Denmark. A clone of the actor Robert Shaw, down to the accent and the savoir-faire. Except, of course, Monk was the real thing. He was married to a Carlsberg beer heiress and rarely appeared at John's without a case of the good stuff for us.

After these three, it becomes more difficult. It is likely Tricia was there. She was a Canadian national, daughter of the former military attaché, with an Iranian boyfriend who fortunately had no sympathy for the revolution. She worked for John at the embassy and he trusted her sufficiently to tell her about us. She would visit from time to time. Of course by this point all of the Canadian nationals remaining on the embassy staff knew about us and presumably any who wished to come would have been at the party. Laverna Dollimore, Ken's secretary, also came frequently. Cora and Kathy became very fond of her and appreciated the opportunity for some girl talk as the majority of our guests were male. There were also several Australian diplomats who were in the know. John organized social events for us once or twice a month so it is impossible for me to remember who was at any particular party. The important point is he wanted us to have normal social interaction, at least to the extent it was possible in the circumstances. One mid-December evening John managed to lay hands on a movie projector and a film, *The Eyes of Laura Mars*. I am a Tommy Lee Jones fan so it is possible we had seen it during the months before leaving for Iran, but regardless it was great fun to eat popcorn and watch street scenes from New York City. The world was still out there.

One social event stood out because of the bigger context. Jim Edward, head of the Canadian security detachment, had left Iran suddenly because he had wandered into the American compound. At the time we were not aware he was performing reconnaissance on behalf of the US government (see Robert Wright's book, described more generally in the afterword, for a broader explanation of the Canadian role in collecting intelligence). The Iranians gave Jim the chance to leave immediately and the only alternative was he would have been declared "persona non grata" and kicked out. Jim was replaced by Claude Gauthier, a tall, barrel-chested, French-Canadian with a strong accent, a great sense of humor and a taste for red wine, at least on the first night we met him. As the evening progressed, Claude approached Cora and Kathy and told them he was an American from the CIA and was going to get us out of Iran. He specifically mentioned a plan to drive us across the border to Turkey.

Cora was a little disconcerted, fearing this new guy might actually be CIA and not enthused by the idea of us being in his care. She found me and I went over to talk to Claude. At that point he was talking to someone else about how he made a killer spaghetti sauce and would prepare it at John's one night, but he only knew the recipe for ten gallons or so of the stuff. I started talking to him and realized he was fairly looped, which served only to make him like most of the others in the room. When he indicated he had replaced Edward, I realized by saying he was an American he was making clear he considered himself one of us and would do whatever he could to insure our safety.

By this time Christmas was around the corner. John obtained a tree and we started decorating it on the 13th, following what I understood was a British tradition connected with the twelve days of Christmas. Every day after John got home, we added a few decorations to the tree. There were a number of Christmas cards on John's mantle but one occupied a place of honor. It was from Prime Minister Joe Clark and contained a personal message of support and best wishes to all of us.

Christmas day itself was truly special. The turkey man finally came through so John surprised us with a 20 pounder (Lee later told me it cost $100). On the down side, there was the traditional Christmas pudding from Harrods Department Store in London. The experience was educational; I had never encountered pudding nearly as hard as a rock. I think we considered it a variant of a fruit cake, which is one of those foods that can perhaps be fairly described as controversial with most people holding strong opinions pro or con. Still there was never any doubt or hesitation we would eat our portions enthusiastically. And again, Lolita laid out a splendid feast.

Lee had some money and very thoughtfully asked John to purchase gifts for each of us on his behalf. He chose worry beads, a middle-eastern aid for people with nervous habits. I am only half joking. As far as I can tell the purpose of worry beads is to give people something to do with their fingers. But they were a perfect choice not only because they were a unique item from that part of the world but because they later became a practical part of our exfiltration kit. They were an ideal souvenir and lent credibility to the idea we had wandered the town. For Zena, he asked John to purchase a Khomeini prayer rug. It was about two feet wide and three feet long, with a black outline of the Ayatollah's stern visage in the center. We had seen them around town before the attack, although I never figured out if they were real prayer rugs or just wall decorations. Either way, we got a good laugh out of it. John and Zena got us a small round box, made of brass with mother of pearl inlay on the top. It was very Iranian in design and so would have been a good choice for a souvenir, making it also useable as part of our exfiltration kit. Cora uses it today to store our collection of Canadian flag lapel pins. Yet again I regretted my poverty which prevented us from purchasing gifts for the others. No one held it against us of course and overall that Christmas may still be the most exceptional of my life.

The New Year holiday followed soon after, but unfortunately my main memory is not a pleasant one. I know we had company and, as always on special days, John and Zena had planned something for us. But whether I drank too much or the food didn't sit well, all I know is I lit a cigar and within minutes felt sick. My New Year's Eve was spent lying on my bed with one foot on the floor to keep the bed from flying away, so I am afraid I can't say much else about the evening. It was an inauspicious beginning to the new year.

While Jimmy Carter was famously wrong in describing Iran itself as an "island of stability," we had found our own island in miniature, not to say there were not a few scary moments. One winter afternoon Bob was sunning himself after exercising in the courtyard when a helicopter zoomed low over the house. Bob immediately jumped up from the lounge chair and flew inside the den. The helicopter continued circling the neighborhood and Zena, visibly upset, came down from upstairs to call John at the embassy.

He knew nothing about it but pointed out a helicopter was not a very good way to find people hiding in a house. A few minutes later, it moved away and slowly we relaxed. John was right about the effectiveness of using a helicopter as a search tool and as we thought more about it we realized we had overreacted. John later reported a mullah had been assassinated in the area and the chopper was trying to track the motorcycle-riding attackers.

Once in a while someone would ring the doorbell unexpectedly and we would secure the den by closing the curtains to the courtyard and the door from the hall. I have already mentioned the occasional trips to Roger's apartment necessitated by potential homebuyers or repairmen. Still, considering our little island was surrounded by very hostile seas and included a gardener who would have liked nothing better than to turn us in to his komiteh buddies, it was a relatively tranquil existence.

## 12. See Ya Later, Exfiltrator

As the New Year unfolded, I increasingly believed the hostages were unfortunately in for a long period of captivity. The terrorists staged another propaganda show for Christmas. They invited three American ministers known for their advocacy of leftist political causes. We did not view the film until we were back at the Department, which was probably a good thing as anyone could see most of the hostages knew very well the event was staged to disguise the horrendous conditions under which they were being held. The terrorists initially demanded payment of $21,500 for rights to the film and a guarantee the buying network would air the entire program. There were no takers so in the end the networks were given access and each showed portions a few days after Christmas.[1] What we were able to learn about the holiday travesty from our usual news sources was depressing but not unexpected. At least we knew most of the hostages had been seen and appeared to be in reasonably good physical health. At the same time the entire episode further highlighted the leverage the hostages gave to the terrorists and their mullah buddies, who were using them to increase their own hold on authority in Iran. That led to the inescapable conclusion it was time for us to go. As if I needed further proof, it also seemed clear humiliating the great Satan was irresistible to nearly everyone, from the mobs assembling almost daily in front of the embassy compound to the highest authority, Khomeini himself. The likelihood of a negotiated release seemed miniscule.

Since the early plan to have us escorted to the airport by a group of friendly ambassadors, no one had directly talked to us about how we might leave. I think we all assumed it would be as Canadians, but beyond that there were too many options and we ourselves had too little information about the realities on the ground throughout the country. Was it possible, as Claude suggested the first night we met him, to get across by land? We just didn't know. On the other

---

1. Mark Bowden, Guests of the Ayatollah (New York, Grove Press, 2006), 277

hand certain facts were clear. First and foremost, our situation was now separate from that of the hostages. Even in the unlikely case a diplomatic breakthrough occurred and the hostages were released, having us show up unexpectedly could blow up the entire plan for reasons I have outlined previously. The Iranians might conclude the failure of the Carter administration to acknowledge our existence meant it had negotiated in bad faith. Were an agreement to be reached it would almost certainly rest on a knife's edge, with the slightest misstep having the potential to destroy the deal. It was also obvious to me time was not our friend. With every passing day the odds of our being discovered increased slightly. With the landlord wanting to sell John's house we had from time to time to go to Roger's. What if there was an auto accident, hardly a rarity in Tehran's terrible traffic? What if one of us became ill and required hospitalization?

As I wrote earlier, the release of most of the women hostages and the naming of the remaining two could raise questions about the whereabouts of Cora and Kathy. Although we did not know at the time, some members of the media figured out there were a few Americans on the loose. We also later learned about a mid-January telephone call to the Taylor residence. Someone speaking with a "vaguely North American" accent had asked to speak with Joe Stafford. Pat Taylor told him there was no one by that name there, but this could not be a simple wrong number. The caller verified he had reached the residence of the Canadian ambassador, and then once again asked for Joe. He seemed insistent.[2]

The optimistic explanation was someone in the media figured out Joe was somewhere in Tehran and was guessing where an American might hide. By the time this call took place the planning for our departure was well underway, but the call highlighted that our governments were right to be concerned about what the media might know. While we ourselves were purposely left in the dark, the Department and the Canadian government, presumably including Taylor, were aware some reporters knew not all of the embassy staff had been captured. Both governments had, so far successfully, persuaded those reporters who knew the story to sit on it. The US government also knew about other publicity that could have seriously

---

2. Pat Taylor interview, Escape from Iran: The Inside Story

compromised us. For example, Lee's mother was not initially told his being in hiding in Tehran needed to be kept secret, so she shared the information with a local Idaho paper.[3] I remain baffled how this report, not to mention the nationally broadcast King interview on CBS news, failed to trigger broader interest in the possibility of embassy staffers on the loose in Tehran. Still, this telephone call marked a new phase. It meant yet another reporter had figured out some of us were out and was guessing where we might be, or one of those already in the know had linked us with the Canadians (to my knowledge, our governments knew of only one who had definitely made the connection and there would have been no reason for him to make the call). Either way, it was an escalation of the risk of media exposure.

Our parents had been invited to the briefing State put on for hostage families, yet our names were never mentioned in press reports nor had we been shown on any of the propaganda clips. Our families, unlike Lee's, had been told not to say anything about our situation, but it put them, and therefore potentially us, in an awkward position. They had to be on guard all the time. My older sister Mary had a friend whose husband was a reporter for the local ABC affiliate in Seattle. One evening they were both working on a project for the preschool their kids attended and a news report about the hostages led to a conversation. It was late, Mary was tired, and she stopped herself at the last second from saying something about me.

Although the information was kept from us, our parents were getting occasional contacts from the press. With a name like Lijek mine were easy enough to find. And somewhat surprisingly to me, Amburn, although it sounds like it might be common, isn't. So while I did not know about the press interest in our families I was concerned our absence from any of the propaganda events, along with the Iranian claim all but two women had been released, could compromise our situation. About this time, I approached Bob and suggested we write a cable to State and once we were both satisfied it said the right things, ask Ken to send it through his channels. It would summarize the points above (minus the media issue, about which we could only speculate), and request the Department begin

---

3. Narrator, Ibid.

active efforts to get us out. Bob agreed with the idea and we discussed it also with Lee. If nothing else, playing with the wording gave me something worthwhile to do for a day.

We asked John to tell Ken we would like to meet with him when it was convenient and presented him with the telegram. We were careful to stress we remained overwhelmed by the hospitality of our Canadian hosts and were not reacting to any specific, immediate problem. The telegram spoke for itself. Ken was noncommittal, but he took the hand-written paper and said he would see what he could do. I now know the telegram was never sent, but even so, I believe it served its purpose. At a minimum, it told Taylor we were ready to leave despite whatever risks it might entail. The arguments we used had probably occurred to the Canadian embassy staff as well as those in Ottawa and DC who were working on the Iran situation. Perhaps hearing them from us made a little difference, strengthening the hand of the officials in Ottawa, including Minister of External Affairs Flora MacDonald, who were making the argument to DC it was time to get us out. At the least, I was confident it justified a paragraph in the sitrep (situation report) Taylor would send to Ottawa the following morning.

I do not recall whether Joe Stafford was included in the discussion regarding the telegram as we did not see him on a regular basis. I was aware Joe did not share our desire to leave. He had several times expressed the belief we had an obligation to stay until the hostages were released. He was the only one of the six who felt this way, and all of the arguments we put into the cable when presented in our mutual discussions had no impact on his position. Joe was probably the smartest of us, certainly the best linguist, but on this issue logic seemed to escape him. Of course he may feel the same way about me. Although we have remained friends, our paths since Iran have seldom crossed so the opportunity to delve into this question has never arisen. Besides, I have no reason to believe Joe would be more willing to explain his position now than before. A number of the people who read earlier drafts of this book commented that my inability to clarify the reasons for Joe's attitude was unsatisfying. I totally understand. I can only tell what I know, that Joe's subsequent career confirmed my judgment of him as gutsy, smart and driven. Those personality traits eliminate fear as a factor behind his views. Perhaps more to the point, staying in Tehran was increasingly dangerous as Joe must have understood. So, unless he decides to explain his position, the mystery will remain.

In any case, I believe history has vindicated the judgment of the five. The hostages were held for an additional year and expecting the Canadians to keep us that long would have been unreasonable. Even aside from Murphy's Law, the daily increase in the odds of something going wrong I mentioned earlier, the practical logistics were a problem. The Sheardowns brought with them packaged food, liquor, cigarettes, and similar items sufficient for a three year tour. At the point of our departure, virtually everything had been consumed. Some critical items (to me, anyway), like the cigarettes, had run out some time ago and, as I mentioned earlier, John was buying them at his own expense on the black market. The preparation of the telegram had given me a small sense of having some control or influence over my situation so it was difficult to return to the normal life of sleeping late, making breakfast, reading and playing Scrabble. On the other hand the daily reminders of how fortunate we were in comparison to our colleagues downtown, whether from the newspaper or radio or even a tidbit from John, were more than enough to keep me relatively content. As things transpired, however, it was only a day or two before Taylor came to us with a question, a hint something might be brewing.

He asked whether we would feel comfortable leaving Iran using US passports. I don't recall the exact flow of the conversation, but our collective answer was a version of "you're kidding, right?" We assumed we would have false identities and a cover story, but even so, "Amrika" was the great Satan and visitors from there would be subjected to special scrutiny at any border crossing or even if stopped in the street. Besides, I thought, we were almost unofficial members of the Canadian embassy staff. Surely it would be a small thing to send us passports more appropriate to our new status. I did not actually joke with Ken in that way but I had assumed (and I think the others did also) the Canadian government would issue us Canadian passports. While I did not understand the procedures required, I did consider a Canadian passport was far and away the best protection we could have during the exit process. To this point, no one had mentioned the possibility the CIA might get involved.

We were thinking in terms of a Canadian operation, largely or exclusively staffed by embassy personnel, perhaps with some help from the New Zealanders or other friendlies.

We did not know the passports had been authorized in early January by a secret "Order-in-Council," which had in turn been signed by the Governor General. It required action at the highest levels of the Canadian government of a kind not done since World War II to place those passports in our hands. I assumed the Canadian equivalent of the CIA would do this on its own, but when I later learned what had actually been required it further highlighted the Canadian commitment to our safety. One could argue issuing these passports was also an act of self-protection. It significantly increased our odds of success, while failure, depending on the plan, would almost certainly have made clear to the Iranians the extent of Canadian assistance to us. Yet it is equally true this decision ended whatever slight chance the Canadian government might have of denying high level official involvement were we to be caught. I don't think the expression was used in those days, but the Canadians were now officially "all in." The passports reached Tehran on January 13.[4]

After this discussion with Taylor, we once again returned to the daily grind. For the first time, however, we began to think maybe our days in Tehran were limited. It was time for *the* Scrabble Tournament. Scrabble had been our regular companion from early days at the Sheardown's. We had all improved tremendously as players but who was best remained controversial. So we devised a round-robin format, the specifics of which I no longer remember. What I do remember is it was me against Lee for the championship and I won the deciding game with a score of 475 points. For those who do not play the game, the instructions say a combined point total of 400-500 points among all players is normal. I don't remember Lee's score, but I recall it was a close game so would guess together we easily topped 800 points. I felt comfortable awarding myself the title "Scrabble Champion of North Tehran," given it was unlikely too many others were in competition for it and my score was truly impressive. This critical issue having been decided we once again

---

4. Kenneth Taylor interview, Ibid.

settled into our various routines. In my case, this meant sleeping late, evaluating my scraggly beard for signs it was finally going to turn into something respectable, a late breakfast and holding Bob personally responsible for the meager content of the news.

Another change sometime in early January was the rental of a safe house. As I wrote earlier John's residence was built into the side of a hill with the roof essentially at ground level at the back. Richard Sewell had located a house in the neighborhood behind us and rented it in the name of the New Zealand embassy. It was equipped with some food and water. We were shown where the house was on a map and another copy of the map along with the entrance key were stashed near our back door. I am not sure where this proposal came from. The CIA was already actively involved in planning our departure so perhaps the insurance value of the safe house was suggested by them. Richard provided other assistance to the CIA so the idea seems reasonable to me. I do recall being told US funds were paying for the house. While we all thought the house was a clever idea, it had no impact on our daily living situation. It was not long, however, before our routines were disrupted in a very fundamental way.

One afternoon in mid-January John came home a bit early. He called us into the den, and after offering drinks to everyone and taking a few sips from his Ballantines announced he and Zena were leaving. The emotion in his voice was palpable. He actually apologized to us that they were unable to stick with us until the end. This was crazy. They had already put their lives at risk for us and had been the greatest hosts imaginable for over two months, but this was John's nature. He was a charter member of Tom Brokaw's "greatest generation." He'd been a RAF bomber pilot in World War II and the spirit of that effort had clearly continued to steer his life. In his book, it was simply not right to quit the task before it was completed even if others were ready to carry it on.

While I think we all sensed John's concern he was abandoning us and leaving a job undone, Lee was the first to respond. He thanked John and Zena for everything they had done, said it was important to remember Zena did not have diplomatic status and it was only right he take care of his wife first. We assumed the Sheardowns, while probably not briefed on the specifics of the exfiltration plan, were aware their departure was part of the drawdown in Canadian embassy staffing that had to happen before we could leave. We ourselves were vaguely aware people were leaving but I for one had not yet drawn the connection to the proximity of our own departure. Following Lee's lead we all took turns thanking them and emphasizing they had done above and beyond as far as taking care of us. They had absolutely no reason to feel their departure was in any sense letting us down.

Our comments to them were based on the assumption they knew at least as much as we did about our departure plans. I don't know why we didn't talk more openly. We were reading a lot into Taylor's question about the passports, perhaps too much, but the Sheardown's reassignment looked to us as confirmation of our own impending trip home. We assumed they understood that also. Ironically, I believed they knew more than we did and their concern was only that they should have been allowed to leave with us. It never occurred to me that even my vague premonition of our exit plans was more concrete than what they had been told. In my world, they were the most important Canadians, and it was inconceivable to me they had been kept in the dark. Looking back, I understand why John and Zena were not briefed on the exfiltration plan. This was simply good procedure, "need to know" and all the spook stuff, but it was heartbreaking for them. Furthermore, we now know the decision to pull the Sheardowns from Tehran was driven by domestic political concerns in Canada. The Canadian news showed long lines of visa applicants at the embassy and questions were raised in parliament as to why the Canadian government was continuing to provide visa services at a time when the Iranians were holding diplomats hostage. This was part of a broader political problem, again something wisely kept from us.

The Minister of External Affairs, Flora MacDonald, on the instructions of Prime Minister Joe Clark, had told opposition leader Pierre Trudeau about us. Clark's government was in an awkward position. As a close ally of the US the Canadians would in normal circumstances have been looking for ways to pressure Iran to free the hostages. Because of us, however, it was decided a low key approach made more sense. So while the government did participate with other American allies on certain initiatives, Trudeau missed no opportunity to excoriate Clark for not doing more. It is no credit to Trudeau, even knowing his antics could endanger us, he continued to harass the government just as before. Trudeau himself was not exactly the most pro-American leader in Canadian history, but during these critical months he made himself sound like the greatest ally we had.

The Canadians decided to relocate visa operations to Kuwait, a nation with a significant Shia population. This decision presumably made sense for operational reasons, but it did not take into account the possible risk to the Sheardowns should we manage to escape Iran and their role in the escape become publicly known. Fortunately, they were called back to Ottawa and were in Malta when news of our escape broke. They heard it first from the media. No one in official Ottawa had thought to tell them, despite the fact we would have, without hesitation, named them the key figures in our escape. It goes back to John's initial welcome,

"Why didn't you call sooner?"

That was fundamental to our decision to impose ourselves on the Sheardowns and subsequently the Canadian government.

We had to spend some time hiding in our rooms over the following days as the packers came to collect John and Zena's personal effects. Since the furniture belonged to the Canadian government we were not going to be deprived of our beds or the sofas in the den. The Zenith radio remained but most of the books were gone, although Roger had a great collection of history books able to keep me going for months if not years. Hiding was a bother but not particularly scary. The packers were told there were no personal possessions in our wing of the house, which made sense as in theory these extra bedrooms would rarely be used. Staying out of sight was the least of our worries. John had become like a father to us. We looked forward to his return home every evening and the news he would bring. We did not realize to what degree we had come to depend on our evening routine as the most important part of the day. Of course we also wondered what arrangements would be made to keep us safe after Zena was gone. She answered the phone and the door during the days, a critical task given our situation. And she would have been the one to try to fend off any nosy komiteh types had, for example, the gardener somehow become suspicious.

On January 19, the day before the Sheardowns were to leave, we had a farewell dinner. Roger came over also. Although it was a sad event for us, we were determined to show no signs of our unease. We already knew how badly John and Zena felt about what they considered their abandonment of us and we were not going to do anything to make the situation more difficult. But again, we thought they knew, at least in general terms, that we would try to follow them out of Iran before long. We did our best to keep the tone light, talking about how the next time we met this would all seem like a bad dream. After dinner we took a couple of photographs in the den, with five of us piled on top of each other on the sofa and Lee and Roger leaning up against the ends. John had a camera with a timer and it was set on the desk next to the radio. Unfortunately, it used 110 film, which created a small, low resolution negative that cannot be blown up without critical loss of detail. Still, the small photo clearly shows the seven of us smiling. In my case at least the smile was not forced. I was happy for John and Zena and reasonably certain we would be seeing them again before long.

The Sheardowns left the next day. The actual goodbye was brief. The men shook hands with John and gave Zena a quick hug, and Cora hugged both. No tears and rather formal. In this case a "stiff upper lip" was the best protection against an excess of emotion that would have embarrassed John and Zena as well as making them feel even worse. We said our farewells in the den because their bags were already by the front door and we could not risk being seen by the local employee driver who was coming to take them to the airport. A final reminder of their absence was the pile of crates stacked in one of the basement rooms, containing their personal effects, which I passed on the way to the laundry. I guessed they would not be shipped until the Sheardowns future assignment was clarified.

We shifted emotional gears quickly from sadness to fear. Once John and Zena were gone we soon realized being on our own in the house was a problem. While some things could be anticipated, others could not. For example, one day when John was home a man came to the door asking to use the phone. His car had broken down on the street out front. No problem for John. Probably not a problem for us even, but it was the kind of chance we did not need to take. We had been instructed not to answer the phone or the door, but what if the landlord came by to have some repairs done? If no one answered he might let himself in. The gardener was once again a concern. As far as he knew the house was empty during the days so we had to take special care to remain quiet. Or what if there were some kind of emergency and we needed to evacuate? How would Roger let us know if we couldn't answer the phone? The safe house was a good idea, but considerably less useful if we could not be alerted to go there. Roger moved into the house the evening the Sheardowns left. Despite our misgivings we coped on our own for the first two days. The second day was more nerve-wracking than the first and finally we voiced our fears to Roger. The next day Junior Gosse, a Canadian Forces military policeman, was at the house when Roger left. Junior was from Newfoundland, a Newfie as he called himself. He was now a member of our very closed little world. Conversation with a new person helped pass the time and we learned some things about that part of Canada. Having him there was a huge relief.

We were starting to fall into our new routine when Ken came over one evening and announced we were going to have visitors. The next evening, January 26, Kevin Costa Harkins and his associate, whom I remember only as Julio, arrived with Ken and Roger. Harkins was the cover name for Antonio Mendez, a CIA officer whose specialties included exfiltration, i.e. moving people across borders without the knowledge of the host government. We never did learn anything about his associate. We assumed Julio was also a cover name. We have subsequently gotten to know the real Tony, but at the time it would have been poor tradecraft to give us his real name. The Staffords were already with us, driven over by Richard Sewell. I did not know who might be aware of Joe's reluctance to leave, whether he had shared his concerns with Taylor. If he had, then they most certainly would have been relayed to Mendez.

Tony looked about forty, average height and build, with black or very dark brown hair and a small mustache. He had a slightly dark complexion, someone who would not stand out in a crowd, except perhaps in Scandinavia or Africa. We soon learned his skill with makeup would undoubtedly have permitted him to work in those places as well. As we introduced ourselves it was clear he was studying each of us, appraising our ability to pull off the exfiltration. We were doing the same, wondering what kind of person would do this type of work for a living. We moved into the den and Mendez explained three different cover stories had been prepared and then proceeded to summarize each.

Option one was we were a group of nutritionists from a Canadian university. I think option two made us businessmen, presumably oil related in some way. I must admit I have only a vague recollection of these first two because they were clearly inferior to option three: the Hollywood scenario. At an earlier point there was discussion of us being a group of unemployed international school teachers, but I am not sure whether that made it into the final three. It was clearly the worst idea if only because there were no international schools open in Iran and anyone remotely connected to the field would have known this. So the selection process was simple, to me anyway. While the choice was technically ours, as Mendez laid out the supporting materials and summarized the proposals, it was immediately obvious the Hollywood option was much more developed. Clearly Tony wanted us to go with it. My feeling was, when you hire a professional you should probably take his advice.

The Hollywood option had us as a location scouting team, in Iran to see Persepolis, the bazaar and possibly other sites for a science fiction film called *Argo: A Cosmic Conflagration*. The CIA had gone so far as to purchase a script and set up a dummy production company in Hollywood. John Chambers, a makeup artist best known for the original *Planet of the Apes* movies as well as the ears for *Star Trek's* Mr. Spock, helped set up the operation. I know there were other people involved in helping Chambers and Mendez, but as Tony has never talked to me about them I can't provide the particulars. While we did not know these details at the time, we were told someone calling the telephone number on my Studio Six Productions business card would be told I was out of the country on business. We had a copy of the script, artist story-boards and a copy of the *Hollywood Reporter* issue with a full page ad announcing the formation of the production company.

This scenario had other advantages as well. It allowed Mendez and Julio to travel with us; each had a job on the team. It made the size of our group reasonable given the specialized nature of each person's work. But far and away its best selling feature was credibility. There was a revolution going on. The country was in chaos. Hollywood people would, to borrow an old phrase, rush in where angels fear to tread. In the reality of revolutionary Iran, Hollywood might not have quite the usual cachet, being considered a source of immorality. Even so, individual Iranians would probably still be impressed to meet someone from one of the most famous places on earth, even if they were mildly ashamed of themselves at the same time. Furthermore, our presence in a potentially hostile place made sense. If we needed Persepolis, we needed Persepolis, and the show must go on revolution or no revolution. I figured if we were detained it was more likely someone would want my business card than to interrogate me.

The one seemingly missing element of the plan was an explanation of what we actually did while in Iran. I have subsequently talked with Tony who indicated we did have this covered.[5] We were supposed to say the Canadian ambassador had informed us the situation in Iran was too difficult for us to do our scouting at this time and we should return at a later date when things had calmed down. This would also help explain our close association with the Canadian embassy in the event we needed to involve them somehow in confirmation of our cover legend. Given we were under stress and the nature of what we called our "alcohol and adrenaline" exit strategy, I will readily admit I may have forgotten this element of the plan, although I do remember telling myself to demand to see the Canadian consul if I were seriously interrogated.

My pseudonym was Joseph Earl Harris. I was the transportation coordinator, married to Teresa Harris, the script writer. My first and middle names as well as the month and day of my birth were those of my father-in-law. This was a clever way to reduce the amount of memorization I needed to do. I assume similar tricks were used for the others. Bob Anders was the location director. Lee was a cameraman. Joe was a producer and Kathy the artist carrying the story-boards as Cora carried the script. In building the team, Tony first obtained from his Hollywood contacts a rough description of the kind of expertise normally present on a scouting crew. His

---

5. Antonio Mendez, interview with the author, November 2, 2011

people then analyzed our files and assigned roles based on what they considered the best match.[6]

I guessed we all saw Mendez was strongly in favor of the Hollywood scenario. Still, we needed to talk among ourselves so we moved to the dining room and had our discussion. After a while, Bob said it was time to vote. As best I can recall it was five votes for Hollywood and one vote, Joe's, for none of the above. None of the above was not a choice and Bob reported we had selected the Hollywood option. Tony removed the small amount of paraphernalia associated with the other scenarios and left us each with one page of information to memorize the next day.

I didn't sleep late on Sunday. Although there was not a lot of information to memorize I wanted to have it down cold. Also, I wanted to watch Joe, hoping he would accept the inevitability of our departure and do his best to become a Hollywood producer. He and Kathy had spent the night, having brought what meager possessions they had at the Taylors with them. Meantime, the Canadians had rounded up suitcases and clothes for our travel. There seemed to be two primary qualifications for including something in my suitcase, an old Samsonite that probably started out brown but was now some vaguely dark color as well as thoroughly scratched and dented: the label had to be non-USA and the item had to be suitable for a male. Otherwise, size did not seem to matter much. Cora, at 5'2", had a wardrobe donor we guessed was six inches taller. I had underwear from a British department store chain, St. Michaels, as well as a men's bikini thong type thing that made great fun at parties for years afterward until it mysteriously disappeared. Probably a good fit for a Hollywood type. Most of my donated clothes were just a bit on the small side, but they would have fit in a pinch. I think the assumption was, if it came to the point they were making us try on the clothing in our suitcases, we were finished anyway. Besides, our checked baggage would theoretically be gone, waiting to be loaded on the airplane. Again, if the authorities were suspicious enough to pull it back, we were probably toast. Cora and I still had our Hartmann carry-ons, the ones we had grabbed at our apartment the morning after the takeover. While made in the USA, we figured the brand was

---

6. Ibid.

widely exported so no one would think anything about a Canadian owning one. The same was true for my briefcase, although I did have to pry off my real initials.

Fortunately the suit I had worn in the rain on the first day, walking to Bob's apartment, was a French-made Yves St. Laurent. There was a US department store label in it, easily removed. I had one good shirt but my initials were on the pocket. Cora expertly removed them, although if one looked closely enough tiny thread holes were still visible. I did have an explanation prepared. I would claim the thread had started to unravel during the trip so rather than have it look bad I had just pulled it all out. We spent the day becoming familiar with the contents of our suitcases and memorizing our new identities. I spent a few minutes in the courtyard, using John's barbecue to burn my checkbook, our real USA passports and the title to the BMW. It was at this point Joe's lack of interest in the plan was becoming painfully obvious. I do not recall I tried to talk to him. I had no new arguments left.

In addition to our Canadian passports, we were given drivers' licenses, health services IDs, and credit cards all courtesy of the Royal Canadian Mounted Police. Tony, on his trips to Ottawa and Los Angeles, picked up miscellaneous items he referred to as "pocket litter." Cora and I had matching Molson's beer key chains as well as assorted restaurant match books and similar stuff. We also had business cards, both our own and some miscellaneous ones we would have picked up on the trip.

Dinner that evening was the kickoff for "alcohol and adrenaline." We had for some time been engaged in what we termed the "scorched earth" program, our intention to leave as little liquor behind as possible. The name almost certainly was suggested by Roger, our history buff. The plan was harder to implement when we didn't know our departure date but John's stockpile was disappearing just in the natural course of things. God forbid, we might have had to institute rationing had not the departure occurred when it did. In any case, the quantities appeared about right. Our group of six was joined by Roger, Ken, and of course Tony and Julio. Additionally we invited Chris Beebe, Richard Sewell and Trolls Monk. Though Trolls was not actively involved in the exit plan, he had been a confidant of Taylor's over the months and a frequent visitor to our house. I always had the feeling, had push come to shove, we could have counted on him to help in whatever way he could. I don't remember what we ate or who cooked. I have to assume Roger was responsible for procuring the food as by this time our in-house stock was confined to canned and boxed items. Even though they had left, John and Zena were with us in spirit, more precisely spirits. It was their wine and liquor we intended to polish off. We had earlier decided the best way to handle the stress of the exfiltration was to do it on adrenaline. We were going to have our party, then practice our identities in mock interrogations and finally grab a couple hours of sleep before the 4:30am departure for the airport.

I do remember the dinner conversation with Tony. He told us he had successfully exfiltrated a number of defectors from the USSR, sometimes including their families, and had done so literally under the noses of the Soviet KGB border guards. In comparison, the Iranians were amateurs and as long as we did our parts there should be no problem getting through Mehrabad Airport. I think he even mentioned a previous exfiltration through Mehrabad a year or so earlier. Along with the adventure stories Mendez put on a little magic show. Using two of the many wine corks scattered around the table, he grasped each between his thumb and index finger, interlocking them almost like magicians use rings. Then, again in a manner similar to the ring trick, he pulled his arms apart while seemingly continuing to hold each cork firmly in his hands. Cora in particular was fascinated with the trick, no doubt helped by pre-dinner cocktails and the wine we'd consumed during the meal. Tony did it multiple times, and despite close observation neither of us could figure out how he was doing it. But then I have always been a sucker for magic tricks and this particular performance was exactly appropriate for the mood of the evening.

At some point Mendez introduced a more serious topic. This was expertly done, inserting a real concern into an otherwise relaxed and unserious conversation. Tony began by noting the CIA, the Canadians and some friendlies had been carefully recording their experiences in departing Iran. This was important both for general information and because there was one potential problem. On deplaning at the airport it was standard practice to issue an arrival card. This was a two part carbonless form with a white original and yellow copy. The original was stapled into the passport; the copy was retained by immigration. Theoretically, upon departure the immigration officer was to pull the yellow from his file and match it with the white. In our case, while the white copy was real, procured by Sewell's airport contact, there was no yellow in the file. We just had to hope the system was too overloaded with little slips of paper to be viable, or better yet, the immigration officer would consider us harmless and not even bother to look for the yellow. Tony was frank. The test runs had led to the conclusion we ought to be okay even without a copy in the file. But that was not an assurance a particular agent on a given day would not look for it. We understood, in an operation of this kind, there could be no certainties. This was a concern, but I was confident the CIA would not be using this plan if their research had led to the conclusion we were not likely to get past immigration.

Although we did not know it at the time we had already dodged a potentially fatal problem. The initial set of six passports pouched to Tehran had a dating error in the Iranian visas, one that showed them being issued after our departure date. Whether the immigration officials would have been sufficiently attentive that morning to discover the error, we will never know as Roger's seemingly limitless knowledge included what he termed the Zoroastrian calendar. He and Taylor were reviewing the documents and Roger saw the mistake. The embassy immediately reported the problem. Tony had wisely pressed the Canadians to issue a spare set of passports for contingency reasons. Tony was already in Frankfurt at this point, but cabled back he would bring the necessary items to prepare the second set for our use. When he sat down to work in Taylor's office, he found his ink pad was dry. He used a bit of Ken's Scotch whisky to dampen the pad. As Tony put it to me later, the exfiltration really was fueled by alcohol.[7]

One minor but nice thing about dinner was we didn't need to clean up. After all, we were abandoning the house in a few hours and the landlord would just have to deal with the mess once it became clear the Canadians were gone. Around 10:00pm, we moved back to the den and began our practice interrogations.

---

7. Ibid.

First we were given a short lecture on Canadianese. Aside from remembering "about" was pronounced more like "aboot" and Toronto should sound closer to the capital of Albania, Tirana, Roger told us to make sure to throw in enough "ehs" at the end of our sentences. Then we saw the other Roger Lucy. Lacking an Iranian immigration officer's uniform he substituted a camouflage jacket that would have been the envy of any pasdar. He barked questions in rapid order: date of birth, place of birth, university attended, interspersed with why did you come to Iran, when did you arrive, then perhaps looping back to an earlier question. In a nearby room Richard Sewell was doing the same thing, with a bit less panache. As we each went through the process our mistakes were noted and we tried to correct them the next time.

The exception was Joe. He did make an effort to take part, but it was obvious his heart wasn't in it. He hadn't practiced much and there was no sense of energy or enthusiasm. During the past weeks I had tried repeatedly both to convince Joe leaving was best for the hostages as well as for us and also to understand his position. Joe was clearly the brains of our group and yet on this issue he was objectively and demonstrably wrong. Now, he was being asked to do a very difficult thing, to take part in a risky enterprise he did not believe in. Furthermore, Joe's personality did not lend itself to the project. He was serious by nature, an intellectual who would have been at home on a university campus. He had a good sense of humor and a dry wit, and certainly did not lack for courage, but the spark of silly exuberance the rest of us had developed was lacking.

I asked Mendez later whether he was seriously concerned about Joe. He indicated he was not; he concluded the rest of us would "jolly" him along. When I asked whether he and Julio were aware before arrival Joe might be a problem, he said they were. There was even the possibility they might need to create a separate exit scenario for him if their observations led them to conclude his participation in *Argo* might end up jeopardizing the chances for everyone else. But once on the ground they decided, despite Joe's lack of enthusiasm for the scenario, there was no need for a separate plan. Tony also noted Joe bought him a tin of caviar at the airport and presented it to him in thanks for his efforts. This gesture would seem to indicate Joe was in the end appreciative of the work done on his behalf.[8]

The evening wore on and around midnight Tony and Julio left. Tehran by night was still dangerous, with roadblocks all too common. Richard Sewell drove them to the hotel. He was an old Tehran hand who had learned the importance of avoiding the street crews. Losing our escorts and Richard to a roadblock would have ended the exfiltration before it began. About 1:00am Cora and I headed to bed. Sleep was difficult. We were wired and we could occasionally hear the ongoing conversation between Joe and Lee from the den below. Lee did not know Joe very well. Although we were a close knit community before the takeover Lee's arrival was too recent. Afterward, when he joined us at the Sheardown's, his opportunities to interact with Joe were limited because the Staffords stayed with the Taylors and visited infrequently. Nevertheless, Lee decided to try to persuade Joe we were doing the right thing by leaving Iran. By this time, the scorched earth policy was virtually complete. Joe and Lee were left with Cointreau to accompany their conversation.

After about ninety minutes, they went to their respective rooms and quiet reigned, briefly. At 3:30am alarms sounded, but we didn't need ours as Lee took care of waking us all by running through the upstairs hallway in his underwear yelling,

"My head. My head."

He was loud enough to wake even Roger, who was in the master suite at the other end of the house. I don't know whether it is possible to be drunk and have a hangover at the same time, but Lee swore he'd managed it. Furthermore, he still smelled of alcohol. Joe presumably did as well, but we didn't see him until he was in a more presentable state. In any case, the plan to exfiltrate on adrenaline was underway. We had to hope Lee and Joe would be able to leave the alcohol smell behind.

We were showered, shaved and in the case of my miserable beard, "mascarad." My experiment failed. After ten weeks the beard was still pitiful. Tony gave me some mascara to make it look fuller and for the first and only time in my life I had a respectable

---

8. Ibid.

beard. We dressed to match our new personas. Cora, who normally used little makeup, applied some she had with her and also used the powders Tony had brought as she'd been instructed. She had some sponge rollers with her so was able to make her hair much curlier than normal. Kathy too did something with her hair. Lee didn't really need to do anything as he was not a recognizable face in the same way as consular section employees. Joe, who unfortunately was one of those consular faces, also did nothing. But the award for inventiveness went to Bob. He was dressed in grey slacks, blue blazer and an ascot around his neck. The shirt was buttoned only half way up, exposing some of his ample chest hair. This was Hollywood flamboyance, or at least as close as we could come with the materials we had. Perhaps the most important bit of "makeup" was the Canadian maple leaf pin each of us wore prominently. Mine was on the lapel of my suit jacket. Maybe it was overkill, but Canadians are a proud people and given the state of relations between Iran and the US it was just common sense for a Canadian national to want to avoid being mistaken for an American.

We carried our ersatz luggage down to John's garage and waited for our ride. At 4:30am the embassy's VW bus pulled into John's garage. The ambassador's driver was behind the wheel. Although he probably knew about us it was time to assume our new identities so we said goodbye to Roger as if we were real Hollywood scouts thanking him for his brief hospitality. We shoved our bags into empty seats or the aisle and clambered aboard. Question one was whether we would make it to the airport without trouble. It was so late it was early. The odds on not hitting a roadblock were reasonable. I figured Ken's driver had to know the best routes. After a few minutes on the road, Bob, with the benefit of his longer time in Tehran, realized we were not heading toward Julio's hotel. He alertly reminded the driver we needed to collect our financial guy, whose real job was to escort us even as Tony went ahead to insure all was well at the airport.

I let my mind wander. A line from the *Wizard of Oz* kept going through my head. Near the end of the film, the good witch, Glenda, tells Dorothy she has always had the power to go home, that all it took was belief in the power. She tells her to say over and over,

"There's no place like home." We had not always had the power to go home, but we had it now, and it was up to us to make sure the plan worked.

# 13. Let's Argau Home

There was little conversation during the drive. The adrenaline was still strong. But the time for exfiltration jokes had passed. It would be foolish to talk openly or play word games in front of the driver. Now it was up to fate, God, whatever one believed in. Tony and the Canadians had done their best to stack the deck in our favor, but as with any human endeavor there was still room for Murphy's Law. A few times I wished we could just keep driving through the comfortable, identity-erasing darkness and never reach Mehrabad airport, but that was not possible. As it was we were fortunate to arrive without incident. Cora used the time to good advantage. She searched her purse and pockets once again and found a ticket from a dry cleaner in one of the pockets of her gray suit. It had her real name on it so she stuffed it between the seat back and bottom cushions of the Volkswagen. It was a piece of genuine pocket litter, one she did not need.

Tony was supposed to be waiting for us inside the terminal. Richard Sewell was responsible for the pick up at his hotel. In fact, Mendez had overslept and Richard's 3:00am phone call woke him. Thanks to Richard's skillful driving and avoidance of roadblocks they reached the airport about 4:30am.[1] The plan was for us to look for Tony. If everything seemed okay to him, he would smile or nod and we would continue into the terminal. If there was a problem we were supposed to turn around as discreetly as possible and return to the van. The driver had been told to wait. Sewell would use his diplomatic airport pass to wander the departure area and keep a general eye on things as well maintain contact with the British Airways representative, who was well placed to know what was happening throughout the terminal. I later learned, not surprisingly, this gentleman was rumored within the expatriate community to be a

---

1. Antonio Mendez with Malcolm McConnell, The Master of Disguise (New York, William Morrow, 1999), 300

British intelligence operative. Richard would also dismiss the driver once he was certain we had no further need for him.

Lee grabbed what he often called his lucky red backpack and his dummy suitcase and shot toward the airport entrance. He wanted to be the first one through. The rest of us followed close behind. Entering the airport was a shock. The lighting was bright. I wanted to be inconspicuous but felt as if there was a spotlight on me. A big part of this was simply that we had not been in a crowded public place for months. My rational brain said no one was paying attention to us. Even in revolutionary Iran there were still plenty of foreigners transiting the airport. It took a moment to regain focus. Our eyes found Mendez. He seemed relaxed so we continued straight into the main terminal area. Each in turn put his or her bags onto the customs counter. The men on the other side were all uniformed. This was a good sign as it meant they were real customs people rather than komiteh zealots. We opened our suitcases. The inspection was perfunctory. I was surprised and annoyed when the inspector used a felt tip pen to write something in Farsi on my carry-on and my briefcase. I smiled and thanked him anyway. Presumably the revolutionary government could not afford inspection stickers. But then I thought if we made it the Farsi inscriptions would be great souvenirs.

We proceeded to check-in at the Swiss Air counter. We did not expect any problems and there were none. Our checked baggage disappeared through an opening in the wall behind the counter. We turned left and proceeded to an immigration checkpoint in the right back corner of the terminal. This was the point of no return. The customs counter was located in the public part of the airport. People could come and go, meeting arriving passengers or transacting business at the ticket counters lining the back wall. Once through immigration there was no exit. Again, the officer was uniformed. Lee engaged him briefly in conversation. He looked at Lee several times and compared him with his photograph. Lee pulled down the corners of his Fu Manchu mustache which apparently was shorter now than in the photograph. It worked. Lee disappeared and we took our turn. He inspected our passports and verified the scrawl on my carry-on items. I thought the beard might raise a question given the apparent concern over Lee's mustache, but again the inspection was perfunctory.

Then we proceeded down a long hallway and made another right turn. At the end of the hall we saw another large room, the departure area, but on our immediate left was an unattended counter. This was part two of immigration where the white and the yellow were supposed to meet. The obvious first thought was to continue past. This was the danger point; if the inspector tried to match the copies we were in trouble. The departure lounge was only ten feet away. Odds were high no one would see us walk past the empty counter. If someone did we could just plead ignorance. How were we supposed to know this counter was important? If we were normal travelers without benefit of a briefing from Tony on the immigration system at Mehrabad, we might well have walked right into the departure area as we had already gone through one passport check. Still, we stopped and waited, hoping someone would appear from the room behind the counter. Cora and I whispered to each other: what do we do? We decided we needed to find the clerk. We did not know whether he was supposed to stamp our passports, something we would need to board our flight later on. Perhaps thirty seconds passed but it seemed an hour.

Cora said excuse me in a loud voice, repeating herself several times. Finally a sleepy-eyed man emerged carrying a teapot. We guessed making tea had kept him busy in the back. He pulled out the white copies, stamped the passports and returned them to us. It was now clear why there were two steps in the immigration process. The first man verified identity while the second was supposed to match up the disembarkation cards. We will never know why he didn't look for the yellow but the multiple scouting trips had proven their value in establishing this procedure wasn't usually followed. We grabbed our passports and walked into the departure area. Outwardly I had to seem indifferent. In my head, I breathed a huge sigh of relief. It was far too soon to start celebrating, but the most critical phase of the process was over. The documents had served their purpose and the white and yellow forms were no longer a threat. In fact, a few minutes later Cora saw Tony and he was holding what appeared to be some white forms. We thought he'd managed to swipe them as he cleared the station, thereby erasing the only documentable proof of our passage. Later, we learned the reality was a little less dramatic. Anders' form fell to the floor as the clerk processed a batch of passports and Tony waited until no one was looking and then picked it up.[2]

There remained one more security check. The airport had a number of arrival/departure lounges; each flight would eventually be assigned to a particular lounge. Our flight would be announced and we would make our way to that lounge and go through security screening. In addition, we had been warned the authorities were on the lookout for valuables. Many Iranians were trying to get their wealth out of the country and to prevent this security personnel were checking for smuggling of valuables such as gold or diamonds. Even the export of Persian rugs was banned. Sometimes the screening included body cavity searches. We hoped as foreigners we would not be suspected of carrying valuables. Having made it through customs and immigration, we would have much preferred to go straight to security and get it over with. But our flight was not departing until 7:00am. There was nothing to do but wait.

We were surprised to see some of the Canadian embassy staff in the lounge. They were even more surprised to see us. Information about our departure plans had been restricted to those with "need to know." For the most part we ignored each other, although Lee could not help himself. One of the staffers had a large maple leaf on his suitcase, and Lee walked past the man and, with a big smile on his face, said "Canadjyen, eh?"[3] The poor man didn't know how to react, in the end he just smiled back. Cora and I had been given some money, both rials and dollars, as well as credit cards (we were never told whether those would work). We did not have much, but our explanation would have been that Julio was our money man and we had only a little bit for personal expenses. We decided to act like real tourists and purchase two tins of caviar. The equivalent quality product went for $300 in the States. This was our last opportunity to enjoy one of the three good things about Iran. There were a few other shops to visit but little of interest. So we walked back into the

---

2. Ibid, 302
3. Lee Shatz interview, Escape from Iran: The Inside Story

main departure area where we saw Joe reading a Farsi newspaper. Maybe he got a signal from Tony or he realized it didn't look right, but he got rid of it. We sat down next to him and Kathy. This was natural as we were supposed to be a group, but when Joe called Cora by her real name for what was at least the second time we decided it would be safer for all if we sat elsewhere.

We saw a couple of revolutionary guards walk past. So far we had not encountered any at the formal checkpoints and it was not clear to us what these men were doing. Tony later indicated they were probably on the lookout for potential smugglers,[4] which meant their focus was on Iranians. About 6:15am, our wait ended. Our flight was announced and we made our way over to the lounge. The security clearance process was mild by current TSA standards. There were a couple of komiteh types there but they seemed interested in the Iranian passengers, looking for contraband I assumed.

As each step brought us closer to departure, the wait became more and more excruciating. The aircraft was already on the ground and we had survived all of the checkpoints. What could possibly go wrong? So far my friend Murphy had left us pretty much alone, but it was time for him to reassert the law. A voice came over the PA system and announced the flight was being delayed due to a mechanical problem. Richard Sewell and his friend the British Airways manager had been shadowing us. He had already asked about the problem and conferred with Tony. Someone grumbled the delay could be three hours. Tony called us together in a corner of the lounge. The problem was relatively minor. It could probably be fixed within an hour. He did mention the possibility of using our alternate tickets. As a precaution we were also ticketed on a British Airways flight departing twenty minutes after the Swiss Air. These tickets would have been used if we learned in advance the Swiss Air flight would be delayed or even canceled for the day. Even so, we could use them now. But we all agreed it would look too strange if we marched out of the departure lounge at this point and moved to another airline. How many people travel with two sets of tickets? Even the Hollywood cover could not provide a reasonable explanation. What about our baggage? Of course we didn't really

---

4. Mendez, 302

care about it, but it would have been difficult to explain why we were sending our suitcases to Zurich and ourselves to London. There was no choice but to wait it out.

This wait was more painful than the previous ones. There was nothing to read, nothing left to talk about. I sat and stared into the glow of dawn. The delay was only thirty minutes. We grabbed our carry-ons and the plastic bag (another of the three good things about Iran, after all, so our purchase was actually a twofer) with the caviar. There were no further formalities. We exited the building and boarded the bus. It took us to the aircraft. A shiny new A-310. I don't know whether Swiss Air maintains the tradition, but back then their aircraft were named after cities or regions in Switzerland. Bob pointed to the name on the plane: Argau. I never learned whether it has any relationship to the original Argo, the ship captained by Jason and crewed by the Argonauts, the heroes of Greek mythology. We did have a couple of heroes in our group, Tony and Julio. So while we Argaunauts had our Jason, actually two of them, the analogy ends there. We were not in search of a Golden Fleece and we were not heroes like the original Argonauts. We were reluctant explorers who simply wanted to get back home. We had the good fortune to come under the protection of real heroes, the Canadians and those who helped them such as Richard Sewell. Still, it was an interesting coincidence, if coincidence it was.

The old saying goes that the best laid plans of mice and men often go astray. Not this time. The plans were well laid and they worked. The last official Canadians followed us out safely later in the day. Claude destroyed the embassy's communications and cryptographic equipment with a sledge hammer. He thereafter became "Sledge." As he departed, Taylor placed a sign at the embassy door indicating it was closed due to a Canadian holiday. The New Zealanders became responsible for Canadian affairs, but their own embassy was attacked four days later. We could only assume it was because they became the representative for Canadian interests. Perhaps to some that relationship implied the New Zealanders must also have had a role in our escape. The attackers guessed right but for the wrong reason. No one was taken hostage, but Chris and Richard were brought home as a preventive measure. The Danes then took over. The Canadian embassy remained closed for eight years.

# Part V

Fleeting Fame

and

A Touch of Fortune

# 14. Ready for Re-Entry

Our seat assignments were scattered throughout the cabin. Cora and I were together near the middle, Tony toward the front. As we settled into our seats, a flight attendant offered to take our caviar and stow it in one of the aircraft refrigerators.

We were airborne.

The captain announced they would try to make up for the time lost due to the malfunction. Though we were no longer on Iranian ground we were still in their airspace. Airplanes are sometimes forced to return because of a mechanical issue. I was pretty sure this wasn't going to happen. I assumed, barring some type of near-catastrophic failure, Tony would get word to the pilot we were aboard and should not be returned to Tehran.

There were no incidents. We counted the minutes until we were out of Iranian airspace. There was no question when this happened. It was twenty-five long minutes and then the beverage carts were rolled into the aisles and alcohol served. Cora and I ordered Bloody Mary's, the first of several in my case. When the carts were gone, Tony leaned into the aisle and hoisted his glass, a silent toast to our mutual success. We raised our glasses in return.

I would be a much better writer if I could describe what I felt during the first moments of freedom. Joy. Relief. Gratitude toward all who had helped us. A bit of guilt too. We were leaving our friends behind. Only an incredible series of events, decisions and stupid, lucky, unforeseeable breaks had brought us to this point. Why could it not have happened for them as well?

Unlike the interminable waiting at Mehrabad Airport the flight passed quickly. We were in approach to Zurich and then on the ground. As we came into the terminal, two men waited for us. Tony and Julio walked over to them, shook hands and exchanged a few words we didn't hear. Then they came back to us. We had time for a quick handshake and goodbye. It was so inadequate considering they might have saved our lives. How odd I don't know Julio's real name. I never met him again. But they were pros and for them it was just another day at the office. Time constraints aside there was never a way to thank them adequately.

The two men who were waiting approached us and introduced themselves. One was Sheldon Krys, the Executive Director of the Bureau of Near Eastern Affairs. Earlier I mentioned briefly how State is organized. The executive director of a bureau is its chief administrative officer. As we were to learn in the coming weeks, Sheldon in addition to all his regular duties was in charge of relations with the hostage families. I never thought to ask him why it was necessary to send someone of his rank to meet us. Perhaps he wanted to come. He had been extensively involved in our situation for months. The other person was Dr. Jerome Korcak, the chief of State's Medical Division, mentioned earlier in connection with the shah's illness. He was sent to make sure we hadn't gone crazy during our time in hiding.

I do not remember whether it was Sheldon or Mendez who took our documents. Unfortunately we were asked to part with our passports and all of the associated identification cards. Some of us managed to keep part of the pocket litter. Cora held on to the *Hollywood Reporter* issue with the ad for *Argo* and a brochure for the Brown Derby restaurant in Hollywood. Our protestations that dual Canadian-American citizenship seemed like a really good idea fell on deaf ears. We were handed newly issued American diplomatic passports we needed to sign. We cleared immigration and went to baggage claim, then through customs again using our new American documentation.

We piled into a white Toyota Lite-Ace van. Sheldon drove to the capital, Bern, a trip of about an hour and a half, and to the residence of the American ambassador. During the trip Cora and I realized we had never retrieved our caviar from the stewardess. When I thought about all the important things that could have gone wrong, it was hard to be too annoyed.

Ambassador Richard Vine, a Georgetown alumnus, greeted us warmly when we arrived. Mrs. Vine showed us to our rooms and we were given a few minutes to wash up before lunch. I don't remember what we ate. I'm sure the food and conversation was good. But what

I remember most is beginning to feel normal. When you live with stress permanently for an extended time, you forget what it's like to relax… just completely and totally relax.

After lunch the ambassador introduced us to his two cute, little finches. He insisted they could speak. We waited and waited but they restricted themselves to chirping. Finally, Ambassador Vine announced they must be intimidated by having eight new people around. He assured us they would talk when the room was empty.

Full normalcy was still to come, however, at least if the Department had its way. After lunch we went to our rooms to rest. We'd hardly slept in two days. The downside of normalcy is it stops the flow of adrenaline. I decided to take a shower but first put my poor excuse for a beard out of its misery. It was either shave or make mascara a permanent part of my morning routine. It was then I noticed my shirt collar was brown. The mascara rubbed off onto the white shirt. This was almost impossible not to notice, but when had it started? I hoped I hadn't walked around Mehrabad Airport with a brown collar, but there was no way to know and it hadn't caused a problem. If it had started coming off while we were still in Iran, I was grateful I didn't know as this would have made it all the harder to act relaxed during the exfiltration. I figured Cora or Tony would have noticed and said something. Apparently no one on our side noticed either. Yet again, it seemed someone up there was looking out for me.

After a shower and a nap we got up and dressed, then went back downstairs. Sheldon had asked us to meet as a group at 4:30pm. It was a bit early so we wandered around the residence main floor and again checked on the finches. Still speechless. We ran into the ambassador who suggested a quick tour of the grounds. It was a mild day for January in Switzerland but there were residual piles of snow here and there and the carp ponds remained covered with ice. We could see the fish swimming around beneath and I was surprised when Vine said they survived the winter trapped like that.

At 4:30 we gathered in the living room. Sheldon was fortyish with medium build and dark hair. He had a habit of clasping his hands in front of his body when speaking. He struck me as very genuine and caring with a dry wit I soon learned could slice through weak logic in a flash. He opened by giving us a symbolic pat on the back for staying calm during the exfiltration and making the choices that allowed us to reach the Canadians and ultimately safety. Then he noted the government was continuing a range of efforts to negotiate the release of the hostages. There was fear knowledge of our escape would seriously complicate those efforts. The result was a plan to send us to Eglin Air Force Base in Florida, where we would live under assumed names until the hostages came home. Apparently State had some kind of facility there and we would be given jobs while we waited.

This was a shock. Not because the concern was unreasonable, but simply because we were living and thinking one day at a time and had not really considered the impact our escape might have. Nor did we know at least one journalist had connected us to the Canadians and would realize the closure of their embassy meant we had left Iran. We also had yet to comprehend how the hostage drama had captured the attention of the world. While I thought this was an intriguing and possibly fun idea both Bob and Lee expressed understandable concerns. Bob's wife was still in Athens. What would she be told? Lee's mother had health issues and he had a serious girlfriend and did not want to keep her in the dark either. Neither one wanted to remain in hiding at least if it meant continued separation from family. As the discussion progressed it became evident we and the Staffords, who did not face these problems to the same degree, were open to the idea. Bob and Lee needed convincing. When all the questions we could think of were asked and answered Sheldon asked Bob and Lee to sleep on it and we would talk more in the morning.

During the meeting, Dr. Korcak, a heavy set man with brown hair and glasses, did a good imitation of the finches, other than the chirping of course. He said nothing but watched intently.

We then moved to the dining room for dinner. A typical ambassador's residence comes with a staff, including a cook. Entertaining foreigners in reasonable style remains one of the fundamental elements of diplomacy and in this case we benefited from the excellent cuisine. Since Lolita left in early January we had gotten used to more rustic cooking. It was a pleasant change to sit down to a really good meal. Ambassador and Mrs. Vine asked many questions, but also made us aware of the degree to which the hostage drama had become an international phenomenon.

As dinner drew to a close the ambassador received a telephone call. He signaled to Sheldon and they left the room. A couple of minutes later Sheldon announced the news of our departure from Iran was hitting the wire services and we were going to leave Bern for Germany as soon as possible. We were asked to collect our belongings and assemble in the entryway. Cora and I needed only a few minutes. Outside of toiletries we hardly had any real clothes (i.e. things we could actually wear as opposed to the "for show" stuff in our suitcases), so there had been no need to unpack.

A Canadian journalist named Jean Pelletier figured out a number of Americans had escaped the embassy takeover and were in hiding with the Canadians. He claimed he did this by close study of the numbers of employees and collecting as much documentation as possible regarding the names of embassy staff. He compared this with the information the terrorists made public. The conclusion we were with the Canadians was a calculation, but confirmed by a contact at the Canadian Embassy in Washington when Pelletier confronted the man with his information and threatened to publish it. He was persuaded to sit on the story because of the obvious danger to the Canadian embassy staff as well as the houseguests.

There is an alternative version of the story. Pelletier's father was the Canadian ambassador in Paris. Early in our stay with the Canadians a telegram making reference to us was mistakenly sent from the Ministry of External Affairs to virtually all Canadian diplomatic posts. Roger Lucy first learned of us from a friend at the embassy in the country where he vacationing. Pelletier insists he did not receive any information from his father and I have no basis to believe otherwise. Several other news organizations also approached the Department with conclusions based on methodology similar to Pelletier's and they also accepted requests to defer publication.

When Pelletier learned the Canadian embassy in Tehran had closed he realized we must be out and his paper, *La Presse* of Montreal, immediately published the story. It was everywhere within hours. But neither Pelletier nor any other reporter knew where we were. Yet. The Department realized reporters would be hunting for us and wanted to present us to the world on its terms.

We loaded up the van. Sheldon drove with Dr. Korcak next to him. The six of us filled the remaining two rows of seats and our luggage the back. The little Lite-Ace was completely full. Perhaps the most dangerous part of our journey had begun. With its 1.6 liter four cylinder engine the van was incapable of maintaining autobahn speeds. Sheldon stayed in the right (slow) lane, but on some hills we were barely capable of doing 40 miles per hour while traffic in the left lane was going double that or more.

Once we were underway Sheldon explained the government did not want us found in Switzerland. There were a limited number of flights out of Tehran and while we could theoretically be anywhere an enterprising reporter might figure it out. I do not think we had entered Switzerland illegally. The passports used for entry were genuine. But the Swiss were now managing our affairs in Iran and it was critical there be no perception they were somehow involved in the exfiltration. We were told to be vague about our route of travel out of Iran. As long as our having been in Switzerland was not officially confirmed the Swiss government was under no obligation to react and Swiss neutrality was preserved.

We crossed into Germany at a small border station on a two-lane road. It was 11:00pm. As we entered Germany we heard a news bulletin on American Forces radio saying we were en route to Germany. Good timing.

It was still January 28th, amazing because early the same morning we had awoken in Tehran. We had covered not only a great physical distance but changed the very nature of our lives. The border guard did not seem particularly attentive, which was good because our passports were not quite normal. For some reason State chose to use Xerox copies of our photographs rather than color as is required by US passport regulations. The passports were diplomatic, however, and presumably that overcame any curiosity the irregular photos might arouse. We had no difficulties crossing and soon were on the A5 autobahn headed north to the US Air Force base at Rhein-Main, Germany. With a few stops for breaks and drinks, the trip lasted much of the night. Though I slept fitfully I was repeatedly nudged into semi-consciousness by the sound of cars blasting past us. Now that we were in the land of no speed limits they were often traveling three times faster than our little van could manage. I chuckled to think we might be rear-ended on the autobahn because State wanted to save a few bucks on the van rental. I said a silent prayer of thanks as we pulled up to the security gate at the air base.

In those days, Rhein-Main was one of the key US Air Force facilities in Europe. It was home of the 8th Air Force. Situated on the south side of the civilian Frankfurt airport, they shared the same runway, the longest in Europe. We were taken to the transient quarters; one wing had been closed off for our use. The base commander came to welcome us and offer any assistance we might need. He said base personnel were aware of our presence and we could leave the hotel without concern as the entire facility was closed to the press. We thanked him, and said our first priority was a shower and a few hours sleep in something that wasn't cramped or moving after which a visit to the base exchange would be great. Since we usually had to do laundry about every three days we were reaching the critical point.

I cannot resist a brief aside (I know, I haven't resisted very many to this point). A very small part of this book was written at the former transient quarters. While working on the manuscript Cora and I had occasion to overnight near Frankfurt airport. Rhein-Main Airbase is long gone, replaced by the civilian airport's cargo terminal. A German hotel chain bought and renovated the transient quarters. As we walked the hallways the building began to look familiar, so we finally asked the desk and they confirmed our hunch.

Sheldon indicated we would be at Rhein-Main for a day or two, long enough to rest, decompress, and catch up on happenings in the outside world. This would also allow time for State to bring our families to Dover Air Force Base in Delaware where we would be reunited with them and more thoroughly briefed and debriefed. He again offered us access to medical care if we felt the need: the base had an Air Force clinic and there was a major Army medical center a half hour away. I am not aware any of us took advantage.

After a shower and a nap we were ready for the exchange. On the trip over I saw yellow ribbons tied around trees and hanging prominently around the base. Sheldon explained the yellow ribbon was the brainchild of Penne Laingen, wife of our Tehran chargé. She in turn got it from the Tony Orlando song in which a yellow ribbon served to welcome home a man returning from prison. This was another step in bringing us up to speed on the impact of the hostage drama back home.

We didn't have any money but Sheldon took care of the expenses. He gave each of us $200 to spend which in those days was a reasonable sum for the purpose, especially at base exchange prices. We each bought a full wardrobe: everything from socks and underwear to shirts to an overcoat with zip-in liner and, in my case, a wonderful pair of fur-lined gloves I still have. We were made to feel like the only customers in the store with sales staff helping us navigate the large and well-stocked exchange. Our fake wardrobes were largely discarded, except for souvenir items like the men's bikini underwear someone with a sense of humor had donated to me. Special mention goes to the small Canadian moose placed in Cora's suitcase. Somewhere along the way one of its ears broke off; figuring out how to reattach it is still on my to-do list.

There was one thing I overlooked in all the excitement: getting a decent haircut. Although I had hair in those days and long hair was still acceptable for men in a business environment, mine looked a bit too much like I had escaped from the 1960's rather than Tehran. I didn't think about it until later, when I saw photographs or video clips of myself.

Later in the day we had a visit from the commander of USAFE, US Air Forces Europe, a four star general. He was very gracious and again we were made to feel like VIPs. While I understood the situation on a practical level, part of me could not help thinking all we had really done aside from being in the wrong place at the wrong time was have a tremendous run of luck. Someone brought over a large stack of magazines and newspapers, some dealing with news of our escape but others providing background on the reaction of people throughout the world to the attack on our embassy. We learned it had spawned a television program, *Nightline*, hosted by Ted Koppel. Walter Cronkite, the anchor of *CBS Evening News* and an icon to many Americans was ending each program with a countdown of the number of days the hostages had been in captivity.

The hostages were to remain in Iran for nearly another year, but the purpose of making us aware of the public and media reaction to the embassy attack was to help prepare us for the ordeal ahead. While our own story made a great sidebar to the hostage drama the media could be expected to play it up far more than it deserved because of its connection to the bigger story. We also saw papers covering the news of our escape. The Iranian reaction was swift, simultaneously silly and sinister. One of the terrorists at the embassy was quoted in a large bold headline in one of the papers,

"That's Illegal, That's Illegal."

Foreign Minister Sadeq Gotbtzadeh, who I can proudly report was expelled from Georgetown University, threatened retaliation against Canadian interests as well as unspecified repercussions for the hostages. In reality he had virtually no influence on those who were holding our people. The comments were intended for the Iranian press and public. I am not aware the situation of the hostages was affected one way or another, nor do I know of any actions taken against individual Canadians. There is no doubt business interests suffered as Canadians were reasonably concerned about traveling to Iran in the aftermath of our escape. There were consequences, however, for Bruce Laingen and the two other Americans enjoying the "hospitality" of the Iranian foreign ministry. Their telephone and telex links to Washington were terminated as well as their ability to meet with other friendly ambassadors in Tehran.[1]

The Iranian government decided to take seriously the terrorist's allegation of illegality by lodging a complaint against Canada in the United Nations Security Council. The technical basis for the complaint was the Canadian prime minister had approved the use of genuine Canadian passports with forged Iranian visas.[2] I assumed this was intended for domestic consumption in Iran. There it would be seen as further proof the United Nations and the institutions of international law were biased against the Islamic republic.

Far more sinister were actions taken against Canadian Embassy and ambassadorial residence local employees. Ken was concerned

1. Robert Wright, 294
2. Ibid, 313

about this from the beginning and included in his February 1 press statement the comment that local staff were not involved in sheltering us and did not aid our escape. Four months later, however, three employees were arrested and though ultimately released without further harassment were interrogated violently. The immediate cause for this action appears to have been an accusation by another embassy local.[3]

I think we all understood implicitly we were not to discuss the CIA's role in our escape. This would have triggered a much more explosive reaction from the Iranians, given the history of CIA involvement in Iran as well as the accusation the embassy itself was a "nest of spies." Furthermore, after joining the Foreign Service we had all been through the standard briefings about protecting intelligence personnel as well as "sources and methods." Nevertheless, Sheldon cautioned us not to talk to anyone about anything until we got to Dover and received a fuller briefing on what we should and should not say.

It is not clear to me whether the exfiltration had any impact on diplomatic efforts to free the hostages. Having read several accounts of the secret efforts the Carter administration was making I do not believe there was any lasting damage. Still, the plan to keep us undercover in Florida did make sense. The Iranians were unpredictable, particularly the terrorists in the embassy compound, so better not to take the chance.

While we were absorbing these facts Sheldon worked to get us home. A commercial flight was impractical for a host of reasons. The commander of USAFE told Sheldon his personal aircraft was unfortunately unavailable due to routine but major maintenance. There was a prison flight heading to Dover the next day. It carried servicemen being returned to the US to serve time for various offenses. Sheldon turned down the idea of putting us on that plane; bad optics given the expected press coverage of our return to the US. While there would be no press in Dover the news of how we returned was almost certainly going to be public and could reflect badly on the State Department.

---

3. Ibid, 326-7

We spent one night and most of the following day at Rhein-Main. Somehow, the mechanics managed to put the USAFE commander's aircraft back together by the afternoon of the second day. We packed our new clothing into our old suitcases and after an emotional send-off from the military community in the Frankfurt area, which turned out in force to wave goodbye, boarded the aircraft.

The Boeing C-135 was a VIP version of the long-serving KC-135 tanker aircraft. It was designed to carry twenty people in high style It included both a number of seating sections where four passengers faced each other across a table and bunks in the rear for sleeping. The only drawback was there were very few windows, presumably because of its tanker origins. This was a small problem, however, as there normally isn't much to see at 35,000 feet. We mostly played cards or read books. A few people took advantage of the time to doze; we were still short of sleep. The friendly and gracious cabin crew provided drinks and snacks as well as the dinner meal.

Because we gained six hours on the time change the eight hour flight brought us to Dover in the early evening of January 30th. Families and some Department officials were awaiting our arrival. I will not try to describe the reunion with our family members except for with my own parents. I was too busy with them to pay much attention to what was happening around me. We Lijeks are not much given to public displays of emotion or lots of hugs and kisses. Still, I loved my parents deeply and it was great to see them after all we and they had been through. We had both been in difficult situations if fundamentally different ones. We were worried about being caught; they were worried about us as well as the possibility of inadvertently saying something that might reveal our actual situation. I never did ask them whether they had problems fending off questions about our lack of visibility among the hostages.

My father, Frank, was sixty-one years old, an executive with the Northrop Aircraft Corporation. He was short, 5'4", with a bit of a paunch and silver gray hair combed straight back. He had let it grow a bit longer since I had last seen him. Perhaps a touch of jealousy here; I obviously did not inherit his thick hair, although I did inherit his poor eyesight as we both wore glasses. My mother was nearly 5'6", tall for a woman of her generation. She had been very attractive in her youth as witnessed by photographs from Algiers where she had been a refugee during World War II. She and her mother escaped from Poland just as the German and Russian invaders were bringing their lines together. Her given name was Wanda, but she had acquired the nickname Lila and that was what my dad called her. She was then fifty-five and her natural blonde hair was turning white. But it remained possible to see why my father was smitten and kept the relationship going through three more years of war as well as the paper drill involved in bringing my mother, who had ended up in London as a displaced person, to the States after the war.

I greeted Cora's parents also and she mine. Her father, Joe, was retired from the Army, a Tennessee boy who had joined up to get away from the temptations of a lower class lifestyle in the South. He was 5'8" with hair beginning to turn white. Old photos showed him as a very slight young man, but age and lifestyle had caused him to gain weight, hardly a rare thing as I can personally testify. He had met Cora's mother, a tiny Japanese woman seven years his senior, while recovering from a Korean War injury in a US Army hospital in Japan. He and Setsuko fought through the military bureaucracy which at the time no longer prohibited marriages between American soldiers and Japanese women, but still did much to discourage them, as well as some resistance from both families. They too had dealt successfully with the press questions. In fact, given they lived in northern New Jersey and Joe worked in New York City the media exposure might have been greater. I do not recall we talked about the issue. Although our soon to come experience with the media left me wondering why they were not badgered constantly about issues such as our absence from the Christmas videos, I can only say this remains one of the several mysteries surrounding the media coverage of our situation. It is similar to the failure to follow up on Kim King's appearance on the evening news when he told the world we were hiding somewhere in Tehran.

The primary representative from the State Department was David Newsom, Undersecretary for Political Affairs and the third-ranking officer of the Department. Henry Precht was also there assisting Newsom. He introduced himself to all of us, but said the evening was for our families and we would talk the next day. We were also greeted by the base commander and a few other officials who would be responsible for our care during the stay in Dover.

We were escorted to the visiting officers' quarters. Our families were already lodged there. For the evening we broke into family groups. We talked both about our experiences and asked about family members. Cora was an only child but I had a brother and two sisters. As we had been allowed to exchange letters we and they did have a sense for how things were. Still, it was gratifying to learn that Sheldon, and in particular his alter ego, Ralph Frank, had done an excellent job of keeping our families informed of our situation. We did not talk to them about the CIA role in our departure. It was to be many years before we felt comfortable doing so, even knowing they could be trusted to keep it to themselves. Cora and I felt it was simpler just to stick to one version of events so there would be no confusion about what had been said to whom. When I finally did tell my parents the entire story some years later, my mother was annoyed we hadn't disclosed everything earlier.

Although Cora's parents had come from close by, mine had journeyed across the country on short notice. Furthermore, we were all feeling the stress of the situation. Even though we were temporary VIPs and being given outstanding treatment by everyone, none of us was used to the idea. We felt uncomfortable and stressed. So while it might have been more normal to sit up half the night talking we went to bed on the early side. We anticipated a busy and perhaps difficult day to come.

The following morning after breakfast with our families, we met with David Newsom and Henry Precht. Newsom was thin, medium height, balding but with some wisps of gray hair. He was well dressed and carried himself like a man with long experience in dealing with difficult situations. He opened by congratulating us on our escape, then emphasized it was critical we conduct ourselves in such a way as to minimize the damage to on-going efforts to free the hostages. He did not detail those efforts, but stressed anything that antagonized the Iranians was not in the best interest of the hostages.

At the top of the list was any mention of the CIA's role in our departure. Given the extreme sensitivity of the Iranians to CIA involvement in their country we were asked to give all credit to the Canadians and be as vague as possible regarding the details of the exfiltration. It was fine to talk about the Canadian passports and that we left as a group of Canadian business persons interested in a possible venture in Iran. In effect, we were to claim we had used one of the discarded scenarios, but the less said, the better. We could talk freely about our time with the Canadians, how we had managed to get out of the embassy compound as well as how we connected with the Canadians.

Newsom also indicated we should refrain from criticizing the administration or its efforts to free the hostages. I am not sure why he assumed we would want to do this. Presumably he figured we viewed the decision to admit the shah for medical treatment as a serious mistake, reflecting a lack of concern for its impact on the safety of the embassy staff. It is also possible Ken Taylor submitted reports on our "mental state" which might have included some of the comments I made about administration policy.

Lastly, he said the Department would prefer we disappear as quickly as possible, but the media frenzy was such it was impossible to keep us away from the press. State would help us cope to the extent possible. This help would come in the form of a controlled environment where we and the Department's public affairs staff could manage both the number of interviews and the press outlets with which we spoke. Furthermore, it was his hope to limit the intense media exposure to several days.

Sheldon, who to this point had sat quietly in the back of the room, indicated we and our families would be flown to Andrews Air Force Base the following morning, February 1st. We would then travel to the State Department building where we would be greeted by employees and make a press appearance. Also, we were told State had rented an entire floor at a hotel in Arlington, VA, not far from the Department, where we would stay for the next couple of days. This would allow State better control over press access to us. Family members were welcome to remain with us at the hotel, although they were under no obligation to stay longer than they wished.

None of the briefing information was surprising. We certainly understood the need to keep the CIA role secret. As far as criticism of the administration this was difficult for me. During the coming days I would have ample opportunities to express my opinion. No doubt journalists would be asking what we thought about the decision to admit the shah as well as Carter's actions following the embassy takeover. I believe Precht understood I had strong feelings. I had already expressed some of them to him during his October visit to the embassy. Later he approached me one-on-one and asked me what I was going to do. I told him I would toe the line. Despite what some might call an inauspicious beginning to my Foreign Service career, I was not prepared to resign and I accepted I had no choice as an employee except to salute and obey. I did not have to endorse policies with which I disagreed, but I could decline to answer certain questions or answer them in a noncommittal way.

I should also admit I had modified my original criticism of Carter's declaration that the safety of the hostages was his prime concern. I still believed saying it when he did was not good strategy. On the other hand now I had read some of the press coverage and understood better the public reaction. I realized no matter what the President might have said, the Iranians were savvy enough to understand the value of the hostages was just as great in American domestic politics as in Iranian. It would have been very hard though probably not impossible for the President to stake out the position that overall US interests might outweigh the safety of the hostages. As a presidential candidate, Ronald Reagan managed to strike this balance. There is ample evidence the Iranians were concerned he would pursue a more aggressive policy. But Carter was not Reagan, and convincing the Iranians this was his administration's view would have been difficult, although it might well have shortened the crisis. So while I continued to believe a more aggressive policy would have been better, I realized I did not have the information to make specific criticisms. Henry left comfortable I was not going to throw any bombs on national television.

That evening we watched a report from Ted Koppel, the ABC diplomatic correspondent, in which he summarized our situation. He stated correctly most of us had escaped out a back gate of the compound (not really an accurate description of the consulate entrance, but close enough), and we had taken refuge with two different Western embassies before reaching the Canadians. Given Lee was with the Swedes and we overnighted with the British, that was technically true although it implied a situation somewhat different from the reality.

ABC also televised a news conference with Flora MacDonald, the Canadian Minister of External Affairs. She implied we had been withdrawn from Iran as part of the drawdown of the Canadian embassy. This left me mildly confused because at another point it was noted we did not have Canadian diplomatic passports so would not have been reasonably considered as part of the embassy staff. I thought the implication was we were not sent out of Iran on our own but rather in the company of Canadian embassy employees. While not technically true it came reasonably close to describing the mechanism of our departure. Some of their staffers were at the airport that morning; she simply left out the part about our escorts. She also emphasized the preparations for the Iranian presidential elections seemed like a good source of distraction making the Iranians less likely to pay attention to the actions of a foreign embassy.

Other than a visit from the governor of Delaware, Pete DuPont, the only task for the day was to prepare statements for the employee greeting and the press conference. Since Joe remained ambivalent about the departure and Lee was uninterested, Bob and I did most of the drafting. The others listened and made occasional suggestions. Both statements were easy to prepare as there was little of substance we could say. We showed them to somebody from the press office and got an okay not long after. The rest of the day was ours. We did a little more shopping at the base exchange. Somehow, again, the need for a haircut eluded my consciousness. Unfortunately, this was the last opportunity, because once we hit Washington there was no time. We talked with our families more about their experiences as "hostage" parents. We learned one of Cora's letters had arrived at her parent's home with a Canadian stamp on it. While there was no chance Cora's parents were going to reveal our location, this was another of the little mistakes that might in other circumstances have revealed our location. Clearly, luck was with us, or as I have said many times, someone up there was looking out for me.

# 15. Like Wow, Man

The following morning, we collected our expanding supply of clothing. I think we abandoned the last of the filler the Canadians had provided for the exfiltration; most had already been dumped in Frankfurt. It was now time to head for Washington, DC and face the media onslaught. It was the first of February, still only a few days since we had left Iran. In many ways it was mind-numbing to think how far we had come. It was not so much in terms of physical distance but more how radically our circumstances had changed. From the boredom of hiding to the exhilaration of the exfiltration to finding ourselves the objects of world-wide media attention. It was almost too much to believe except it was really happening. One good thing was I did not have time to feel intimidated.

The Special Air Mission fleet had sent a modified DC-9 to pick us up. This was referred to by some as Air Force Two because it was often used by Vice President Walter Mondale for domestic travel, but I learned later the aircraft actually gets the designation only when the vice-president is using it. In any case it was very luxurious and made the C-135 look positively shabby in comparison. It is easy to get spoiled although we knew it would be our last flight of this kind.

The flight itself took about forty minutes. When the aircraft reached the parking stand at Andrews Air Force Base and the stairs were wheeled into place a rented city bus pulled up. Not exactly a limo, but it served the purpose, and we were all able to ride together. The official greeter was Harry Barnes, the Director-General of the Foreign Service. By now it is probably apparent the State Department has a thing for titles and this was definitely one of the better ones. Perhaps there is some history that explains why State would award its chief personnel officer such an extravagant moniker, but I do not know it.

Barnes was very tall, at least 6'6", thin and gangly. I noticed later that he had a hard time fitting into the bus seats. He had a preference for those that faced the aisle so he did not have to contort his legs. He spoke with a slight southern drawl as he greeted each of us and our family members at the bottom of the stairway. Also present was Barbara Watson, a distinguished looking elderly woman who was head of Consular Affairs. Her presence was appropriate as, with the exception of Lee, we were all performing consular work. We were then directed onto the bus for the fifteen mile trip to the main Department of State building. We spread out among the seats in family groups and even with the staffers there were more seats than people. We moved around a bit during the forty-five minute drive from the Maryland suburbs to Foggy Bottom, as the section of DC where the Department was located is called.

Barnes spoke with me for a few minutes regarding an onward assignment. Sheldon had earlier mentioned he might meet the flight and, if so, would probably give me an opportunity to express a preference. Cora and I had a little time to think about where we might want to go. I told him New Zealand would be my first choice. We had bonded with the two New Zealanders during our time with the Canadians and the description of their homeland was very enticing. Barnes was noncommittal, as of course he did not know what positions were available, but promised to do everything possible. He also spoke with Joe and Bob, presumably asking the same question. I don't think any of the three of us were seriously concerned about onward assignments yet, but it was extremely rare for a first tour officer or almost anyone for that matter to have an opportunity to make such a request directly to the man himself. There was no harm in putting my preference on the record.

The bus pulled up at what is known as the Diplomatic Entrance. This is the formal entrance to what we called main State (main as opposed to the myriad annex buildings). The entrance was routinely used by foreign ambassadors or even heads of state. It was also the standard backdrop for TV news correspondents to record their on-air segments, such as the Koppel report we had watched the previous evening. It was attractive with marble walls and floors. Along the glass wall opposite the entrance was a display of flags of all the nations with which we had diplomatic relations. The entrance was surrounded on three sides, the exception being the side with the flags, by a combination balcony and walkway, as the lobby had a ceiling which extended at least as high as the third floor. Both the ground floor and the balcony were completely packed with employees who had come to welcome us home. The exception was an area to our right, in front of the marble plaque inscribed with the names of employees who died in the line of duty (a second plaque has since been added to accommodate the violence of recent decades). Here a temporary podium had been erected. We were escorted through the crowd to an area surrounding the podium, where we were to stand and Bob to speak. The Canadian ambassador to the US, Gilles Mathieu, was already there and we quickly introduced ourselves.

Bob had previously worked in the public relations office and there was a large contingent of employees from that office with signs specifically welcoming Bob. The rest of us settled for the numerous yellow ribbons, "Thanks Canada" and "Welcome Home" signs taped up all around or waved by people in the crowd. Bob read the first of the two speeches we had prepared in Dover. He thanked everyone for coming to greet us with a special nod to his friends in public affairs. He expressed our gratitude for the support given our families and especially to those of the real hostages. He asked everyone to continue working for the release of the hostages and that we should remember them and their families in our prayers. It was all pretty general stuff, but this was basically a pep rally so it would have been difficult to say anything more substantive. Besides, as had been made clear to us many times in the preceding days, the Department did not want substance. He ended by praising and thanking the Canadians. Then someone introduced Ambassador Mathieu which drew the loudest cheer. He spoke briefly or tried to as the crowd repeatedly interrupted with applause.

Then we were whisked away to the offices of the Department spokesman, Hodding Carter III. Carter, no relation to the President, had worked for him in Georgia and was definitely one of the inner circle. The fact he ended up at State was a bit puzzling, but either he wanted the job or the President wanted his own man there. Carter was in his mid-thirties with longish brown hair and medium build. He had a strong southern accent and was friendly and business-like at the same time. He gave us a quick briefing on what would come next. The Department was calling it a "press appearance" since there would be no questions. The press corps, as many as could fit into the Department's Dean Acheson auditorium, the largest conference room in the building, was already waiting for us. We walked out on the stage proudly still wearing the Canadian flag lapel pins that had accompanied us through Mehrabad airport. We each introduced ourselves then Bob read the prepared statement. The event was carried live on television, and Carter cautioned us to keep our heads up because looking down would appear on camera as if you were dozing. Unfortunately, I quickly forgot. When I watched the footage later I saw myself several times looking as if I had fallen asleep.

As the statement is short, I am including it here:

"Good afternoon. We thank you for this opportunity to meet with you and to say how very happy we are to be home again. We have already met with our families, and we were delighted to find that they are all well.

"We are deeply grateful to the United States government and the many volunteers for their steadfast support and assistance to our families and to the families of the hostages who remain in Tehran. It was very reassuring to know that our families were constantly kept informed. As you already know, the government of Canada and its representatives in Tehran made it possible for us to avoid capture and eventually to leave Iran. When the embassy was overrun on November 4 five of us were working in the consular section at the rear of the embassy compound, some distance from the chancery where the main attack was centered. Thus we were able to leave the premises unobserved. We made our way to our homes or the homes of friends. As the situation became more tense, we were able to move to Canadian premises where we remained in hiding. Lee Schatz, the agricultural attaché, worked in an office off the compound in a building on the same street as the embassy. Thus he was not trapped with the others and he too joined us at the Canadians. It is difficult to fully express our appreciation for the risks the Canadians took to insure our safety and comfort. They made us feel a part of their family, especially at times such as Christmas, when our spirits needed a boost. We thank them for their brave support.

"Most of our days were spent following events in the world. We had no contact with Washington except to send word through the

Canadians that we were safe and well. We avidly read newspapers and listened to overseas radio broadcasts. Also, during the course of the three months, we played Scrabble to the point where some of us could identify the letter on the front by the shape of the grain on the back of the tile.

"From the radio and newspapers available to us we knew that Americans were united in their demand that the hostages be freed. This realization gave us strength and courage.

"As we have said, we are glad to be home and grateful for your concern. However, the detention of our friends and colleagues continues. Although the information the hostages receive might be very limited, any knowledge of your efforts surely serves as the strongest source of hope for them. We must not and will not forget them. On behalf of those remaining in Tehran we thank you for all that has been done. We will now join you in these continuing efforts in doing everything possible to assure the return of the fifty hostages in the compound and our three colleagues in the foreign ministry.

"Because of the sensitivity of the situation we know you will understand that we cannot take questions at this time or give details beyond the bare outline. We have first and foremost in our minds the continued safety and hopes for an early release of the hostages in the compound. We are certain that you understand and agree with our desire to do nothing which would jeopardize the hostages or our benefactors.

"In this same spirit we wish to express our thanks to the press. We understand that various aspects of our situation during the last three months were known to some members of the press. We are extremely appreciative of their responsible handling of this information. We know that it was based on their desire to maintain our safety.

"Thank you very much."[1]

Cora and I ended up with the speech text, signed by all six houseguests as well as Sheldon Krys. The statement was aimed primarily at the American public but rightly mentioned and thanked the press as well.

---

1. Document in possession of the author.

The reference to Scrabble yielded an unexpected benefit. What Bob said was true. In those days the tiles were made of wood and some had distinctive grain patterns. A few weeks later each of us received a warm letter from the president of the company along with a deluxe edition of the game.

Meantime, our families had already been taken to the hotel in Virginia. The Department is two minutes from a bridge over the Potomac River on the far side of which is Arlington. As I mentioned earlier, State had rented a floor in a hotel. The media were already there waiting but our families had been smuggled in using the freight elevator.

After the press briefing we returned to Carter's office. He thanked Bob for a good job in presenting the statement. He also talked a bit about what we should expect once we got to Arlington. Although the Department wanted this story off the front pages as quickly as possible, the media sharks were circling and there was no alternative except to toss them some red meat, i.e. us. The media would get to us one way or another. If they were not allowed access to us now they would follow us over the coming weeks and continue to camp out in front of our relatives' homes, which might have the perverse effect of dragging out interest in our story. While there would probably be some of that regardless, the best strategy was to give the press reasonable access to us for a limited time. Once that was over it would be easier to make the argument we had said all we could. Now we should be left in peace to rest and relax along with our families.

We were given some basic guidelines for dealing with the press such as the meaning of certain terms like background and deep background. We were also asked to stay away from any subject areas with policy implications. We were to do our best to keep this a human interest story with a "Thanks, Canada" angle.

At some point in the day we were also given a four page document entitled "Public Relations Guidance for Iranian Escapees and Freed Hostages."[2] I guessed it had been written several months earlier when the Iranians released the thirteen female and minority hostages and the title now updated to include us. Its main relevance

2. Document in possession of the author.

was the finding that our experience was considered classified information at least until the hostages were released. Needless to say, we understood far better than the people who wrote the memo as they were not privy to the real story.

It also said we should not speak or write about our experiences without official permission, and we should refrain from giving interviews. This was a bit strange since the Department itself was arranging interviews for us, but I understood the intent. We should not continue to seek media attention once this initial period was over. It went on to cover compensation for speaking and writing (not allowed while the hostages were still held), and ended with an explanation that for purposes of this event we were considered "public persons." This designation severely limited our rights in various ways. We could not prevent anyone from writing about us or publishing photos or video footage of us. There was a lot of legalese regarding our remaining privacy rights. Finally, we could not sue for libel, or more exactly, if we did sue we would have to prove deliberate malicious intent, a very high standard.

All of this was a bit irritating but not surprising. I don't think any of us had planned to sell our stories, particularly as the highly classified nature of the real version made it necessary to keep everything as vague as possible. But there was a feeling of being exposed as the document made clear our privacy rights were severely curtailed. The plan to disappear as quickly as we reasonably could might be more difficult than we had imagined.

We were then told about Jean Pelletier. I have written previously how he may have learned of our existence. At this time, however, all we knew was he had figured out we were in hiding with the Canadians and had chosen to keep the story secret. He waited until he had confirmation the Canadian embassy in Tehran had closed before he let the story be published. Although he still had the benefit of breaking the news it was certainly not the exclusive he could have had if he published when he first learned of us. He had asked for an opportunity to meet with us and for our part we were happy to have a chance to thank him personally for putting our safety ahead of a good story. Hodding Carter himself walked us to a nearby room where Pelletier watched a video feed of the press conference and was now waiting. We introduced ourselves and said our thanks.

Oddly enough I have no recollection of him requesting an interview with us. It would certainly have been a reasonable request in the circumstances, especially as he went on to write a book, but perhaps he was more focused on the Canadian story.

While some in the US government were grateful to Pelletier for holding the story as long as he did, others believed he should have sat on it longer. There were press reports the President himself had asked several US media outlets to refrain from going public even once we were out both to protect the hostages and to avoid disruption to whatever diplomatic efforts were ongoing. Personally, I think Pelletier's decision was reasonable. What strikes me as odd is apparently he was not the first to figure out we were out and in hiding with the Canadians, so why we were given the opportunity to thank him and not the others is unclear. Perhaps he was the only one who asked. By holding the story until we and the Canadians were safe he made sure no one was directly harmed by its publication. Beyond this things get complicated. Presumably Pelletier knew he wasn't the only one sitting on the story so waiting increased the risk all his hard work would come to nothing. With the hostage drama itself seemingly set to continue indefinitely it is unclear there would ever have been a time to publish that would have been acceptable to everyone, at least not until the hostages were freed.

Following the meeting, Sheldon escorted us to lunch. It was in the formal dining room, a facility on the sixth floor normally reserved for the big shots. I probably should explain that State, being very hierarchical, assigned office space by rank. Main State had seven floors plus a basement. The seventh floor was where the secretary, deputy secretary and the other most senior officials had their offices. The next tier of officialdom was on the sixth floor. Generally, if you didn't rate at least the sixth floor, you didn't rate. I must admit I always found this system strange. To me it would have been more logical to put an office or bureau in one section of the building so the space would be contiguous. Instead, if we needed to see our own assistant secretary we still had to make the trek to the sixth floor regardless of where the rest of the bureau was situated. This explains why the sixth floor dining room was where it was. If your office was below the sixth floor, you probably couldn't eat there except as an invited guest.

We had a nice lunch with real tableware and cloth napkins. It was to be many years before I made it back, still as a guest, to that facility. Then we were taken to meet Secretary of State Cyrus Vance. Vance was tall and lean, with thick graying hair parted firmly on the right side. He was in his early sixties but looked younger and still had a slight trace of a West Virginia accent. He was a true gentleman, a veteran diplomat who greeted us graciously, saying our situation had never been far from his thoughts during the past months even as the administration necessarily focused on the release of the hostages. He echoed what others had already told us, the best thing we could do for our compatriots was to exercise caution in our press contacts, being careful to say nothing inflammatory. He reiterated the government was continuing to explore every diplomatic avenue to try to negotiate the hostages' release, but our ability to do so was severely limited by the intransigence of the Ayatollah Khomeini and the vagueness of the current governmental structure in Iran. These were things we understood but hearing them from America's chief diplomat was still sobering. There was no good news for the hostages.

An aide came in and whispered something to the Secretary. He turned to us and said the President wanted to see us. As we exited the office his security detail joined our group and we took an elevator down to the parking garage. There were two vehicles waiting. The Secretary climbed into his limousine and invited some of us to join him. Even though the vehicle was a long wheelbase black Cadillac, only five people could sit in the back and his driver and a security officer filled the front. The rest of us piled into a Ford LTD.

The White House is only a few minutes' drive from the State Department, so as with much of what we had done that day, there was little opportunity to think about the fact we were soon going to meet the leader of the free world. I could not help but consider he was also supposed to be the most powerful man in the world. As far as the hostages were concerned, an intransigent old man in Tehran had to this point held him to a stalemate. One could argue the ayatollah was winning, in the sense the hostage crisis was helping him accomplish his domestic agenda of turning Iran into a theocratic state. Meantime, the President was facing a potential primary challenge from Senator Ted Kennedy of Massachusetts. If he did not bring the hostages home safely by November, the general election could be problematic also.

We pulled into the White House main entrance on Pennsylvania Avenue. I had twice attended social events at the White House while in college, but this was clearly different. In addition to our using the formal entrance there was no metal detector or ID check. Entering as part of the secretary of state's entourage eliminated those requirements. As we proceeded into the west wing we were met by Hamilton Jordan, the chief of staff. He knocked on the Oval Office door and without waiting for a response opened it and led us in. The President was sitting behind his desk which has its back to the three windows in the oval shaped wall. He arose immediately and walked over to greet us. We each introduced ourselves and the President welcomed us and invited us to seat ourselves on the two sofas that faced each other near the center of the office. He himself sat on one of the armchairs angling toward the sofas.

Secretary Vance said goodbye to us and exited the room with Jordan, leaving us alone with the President. There is something strange about meeting someone you have seen and heard on television for many years. It is almost as if you develop certain expectations of how he will be in person. Of course he looked much the same as I expected: mid-fifties, brown hair just graying at the edges, the big warm smile. And the personality appeared to match the smile. He asked us how we had been treated so far and we replied everyone with whom we had come in contact had treated us exceptionally well. We were overwhelmed by everything from the anticipated media madness to the VIP treatment. The President then asked about the exfiltration, the first time we were able to speak about it since reaching Switzerland. He indicated he had personally authorized the operation after considerable thought, and that no one, except perhaps we ourselves was more pleased with how it had turned out. This gave us the opportunity to say some good things about Tony and Julio and what we considered the genius of the plan.

There is no question in my mind the Carter administration seriously mishandled the Iran crisis. I have not been reticent with my criticisms throughout the book. At the same time, however, I must acknowledge Carter as a human being appeared to have a genuine concern for us and for the hostages. When he said in the first days following the takeover that the safe return of the hostages was his highest priority, he spoke from the heart. While it may have been poor tactics it was genuine. Cora likes to say Carter would have made a good neighbor for many of the same reasons he was a poor President. I think it is also true this was a different Carter than the one we have with us today. For whatever reason, perhaps because of losing the election to Reagan, he has become a bitter man and a defender of dictators such as Venezuela's Hugo Chavez, exactly the kind of human rights violator he would have opposed while President.

Carter spoke with us for about thirty minutes. While much of the half hour is now a blur, due equally to the nervous excitement of the moment as the passage of years, I remember he gave us a brief tour of the Oval Office showing us some of the things he found particularly interesting. The one item that stands out in memory was an image of a cat embroidered from silk, a gift from the Chinese government during his state visit there. The threads that made up the body of the cat were so thin you could see through the cat itself, while the surrounding threads that held the image in its wooden frame were so fine they were hardly visible. In addition to being semi-transparent the cat was created in such a manner it could be viewed equally well from either side. The President knelt on a chair in order to grab the frame from its place on the shelf behind the chair so we could get a closer view. The action of the President when he did that remains indelible in my memory. There was something particularly human and touching in his simple appreciation for this beautiful work of art and his desire to share it with us.

Our visit ended with a round of photographs as the media were called in. We knew the President wanted to be seen with us because it was a small way to deflect, at least temporarily, public frustration with the lack of progress in bringing the hostages home. We later heard some in the group of women and African-American hostages released the previous Thanksgiving did not want to meet with Carter, presumably because they held him responsible for the mistakes leading to the takeover. I have always suspected that is the reason why we were not told ahead of time about the plan for us to go to the Oval Office. I do not think they needed to worry. Even I, perhaps the least disposed in our group to want to boost the President's poll ratings, realized he had gone out on a limb in authorizing our rescue. Its failure would have been a political disaster for him and it took guts to make the call, especially as some of his key advisers were against the attempt. I think we owed him a personal thank-you. The photos were taken and made their way into newspapers and magazines around the nation. The President introduced us as "six brave Americans" and added, "We all love you."[3]

As Secretary Vance had already returned to the Department we were met by another vehicle and driver. Our luggage had been moved from the aircraft that brought us from Dover to this van and it was time for us to move to the hotel. It was rush hour and it took the better part of an hour for us to cover the five miles to Arlington. We came in through a side entrance so we did not have to run a media gauntlet. The rooms were already assigned and Ralph Frank gave us our keys as we rode up the freight elevator to the secure floor. I am not sure what we did for dinner. I assume we ordered from room service as we were safe only on our floor. The rest of the hotel was crawling with media and it would have been a bad idea to go to any of the restaurants.

I had already said goodbye to my parents. My father needed to get back to work and neither he nor my mother were particularly interested in the media circus. They had been living with it for some months already, as some of the notes and clippings I later found in my mother's papers testify. It was our turn. Cora's parents had also gone home. Of course both would have to continue to deal with local reporters where they lived.

After dinner we met with some of the public affairs people from State to talk about the next day. There were numerous requests for interviews. For Cora and me, it was usually for the two of us together. The same was probably true for Joe and Kathy. We largely lost track of them as well as Bob and Lee over the next couple of days. I am not even sure Lee came to the hotel. Since he was not a

---

3. "A Daring Escape from Iran," Newsweek, February 11, 1980, 29

State employee Lee was under no obligation to cooperate with the Department's press people. In any case, it appeared the press office had negotiated with the media who would talk to whom. While I presume some of the requests were to meet with all six of us, those were turned down in the interest of "spreading the wealth."

The print media were easy. We would sit down with a reporter, answer some questions, then they would snap a few photos. TV was different. Most of the interviews were live. I thought it would be scary, but I soon enough got used to the drill. The questions were not particularly difficult. They tended to ask whether we were scared during the exfiltration, how we passed the time while hiding with the Canadians, how did we make contact with the Canadians in the first place and what did we think now about Canadians in general and Taylor in particular. It was easy to forget there might be millions of people watching, and as I was actually engaged in the conversation I didn't have to worry about letting my head droop and looking as though I were asleep. Cora let me do most of the talking anyway. I don't think she was ever as comfortable with it as I was.

At this point I remember distinctly only one of the interviews, with Steve Bell from *ABC Morning News*, the predecessor of *Good Morning America*. Even before meeting him I considered Bell a professional and objective interviewer. I was pleased to have the opportunity to be interviewed by him. I believe it was set for the second morning and final day of our stay at the secure hotel. As I expected, he tried to move the conversation beyond the fluff, asking whether we had any hard feelings toward the administration because of the decision to admit the shah. We were already telling lies about the exfiltration itself and much as I would have liked to tell the truth, I accepted criticism of the administration would not benefit the hostages. I think our standard answer became something like:

"It was a difficult decision in a complex situation."

Despite the fact I have a substantial archive of news reports from the days following our return to Washington, I cannot find any articles based on the interviews we did during those two days. Both *Time* and *Newsweek* had reasonably extensive coverage of our escape, but both relied largely on the account Kim King had earlier provided. Of course in Kim's account he generally claimed credit for our escape from the consulate building, going so far as to state he was the one who inspected the street through my window (not possible due to its construction) and then opened the rolling shutter door (not possible because Lopez had the key). In any case, I suppose it is all to the good the media in general did not push hard to establish what had really happened. The only hint of CIA involvement was the acknowledgment the agency had doctored the passports issued by the Canadians, putting in visas and entry and exit stamps to make it appear we had stopped at a number of destinations before reaching Tehran.[4]

The ABC news report for that evening, another from Ted Koppel, showed footage of our arrival at main State aboard the Metro buses. There were a few excerpts from the welcome ceremony including the comment that the biggest applause went to the Canadian ambassador to the US, Gilles Mathieu. Then there were a couple of segments of Bob's speech to the press, including a shot of me appearing to doze, though I did manage to look up just as the camera panned away. Lastly, Koppel switched to the White House visit televising the final moments when we had our photos taken with the President. This summary comes not from memory, but rather from an ABC VHS tape entitled *America Held Hostage: As it Happened*.[5] Perhaps equally interesting is the next report on this tape is from mid-March, which confirms we were successful in getting ourselves off the news. I guess there was a limit on how much "Thanks, Canada" the media was willing to broadcast although the actual process of Americans thanking Canadians went on for much longer.

With one exception the media people we dealt with during the time we were at the hotel were polite, professional and respectful of the constraints we were under. Since our story was reported primarily from a human interest angle I can even say they seemed to enjoy the opportunity to report something positive in what was otherwise an increasingly dismal situation. As always, there was the exception. A reporter from one of the tabloids was stalking us when we were on the press floor and he finally cornered Cora and me as we were

---

4. Ibid, 26-9

5. "America Held Hostage: As It Happened," ABC News, video excerpts from news broadcasts, released in 1994, in possession of the author.

leaving an interview. He wanted an interview as well even though the Department press people had not blessed his request and passed it on to us. When we said he would have to work through public affairs, he threatened to harass us and our families until we agreed. We did take up his request with someone from the press office. He confirmed we were right to turn down the interview and advised us not to worry about the threat. He promised to talk to the reporter, but noted also as a practical matter it was unlikely he would actually try to act on the threat. It wasn't worth his time. As it happened, that turned out to be true. We never heard from him again.

# 16. Lying for One's Country

Sir Henry Wotton, a 17th century British diplomat, is credited with the aphorism that an ambassador is an "honest gentlemen sent to lie abroad for the good of his country." We, and the Canadians, were to modify this adage slightly over the coming months, and ultimately years, as we lied to our own people as well as to foreigners. While initially this was primarily to protect the hostages, after their release it continued to be necessary in the interests of safeguarding what the intelligence community terms "sources and methods." Furthermore, the Canadians were engaged in a low key attempt to rebuild their trade relations with Iran and the extent of their cooperation with the CIA would have seriously undermined the effort.

Aside from Flora MacDonald's news conference, Ken Taylor himself also appeared before the press in Ottawa on February 1. Taylor's account was necessarily similar to the others. He talked in very general terms about the issuance of the Canadian passports but the most interesting item in his statement was regarding the telephone call made to his residence in Tehran on or about January 19, the caller asking for Joe Stafford. Taylor acknowledged he was aware a number of news organizations had information about us, but fudged the question whether he thought the call came from one of those organizations. I was surprised he noted the first compromise of our status, presumably the breakthrough by Pelletier, was as early as December 10. There was also discussion of his friendship with Peter Jennings, a Canadian who at the time was the anchorman for *ABC Evening News*. Jennings had visited Iran during January as part of his coverage of the hostage crisis and had dinner at the Taylor residence even as Joe and Kathy were hiding there. Taylor insisted he had remained mum. He declined to answer questions about our falsified identifies or professions although he did confirm the passports were not diplomatic.[1]

---

1. Canadian Embassy, Washington, DC, Press Release dated February 4, 1980, in possession of the author.

After two nights at the Arlington hotel, the Department told us to semi-disappear. February 1st was a Friday. There was enough press interest in us they were willing to hang around on Saturday. But by Sunday it was time to move on. We were issued temporary duty orders which would permit us to obtain reimbursement for meals and lodging. This was normal since for all practical purposes we no longer had a permanent assignment. There were still some things State wanted us to do, but constant press availability was not one of them. So we and the Staffords looked for a place to stay. We found the Wilson Motel and Apartments, an older complex of brick duplex buildings located, not surprisingly, on Wilson Boulevard. Wilson was one of the main streets in Arlington with frequent bus service to the subway station in Rosslyn, which was important since we did not have a car. It was not exactly four star, but the units seemed clean enough and our now finely honed instincts told us we would not be looked for there. Some of the rooms were configured as motel rooms and others as short term apartments, but both had small kitchens and enough cooking gear we could feed ourselves. We opted for the motel-type room as it came with daily maid service and was still within per diem.

There was a convenience store within walking distance and we picked up some basics so we could at least have breakfast. After subsisting on restaurant food for more than a week I was looking forward to the simplicity of a glass of milk and toast for breakfast.

By this time Lee and Bob had gone their separate ways. Bob, being married, wanted to spend time with his wife Linda. They had family in the DC area. I am not sure what Lee was doing, but I knew he had a long-time girlfriend and his mother was having some health issues so clearly he had higher priorities than assisting the Department's public relations effort. One part of that effort was for us to pay a visit to the Canadian embassy in Washington and officially thank the people of Canada for what their government had done on our behalf. The visit had been set for mid-morning on Monday, February 4. We made our way to the Department where we connected with Bob and were given a car and driver to take us over to the Canadians. Lee had not appeared but we assumed he would meet us there. When we arrived, there was no sign of him.

This was embarrassing because we did not have a ready explanation for his absence. Fortunately, the Canadians may have been equally embarrassed because the ambassador was not there, having proceeded to a prior out-of-town engagement. In any case, Kathy made up an excuse for Lee's absence which I no longer remember and the event worked out fine. The media did not notice the hick-ups. Bob made his usual good statement once again putting his public relations expertise to work and the Canadians presented us with copies of a beautiful coffee table book created for the US bicentennial, called <u>Between Friends</u>. The entire visit took about an hour and certainly seemed an appropriately formal if small way to thank the Canadian government and people for the risks taken on our behalf.

One of us, not me, ran into Lee sometime later. The explanation presented was Lee had met some Canadians in a bar and had thanked them. He said he figured this was a sufficient expression of his thanks to Canada and therefore exempted him from showing up at the embassy. I don't remember who it was that spoke with Lee, but I understood they pointed out the obvious, It was both a question of thanking Canada in a formal way (presumably there was no press coverage of his bar encounter) and also leaving one's colleagues in an awkward position.

I received an interesting offer about this time. During my college days I had been friendly with John T. (Terry) Dolan and Roger Stone. Both were political activists and after college they formed what I understand to be the first political action committee or PAC, known as the National Conservative Political Action Coalition. I guess this makes them pioneers of a sort. Terry passed a letter through the Department suggesting I resign and go on a speaking tour they would organize. The purpose of the tour would be to criticize the administration for its mismanagement of the crisis and Terry knew me well enough to judge I would have a lot to say on the subject. With the election coming up this could be helpful to Republican candidates in general and the presidential nominee in particular. While I did give passing thought to the proposal, as I mentioned earlier, I was still interested in a State Department career. Also, while there were things I would like to say, I had to keep perspective on what would help the hostages far more than on what would hurt the administration. Then there was the not so minor point that some of the people who were most insistent the US government had a moral obligation to admit the shah, such as Henry Kissinger, were themselves Republicans. So despite the temptation, I turned down the offer.

Our next and perhaps final official public relations act was to make a trip to Canada. CTV (I tried to find out what the initials actually stand for, but contrary to popular impression in Canada, Wikipedia says it is not an acronym for Canadian Television) had a morning show called *Canada AM*. They invited us to appear, directing the invitation through the State Department where we assumed it had received all of the necessary clearances. We were issued no-cost travel orders by the Near East Bureau. This made the trip official business even though CTV paid our expenses, including plane tickets routing us through Pittsburgh. I remember this well because the immigration officers recognized us and gave us a special welcome as we passed through. We flew from there to Toronto and spent the afternoon seeing a very small slice of this wonderful city. It was early to bed as we had to get up at 4:00am in order to make it to the studio on time.

Also in the afternoon we gave a brief interview to a reporter from the *Toronto Star* which turned into a front page article comparing Ken Taylor to Sir William Stevenson, the World War II spymaster who played a major role in the success of British intelligence and special operations efforts against the Nazis. I did mention one of the books being passed around the Sheardown's house was A Man Called Intrepid, a biography of Stevenson. This was all fine and we had no desire to take anything away from Ken, but it was becoming increasingly clear the media seemed unable to spread its focus beyond the handsome and dashing ambassador. We also talked about the Sheardowns and how important they were, yet all that made it into the article was Bob Anders had a "contact" at the Canadian embassy.[2]

As should be clear from this book, John and Zena Sheardown

---

2. Gillian Cosgrove, "Our Guests in Iran Drop In on Metro," Toronto Star, February 6, 1980, 1

were critical to us finding our way to the Canadians as well as our care, feeding and psychological well-being during the nearly three months we were in hiding with them. We were anxious the Sheardowns not be forgotten. I now realize the comparison to Stevenson was more accurate than the author of the article could have guessed. Thanks to the work of Robert Wright, we know Taylor was involved in a range of intelligence work intended to help the hostages, aside from everything he was doing for us. But this information wasn't known at the time and the press was captivated by the Taylor persona as much as by his known accomplishments.

The TV interview itself was pretty routine, lots of opportunities to thank Canada and to make special mention of the Sheardowns. Of course we also spoke highly of Joe Clark, the Prime Minister. How could we not? He had, without a moment's hesitation we were told, made the decision to support Taylor's desire to take us in. He did not weigh the consequences for Canadian commercial interests, for example. At this time we did not know about Trudeau's despicable behavior. If we had the temptation to say something more overtly political might have been overwhelming, but it seemed to me we restricted our comments to a factual description of what Clark had done and the psychological importance to us of knowing our presence at the Canadian mission had been approved at the highest level.

This was insufficiently restrained, at least in the opinion of some presumably pro-Trudeau hack in the Canadian Ministry of External Affairs. Before we left the studio, we received a telephone call from the Canadian Desk at the Department telling us the ministry had complained we were interfering in Canadian domestic affairs. The caller suggested we should get on the first plane home. I responded our visit had been cleared within the Department and we did not have any further press events scheduled in any case. Personally, I didn't see much difference between our comments and the telephone call President Carter had made to Clark thanking him for helping us. For that matter, Clark himself showed his class by refusing to use his role in our escape in his campaign.

We returned to Washington later the same day, carrying souvenir Canada AM coffee mugs as compensation for our time. This was the last public appearance we were to make, for a while anyway. Once we returned to Washington, it was strongly suggested we really disappear for a while. The Near East Bureau presented us with a new set of travel orders, valid for thirty days, that authorized lodging and per diem. The location was not specified. We collected our belongings, checked out of the motel, and headed to National (now Reagan) Airport. For the first and only time in my life I went to an airport without a ticket and even without a clear destination in mind. Cora and I talked in the taxi and we decided a low profile place to hide would be with my room-mate from college, Craig Gardner. He lived outside Chicago and it seemed unlikely the press would think to look for us there. So I called Craig from the airport, he said fine, and we purchased one way tickets to O'Hare Airport on the next flight.

While we were taking the first steps toward retirement from the limelight Taylor was just beginning his road show. Pat Taylor estimated he made over a thousand public appearances.[3] It seemed everyone wanted to thank Canada and Ken was the obvious choice. The Ministry of External Affairs decided there was no better use for his time than to crisscross the USA from the Big Apple to Rotary clubs in small towns. I suspect the Carter administration was pleased too. These appearances reminded Americans, even while the hostages remained in captivity, there was at least one bright spot in the affair.

This speaking tour and related public relations efforts were later to become a basis for criticism and accusations of grandstanding. This is bunk. I think Ken made a reasonable effort to share the limelight by mentioning the Sheardowns and other embassy staff. I know for certain we mentioned the Sheardowns in the *Toronto Star* interview to no purpose, so it doesn't surprise me that Ken's efforts were no more successful. Roger Lucy was initially told to avoid the press but was happy to remain in the background. The Sheardowns did have a number of complaints that to me seem valid. These range from the fact the ministry sent them to Kuwait from Tehran, hardly a safe haven given its heavily Shia population, to the lack of compensation for the cost of keeping us fed. John was paid Canadian $1.65 per

---

3. Robert Wright, 309

day per head. While it would have been unreasonable to expect Canadian taxpayers to cover our liquor and cigarettes, food alone cost more than that. Of course we offered to reimburse John, but he would not hear of it. I think it was less the amount offered than that it was part of a pattern he and Zena justifiably found difficult to understand and accept. Another example was the Sheardowns were given no notice of our departure, and learned of it from a BBC radio broadcast. I mentioned earlier they believed they deserved to know about the exfiltration plan. That can be argued both ways, but there is no doubt it added to the feeling their role was being deliberately undervalued.

I can no longer recall for certain all the destinations we visited during our thirty day taxpayer-funded dodge the press tour. I do recall, since we were paying the airfare, we did follow a logical progression west. The next stop was probably my sister in Seattle. She had received some press attention, but by the second week in February it had largely faded. After that it would probably have been safe to head to my parents in Huntington Beach, CA. My brother and younger sister also lived nearby. The last stop would likely have been Cora's parents' home in Oceanport, NJ. This would have been early March, more than a month after our return and the New York area media would have been among the first to move on to other stories. Our strategy worked. We did avoid the press and therefore further need to lie for our country.

# 17. What Now?

Our thirty day travel orders expired. It was time to return to Washington. Technically we were still assigned to the embassy in Tehran and it was necessary to make some decisions regarding an onward assignment. I was not ready to leave Washington quite yet. There were a number of administrative and other details that needed attention. But untenured junior officers are expected to demonstrate their suitability for the Foreign Service by serving abroad and despite what most would agree was a poor start to my career, I had not lost the desire to see the world, at least the part of it that was not heavily Muslim. On the other hand, both Cora and I wanted to be in the US when the hostages returned. I talked to Sheldon Krys about our dilemma. He promised the Near East bureau would fund our travel back to DC from wherever we ended up so we could see our friends when they were finally released.

I needed to have something more specific than non-Islamic to say to Richard Masters, who was still in charge of untenured junior officers, and Bill Hudson, who was still running administrative officer assignments. I did talk to them about my conversation with the Director-General on the bus from Andrews Air Force Base, but was told there was nothing available in New Zealand. The first question that needed answering was whether the aborted first tour in Tehran was sufficient to meet the general requirement all new officers serve a consular tour. I argued it was, noting I had worked, albeit briefly, in all three areas of consular work, immigration, tourist visas and services to Americans. Bill supported me and eventually I was offered a position as a general services officer in Hong Kong.

Before I let go of New Zealand, I should mention it appears I was misled by someone regarding the availability of a position at the embassy in Wellington. Several years later while serving in Kathmandu, I ended up working for the man who would have been my boss if I had succeeded in getting New Zealand. He told me there was an appropriate vacancy in his section and the Department sent him a bozo who proved unsatisfactory. I would like to think this was a misunderstanding. Perhaps I waited too long to try to make good on the Director-General's claimed willingness to do what he could, presumably a lot, to get me to New Zealand.

At the time I had no choice but to accept personnel's assurance and so went to the Foreign Service Lounge to research Hong Kong. I understand the lounge still exists in a different form, but in those days it was a very useful institution. Officers between assignments could have mail forwarded there and everything that would normally have gone to Tehran was held for me. This saved the bother of making temporary changes of address. The lounge also provided telephone booths from which we transients could make calls and even typewriters for filling out forms or drafting memos were available. In addition they kept post reports. Each overseas embassy or stand-alone consulate in the case of Hong Kong was required to submit a periodic description of what life there was like. In practice the post report tended to be a recruiting tool, emphasizing the good points and glossing over the bad, which was saved for another periodic report designed to justify hardship pay.

I took the post report home and Cora and I both read through it. It certainly sounded exotic and even the negatives appeared to apply more to families with children than to couples or singles. So I accepted the assignment. The job opened in June which seemed about right to us in terms of when to leave DC. So the next question was what to do with me during the intervening months and the answer was training, training and more training. There was no language requirement, at least not for my job, but I was going into my first administrative assignment so it was appropriate to put me through the general services officer course.

I mentioned earlier that Tehran's supervisory general services officer, Gary Lee, was in our building on the day of the takeover. General services is a sub-specialty of administration, and includes everything from building maintenance to procurement and purchasing, to supply management and inventory control. Hong Kong was a large post with four Americans working in this area and I was assigned to the building maintenance job. Even the Department of State did not believe an administrative generalist like me could be taught anything more than the basics of building maintenance in a couple of weeks. I had a very skilled and knowledgeable local employee working with me. As in my first Tehran job, our relationship reminded me very much of how I felt as a second lieutenant when I moved into my first real Army job. The sergeant-major ran the place and it was my job to try to meld the taskings I was getting from up the chain of command with the realities of resource and other constraints that were coming from below.

In addition to the general services course both Cora and I were assigned to area studies. As with our previous go-round prior to heading for Iran this course covered a broad swath of the world: China, Taiwan, Hong Kong and several other countries. There was not much focus on Hong Kong. But it was interesting and it helped keep the per diem money flowing.

The general services training lasted four weeks and area studies two so I was assigned to the Budget and Fiscal management course as well. This was six weeks long and it carried me through to the point where we were ready to depart for Hong Kong. This course was not directly relevant to my job as a maintenance officer, but it never hurts to know about money and it definitely came in handy later in my career. Besides, I understood the Department was doing me a favor in giving me an official place to hang my hat while I worked through the issues left from the embassy takeover. As it turned out, one of the people I met through the course, a Tehran alumnus, was on his way to Kathmandu. Largely because of my conversations with him I eventually ended up asking for Nepal as my post-Hong Kong assignment. It was a great decision and one of the more interesting places in which we served.

The Iran Working Group was created in the immediate aftermath of the embassy takeover and continued functioning until the end of the crisis. This was a useful place to volunteer when I had time away from class. In fact, virtually all the employees there were volunteers, some of whom were there rather than working their normal job while others were pulling double duty. I usually worked either the swing shift or the night shift. The swing shift was definitely more interesting as there was more activity than in the middle of the night.

During the first hours of the takeover as we overnighted at the Iran-America Society, we helped maintain an open line to the working group. At that time, it was an impromptu undertaking with temporary staffing, as everyone assumed the crisis would last a day or two. As I described it then it was an adjunct to the operations center. Five months later it was still in the same location. Most working groups last for days or weeks, rarely months, but as the hostage drama dragged on, so did the Iran Working Group's presence there. The operations center was really the only place because of the telephone systems and the ability of center staff to contact Department principals (the working name for big shots) at a moment's notice. The center always knew where everyone was. By this time, however, the working group was very much on the periphery of the serious action. One could almost say the same thing about the State Department itself. The White House was preoccupied with the crisis and had pretty much taken over whatever diplomatic efforts were underway.

As far as I could tell the main functions of the working group while I served there were liaison with hostage families and helping deal with the outpouring of public anger and concern about the hostages. The center conference room had been given to the working group and was filled with stacks of mail from well-wishers around the globe. Much of the work was being handled by volunteers from the Family Liaison Action Group, or FLAG, which was the creation of Penne Laingen and several other hostage spouses. There was too much mail to answer. Letters addressed to particular hostages were forwarded to Iran via the International Committee of the Red Cross. I heard later some of them were actually delivered to the intended recipients, but I presume the terrorists had priorities other than playing mailman, so most of what we sent undoubtedly ended up in the trash. This is especially true because all incoming and outgoing mail had to be censored by the terrorists. They did not want the hostages to know how their ordeal was viewed in the larger world, although the hostages probably realized the mere fact of getting supportive mail from strangers said something independent from the substance of the letters themselves. Other letters, in particular those addressed to hostage families either by name or in general, were forwarded to them. I know Cora's parents and mine received some of this mail and I personally answered some as time allowed.

The Department had a policy of trying to call close relatives of the hostages once a week. Thankfully I did not have to make these calls. Employee volunteers or FLAG members made them with the idea the same person would call regularly and try to establish a rapport with the family member (there were something in the range of 250 persons designated by the Department as family members). This made sense to me. If the point of the call program was to give relatives an opportunity to ask questions or just vent, then it seemed much more effective to have the Department caller build a relationship with the individual over time. Since my work schedule was irregular and temporary I wasn't assigned to any particular families.

That is not to say I did not occasionally speak with relatives who would call during my shift because they heard a rumor or simply wanted to speak with someone. Mostly, however, I helped sort mail and answered calls from people who either wanted information about the hostage crisis or had an idea for resolving it. In these latter cases, I would take down the suggestion and record it in the log. That didn't mean anything, of course, as all calls were logged for the record. It isn't that we were uninterested in outside ideas, but I don't think any proposal called in during my hours would have been effective. The callers, like most of us at State, did not know what was happening at the top. But people were angry and frustrated, which was certainly understandable, so it was our job to lend a sympathetic ear. I do not mean to imply the callers were cranks; the ideas being generated in official Washington were no more effective.

During the months of training, we found ourselves inexpensive furnished lodgings in an older and somewhat shabby building, priced within per diem limits. It was on Lee Highway, another of the major thoroughfares in Arlington with decent bus service to the Rosslyn metro. My training courses were at the Foreign Service Institute in Rosslyn, and if I needed to go to Main State, it was one station to the Foggy Bottom stop, and from there about a fifteen minute walk. There was also the shuttle bus during working hours. At some point I would have to think about buying a car, but as parking in Rosslyn or at State was very pricey that did not enter into the discussion of where to live. Since we were on temporary duty orders our household effects remained in storage at government expense.

Joe and Kathy moved into the same complex. Like us, they remained on temporary duty orders and so were able to leave their effects in storage. They got permission to access their car. The Department does not normally store automobiles but it was impossible to ship a car to Tehran. They were therefore able to secure storage for their early 1960's beige Chevrolet Impala. It was a huge car. Prior to joining the Foreign Service the Staffords had lived in Rome for a while. I had a hard time imagining maneuvering the monster down Rome's narrow streets, but Kathy in particular told wonderful stories of doing exactly that. Not to mention they kept their Tennessee registration during their stay. Kathy did acknowledge she was stopped one time by an Italian police officer about the registration, but she pretended not to understand Italian and after a while the man threw up his hands and let her go. In any case it was particularly helpful to Cora to have an alternative to the bus.

Like me, Joe was working on a new assignment. I recall he asked for Rome and ended up as administrative officer in Palermo, a small consulate in Sicily. Also like me, Joe was spared any further need to do consular work. While he did end up with an assignment in the same country as he had requested, I understand culturally southern Italy is rather distinct from the rest of the country, so Palermo was in a way no closer to Rome than Hong Kong to Wellington. Bob ended up in Oslo. Unlike Joe or me, he did not have as specific an idea of where he wanted to go, just a nice place that would be good for his family. Oslo fit the bill.

Now that we were half settled, we needed clothes. There used to be a Washington area store called Raleigh's. It was expensive but had great sales and as luck would have it one took place shortly after our return to the DC area. So we started rebuilding our wardrobes as well as buying new luggage and other things we would eventually need for Hong Kong.

We had a few administrative details to deal with. The most important was filing a claim for the possessions we lost in Iran.

As I mentioned earlier, I traveled with seven suitcases because air freight forwarders were supposedly unable to operate at the time I went, but Cora was authorized regular air freight. Claims were limited by statute to $15,000. As with many regulations written by Congress where a specific dollar figure is used, no one had bothered to update the limit for inflation, which had been a problem in the 1960's and was again during the Carter administration. Someone in the Department had the truly excellent idea of allowing employees to file a separate claim for an automobile. This was a lifesaver for us because of the BMW.

While I don't remember exact figures our personal effects, clothes, dishes, food and other consumables we had at our apartment, totaled around $8,000. The car was a problem. I submitted a claim for the replacement value even though it exceeded what I paid at the official exchange rate. The Department regulations said that re-imbursement was limited to purchase price. I put a memo on the claim arguing that the definition of "purchase price" should take into account the political situation in Iran that allowed me to buy the car at an advantageous exchange rate (there was no legal requirement to exchange at the official rate so I wasn't engaged in a black market transaction). This is a gross oversimplification: I still have the three page memo I wrote explaining everything, including the customs status of the vehicle and how this affected the agreement. This approach did not work. I was called in to see the head of the office who implied I was trying to cheat the government. How quickly things change. One day the President calls me a hero (I admit I didn't deserve it, but I would have hoped the bureaucracy would accord me a little slack); a month later I am nearly accused of fraud.

It was my fault. Deep down I knew that the request for replacement value reimbursement would not work and my request did put the office manager in a tough spot. I just couldn't stand the thought some mullah was driving my BMW while I was going to have to settle for a Toyota. As I have several times noted, I like cars and losing the second nicest car I'd ever owned after a couple of weeks was annoying. Clearly, in the context of everything else that was happening it was trivial, but I did not see the harm in trying to get the government to compensate me for my actual loss, i.e. a

BMW, I emphasized I hadn't tried to slip anything by anyone and had explicitly called attention to what I was doing and why.

There was a further complication. Most of the purchase had been financed through the Department's credit union. The check had not yet cleared when the embassy was taken over so the credit union stopped payment. But the seller was out of Iran by then and obviously not responsible for what happened to the embassy or the car. I did feel strongly the seller was owed his money. So I was put in the rather odd position of trying to convince the Department to pay me so I could pay the man from whom I had bought the car. In the end they agreed.

This experience should have taught me a lesson, but it would take repeated examples before I grasped the point many Washington officials have no understanding of the requirements of doing business abroad. Iran was not the only country where getting something done often required drinking lots of tea while building relationships. Yes, sometimes it meant you would be asked later for a favor in return. But you could always say no. In the specific case of Iran, I learned during my brief time there that, more often than not, an Iranian with a completely legitimate request still preferred to deal with someone with whom he had established a relationship. I earlier mentioned the relevant Farsi word: partibazi, which refers to the development and use of a network of personal contacts. That was the Iranian way and it is what Massoud did for the embassy. Could it have resulted in a request for a favor? Sure. Would that have been a problem? No, because, as in the case of the revolutionary guard who stopped Rich Queen and me at the roadblock one night, the ultimate decision whether to grant the request was based on US policy and nothing else.

In hindsight, I suppose we should be grateful someone in the bureaucracy at least had the foresight to see the $15,000 limit was unreasonable and permit cars to be claimed separately. This still left us with some significant losses. There was a prohibition on reimbursement for what were termed intangible items. Those included the $600 prepayment on my auto insurance (to an Iranian company so no chance of a refund) and the $400 worth of airline tickets in my safe. We had been planning to visit a friend in Kuwait over Thanksgiving.

I am pretty sure by the time the hostages came home, the limit had been raised to $40,000. In the meantime, I did buy a Toyota, a black Celica. Life without a car was proving difficult and we anticipated being able to ship the Toyota to our next assignment.

Another issue with significant financial consequences for us was Cora's salary. Was she to be paid for the time in hiding or not? Since she was a temporary, hourly employee, a technical argument could be made she wasn't working so was not entitled to pay. Fortunately, in this case our dealings were with Sheldon's office, and they agreed she would be paid as if she had continued to work on the same basis as before the takeover.

There was another important housekeeping task we had to address. I noted earlier I was fortunate to have my checkbook with me when we left the consulate building and was therefore able to send checks for the mortgage payments on our condo. After that first payment sent via the Brits, I asked my dad to handle it, sending him money along with information on how to contact our property manager. Although it was rented the income was not enough to cover the full cost of the mortgage. In addition, the condo had almost as many adventures as we had. The initial tenants were students from some country in North Africa. They were evicted because they were keeping goats in the unit (please note, this was the twentieth floor of a high rise building) or performing ritual sacrifices or perhaps both. I never did get a full explanation from Jim Hill, the property manager. The second tenant was a high ranking government official in the process of a divorce. He committed suicide. We did not want to know whether he did it in our unit or not. Hill was savvy enough to get a financial guarantee from the embassy sponsoring the students, and he didn't charge us a finder's fee for the second tenant because the first stayed such a short time. Nor did he charge us for the third tenant, a CIA secretary who stayed for several years and ultimately bought the place from us.

Because of all this chaos, we definitely wanted to meet with Hill. The newest tenant had just moved in and we wanted to see the file, just to satisfy ourselves we finally had a keeper. There was also a second issue. I had recommended Jim to Don Cooke, who owned a condo about a mile away from ours. Unlike me, unfortunately,

Don was unable to send any checks to cover his mortgage shortfall and I wanted to make sure Hill was able to deal with this. He was covering the shortfall himself. I offered to talk to the Department to find out whether they could do something, or to help cover it myself. He said he considered it an honor to be able to help one of the hostages and absolutely refused to entertain my suggestions. He was confident Don would settle everything when he could and in the meantime it was not a problem. It was clear we had chosen the right man to look out for our property and recommending him to Don was a good decision.

While it is amazing how much a revolution can screw up one's finances we never forgot we were lucky to be home and fighting bureaucratic battles rather than dealing with the hellish situation the hostages were facing. We had to cope with these practical issues but the situation of the hostages was never far from our thoughts. While everyone was frustrated by the lack of progress in negotiations, we and the thirteen who had been released in November began a series of meetings. I do not remember who hosted, except it was someone with a decent-sized house at their disposal. Nor do I remember who attended except to say enough people came and showed sufficient interest that we had three or four meetings. The purpose of these gatherings was twofold. First, it was an opportunity to talk about our friends. We all felt a certain guilt, not in the sense of being responsible for what had befallen the hostages, but rather in the mold of "there but for the grace of God go I." Even though our freedom had been secured in a way different from those released by the ayatollah, we were all acutely aware it was primarily just luck we were home and they were not.

The second purpose was to consider whether there was anything we could or should do to try to help the hostages. We were pretty sure that as a group we could get an audience, either with someone in the administration or the media. The question was whether we had anything to say. As we were not privy to any of the secret efforts we hoped were underway, either in the diplomatic or military spheres, what we saw was an administration that seemed to have no policy or plan whatsoever other than to threaten severe retaliation if the hostages were harmed. That was good as far as it went, but clearly it did not go very far in terms of the development of a strategy to actually bring the hostages home.

There were other options. One was a naval blockade of Iran's ports with the intent of preventing the regime from selling oil and importing food. The theory was any Iranian government unable to sell oil would not survive. This was hardly risk free, however. Aside from the possibility of retaliation against the hostages the Iranians could try to block the Straits of Hormuz, through which tankers carry much of the world's oil supply. Another possibility was to demand our so-called allies truly enforce the economic sanctions they theoretically supported: an "us or them" strategy. Any country found to be trading with Iran would immediately have its US assets frozen and its ability to sell goods to the US suspended until it agreed to comply fully and completely with trade sanctions. A third option was selective military strikes against Iran's oil infrastructure. Aside from the wells themselves, Iran has been and remains chronically short of domestic refining capacity. If we began to take out that capacity piece by piece we would put tremendous pressure on the regime as Iranians became increasingly unable to buy gas.

These were just some of the ideas we discussed. None were without risk for the hostages, but then it was also true the hostages were in great peril every day they remained in Iran. The physical and emotional stress with which they were living exposed them to various dangers. There remained the possibility one of them might try to escape or simply reach the breaking point, forcing a showdown with the captors.

On April 24th everything changed. This was the day operation Eagle Claw collapsed in a ball of fire in the Iranian desert. Eagle Claw was the code name for the military undertaking to rescue the hostages. It was a complex plan, but at its core was the transport of Delta force "operators" to a point in the Iranian desert where they would meet up with a fleet of helicopters flying in from ships off the coast of Iran. The initial problem was a lack of operational helicopters. Only eight were sent; a minimum of six were required. Carter claims the military chain of command recommended eight; others have said Carter refused to consider more because he wanted to avoid the appearance of an invasion in the event the operation was detected. Whatever the reason for the initial number of helicopters, the operation was canceled when the number of functioning choppers dropped to five. After the abort order an accident occurred; a helicopter crashed into a C-130 transport aircraft loaded with fuel. Eight Americans died and the remaining US forces returned to their bases and ships.

There were of course many other aspects to the plan, including both intelligence gathering and logistical support in Tehran we now know was provided with the assistance of Ken Taylor.[1] As a point of curiosity, I was on duty that day at the Iran Working Group, doing my usual swing shift. I was surprised to see Hal Saunders, the Assistant Secretary of the Bureau of Near Eastern Affairs, come into the operations center, although he did not come by the working group. I did not find out about Eagle Claw until I heard it on the news the next morning, but I assume Saunders came in to read the classified reporting.

Whether the plan was a good idea or even could have worked has been the subject of more than one book (both Wright and Bowden cover it well) and is certainly beyond my expertise. But the failure of Eagle Claw had a major impact on our group discussions because the Iranian reaction included moving many of the hostages away from the embassy compound. The purpose was to make a future rescue attempt impossible, but a secondary result was the hostages were no longer under the centralized control of either the terrorist commanders or perhaps even the Ayatollah Khomeini. This made the idea of trying to put additional economic or diplomatic pressure, let alone taking military action, more problematic. The hostages were increasingly pawns in Iran's domestic political maneuvering and there was no guarantee a decision by the central government to release the hostages, especially if made under some kind of pressure from the US, would have been universally honored. While I understand the terrorists took steps to keep the hostages under their control even as they scattered them around the country, there is no certainty they would have been able to prevent the kidnapping of a hostage by a group opposed to whatever agreement we might

---

1. Ibid, 230 ff

have been able to force upon Khomeini. This development made the possibility of our group doing anything helpful even more remote than it was in the beginning.

Some us took part in a lawsuit against the Iranian government and the Ayatollah Khomeini. The initial suit was filed by a number of the former hostages released before Thanksgiving. Cora and I, our parents and Lee Schatz later joined the suit. Our attorney was John P. Coale, who I understand has been a controversial figure in his career as a plaintiff's attorney, but I think he dealt fairly with us. While the suit asked for lots of money, I never had any serious expectation it would produce any. My hope was by filing the suit we would keep some focus on the need to recompense the hostages for their ordeal. Clearly, there is a limit on what money can do to compensate someone in that kind of situation. But it remains the best means we have. Given the bureaucratic obstacle course we had to maneuver, and my understanding the earlier thirteen encountered many of the same problems although they had been through a far worse experience, I could see little downside in joining the suit.

Iran had billions of dollars worth of assets frozen in the US and eventually there would have to be a resolution of those assets. It would inevitably be a part of the negotiations to free the hostages. I did not believe the suit itself would significantly complicate the ability of our government to meet Iranian demands as the President had the authority to conduct foreign policy under the constitution. He could ignore any court order, although that might make the US government ultimately liable in Iran's place. That was Coale's belief and was, frankly, fine by me. As it turned out, the President did issue an executive order which nullified our suit, but contrary to Coale's thinking, the courts did not find the US was liable for the damages we might otherwise have collected from Iran. As with some other issues I have touched on, a full explanation would require more space than I consider appropriate in this book. But for us, the ultimate outcome was not a surprise or a disappointment. I don't know whether the suit had any bearing on the later decisions of the Commission on Hostage Compensation or even the fact it was decided to create the commission. But more on that later.

The last meeting of the Tehran alumni was an April picnic. We met in a park in West Virginia for lunch. I had been one of the people trying to keep the group focused on the question whether we could do anything to help the hostages. But Eagle Claw was a psychological watershed for me. Its failure convinced me there was no prospect of the hostages coming home anytime soon and our own group could not help. So this was purely a social event. It was interesting primarily because we learned one of our number had gone back into Iran with the Eagle Claw team. We found out soon after our return that one of the employees released earlier had managed to convince the terrorists he was a Marine guard. As he was African-American, they let him go. In fact, he was probably one of the people they would have least wanted to release, but unlike the CIA guys he did not leave a paper trail and his quick thinking to take the place of a Marine guard on leave resulted in an early departure.

A second and far more unusual picnic took place at the farm owned by Tony Mendez. This came about as a result of a chance meeting between Bob Anders and Tony at the Foggy Bottom Metro station. Even CIA operatives have to get to work. I don't know what hoops Tony had to jump through in order to get permission to host the gathering, but it was great fun. In addition to the six of us, he invited two agency people who worked for him, and John Chambers, who had been the primary Hollywood contact for Tony. Chambers said it was an almost unprecedented opportunity to meet the people his expertise had assisted. Most of the time, Tony was exfiltrating moles or covert operatives and for obvious reasons they were made to disappear once they reached our shores. We were different, and for us it was a chance to meet another real hero. While Chambers did not risk his life the way Tony did, he had chosen to share his expertise with an organization that is generally not popular in Hollywood. Public knowledge would certainly not have helped his career.

We had a chance to meet Tony's wife and children, see his art studio, the house that he was building with his own labor and to explore the farm. Tony gave us an expert tour of the Antietam civil war battlefield, and Bob Anders reminded us he had as much hair on his back as we already knew he had on his chest. The ladies in particular gave him a tough time about it as he played tennis minus his shirt on the unusually warm spring day.

During these weeks we also had an interesting dinner at the home of a lady named Leah, whose maiden name was Lijek. An unusual name could be good and bad. On the one hand it got my parents a batch of pistachios courtesy of the immigrant visa applicant I had helped. But it also brought reporters to their door very soon after the attack on the embassy, putting them on the spot even as the Department was figuring out how to deal with the press.

In Leah's case the press got things confused, very confused. Somehow they found her in the hours after our escape became public, even though her married name was different. A reporter called and asked for her reaction to the news her husband had just escaped from Iran. Her answer, as she put it to us at dinner, was something like,

"What? Iran? I thought he was working down at the deli."

Her husband owned a wholesale deli products distribution company in the Silver Spring suburb of Washington. For many years after I would think of the story whenever I saw one of his trucks pass by.

Leah wrote to me through the Department and asked me to call her if I was interested in exploring our family connection. When I did telephone her, she invited her two brothers, Abraham and John, to come down from New York for a dinner at her home. That conversation by itself resolved a little mystery. For many years I had a habit of looking for Lijeks in telephone directories when I would first visit a city. If I found any I could usually plug them in somewhere in the family tree. These two were an exception. But the dinner also left us with a greater mystery, one which remains unsolved. Leah and her family were Jewish and hailed from central Poland. My father's family was Catholic and could document its presence in the former Pomerania in north central Poland, at least as far back as the mid 19th century. Were we related? While there is no way to know for certain my father had an uncanny resemblance to Abraham. Also, Lijek is not a common name in Poland either, as I learned during my assignment there. I never encountered another Lijek, other than relatives, and many Poles thought the name was Czech and were surprised when I told them I was of Polish ancestry.

I regret not making an effort to stay in touch with Leah.

Not long after the dinner it was time to head out. One last event took place on our way to Hong Kong. George Steinbrenner, owner of the New York Yankees, had the generous idea of inviting the six of us and the Canadians to New York for a Yankees/Blue Jays game. The Yankees picked up all the expenses, including rooms at the New York Hilton and limousine transportation. Our seats were in the owner's box. It was a once-in-a-lifetime treat. Reggie Jackson, Mr. October himself, was playing for the Yankees in those days and he came by to say hello. Kathy Stafford complained jokingly she had not received a souvenir hat so he gave her the one he was wearing.

The Yankees clobbered our Toronto guests, 6-0, which was probably not the most diplomatic outcome, but then baseball is not a diplomatic activity. After the game, we went to a bar near the hotel and enjoyed several hours of good conversation. This was the first time we had seen Roger and the Sheardowns since the exfiltration so it was a joyful reunion. Unfortunately it was too short, and the next morning we flew to Los Angeles to begin a roundabout trip to Hong Kong.

# 18. New Place, Lots of the Same Stuff

The trip to Hong Kong was definitely indirect. We first flew to LA to spend a couple of days with my family. Then it was on to Fiji, where we had a glorious week enjoying the beaches and making trips to some of the outlying islands. One of those trips was to a small resort on a private island. The Australian owner came out to meet the boat. I told Cora I had never seen a more contented-looking individual.

From there we flew to Auckland, New Zealand, where we met up with Richard Sewell and Chris Beebe. As I mentioned earlier, their embassy had been attacked four days after we left, perhaps because they had become the protecting power for Canada. Both had been transferred out of Iran. To my knowledge they had not been publicly named for their involvement with us, but I suspect the New Zealand government did not want to take any chances. Had someone somewhere leaked information about how helpful they had been it might have resulted in some kind of retribution beyond the damage inflicted on their embassy.

I can think of no better tour guides. Because we and they had limited time we restricted ourselves to the North Island. Still, we covered everything from the Bay of Islands in the far north to Wellington in the south. Chris had read a restaurant review of a place called the Panorama Seafood Restaurant on Ninety Mile Beach at the far northwest tip of the island, across from the Bay of Islands. The restaurant was run by a Dutch couple, Corry and Henk Kraaijenhof, had seating for perhaps eight people and required advance arrangements for meals. Chris called ahead, but we underestimated how long it would take to get there. Richard, who was driving, began to insist the place existed only in Chris's imagination. As the miles went by, the lights of houses became less and less frequent and still no restaurant. But we did find it and I have the business card to prove it did exist. By the time we arrived it was rather late and we had missed our reservation, but the owners were very hospitable. The restaurant was famous for toheroa, a clam-like shellfish which is unique to New Zealand. I presume Richard and Chris had tasted it previously, but as it is a special delicacy and Chris was something of a gourmet, he figured this restaurant was the place to introduce it to us. The meal was fantastic, well worth the trip.

There were many highlights of our week: the boat trip on the Bay of Islands, considered one of the premier fishing spots in the world, or having our pictures taken in front of an enormous kauri tree with diameters at the base nearing 20' and a height ranging up to 150'. It seemed no matter where we went, we met someone who was either a relative, however distant, of Chris or Richard, or a friend of a relative. In one case we found ourselves invited to a trout breakfast thanks to one of these chance meetings. This was a particular treat because as a game fish trout is not available in restaurants and we were certainly not equipped to catch any ourselves.

I could go on, but as this is not a travelogue I will simply say we had a terrific time and left New Zealand regretting we had not fought harder for that assignment. From there, we went to Sydney, Australia, to visit a high school friend of Cora's. Her father had been in the military and served at Fort Monmouth in New Jersey, where Cora's father had frequently been stationed. It was another wonderful week including a drive to Canberra, the capital. Both Australia and New Zealand remained top choices for future assignments, but not surprisingly they were in great demand and we have not had a chance to visit either one since, let alone to get an assignment.

Then it was on to Hong Kong. As is clear to any student of geography our route to Hong Kong was based on our desire to see friends rather than on physical proximity so we were left with a 4,000 mile journey. We arrived in Hong Kong on June 25th, rested, relaxed and ready for a change of scene. DC was too depressing with constant reminders of the stalemate over the hostages.

I found my new job interesting and my co-workers generally pleasant. It felt good to have a real job again after months of enforced idleness followed by the press mania and ultimately the months of training. Although technically a consulate general subordinate to the embassy in London, as Hong Kong at this time was still a British colony, in reality it was an independent post and quite a large one. It served as a regional hub and headquarters for a number of government agencies due to the excellent air connections and quality of life. It was also our main "China-watching" post. Although we now had formal diplomatic relations with China the process of developing our posts there was slow.

We quickly made friends among the singles and couples in our age group. In fact, we already knew several from the area studies class. The two main activities in Hong Kong were eating and shopping. We fell in with a group of people who liked to try different restaurants on a regular basis. That led to some great meals as well as frequent bouts of gastric upset. As for shopping there was no end of opportunities. The consulate organized factory trips on a regular basis. We and our friends discovered our own favorite places as well.

Cora found a job teaching English to Vietnamese refugees, boat people who had made it through the gauntlet and were now living in special camps. Most of them would end up resettled elsewhere, usually in the US. She also worked temporary secretarial or what we now call information technology jobs in the consulate and eventually landed a position at the Japanese School teaching English. Although it is not necessary to speak a language in order to teach English to people who speak that language (i.e. Cora did not speak Vietnamese), the Japanese school was undoubtedly impressed by her knowledge of their language and culture.

During these months as we were integrating ourselves into the Hong Kong community, Iran would not go away. First and foremost were the hostages. Although there was no *Nightline* or Walter Cronkite counting the days of captivity, reports on the status of the hostages appeared regularly in the papers and the English-language TV news. This was a good thing; we appreciated the fact the hostages remained news even in this relatively distant corner of the world.

In July we heard Richard Queen was being released for medical reasons. The news left me initially puzzled but hopeful. Perhaps Rich had something minor but difficult to diagnose, and with symptoms scary enough the Iranians preferred to get credit for a humanitarian release rather than run the risk of having a hostage die. When I learned it was multiple sclerosis, I was saddened. I did not know much about the disease, but enough to understand it was at best life-changing for Rich. I wrote him a letter, but do not know whether he received it. When we finally saw him after the hostages were released he was doing very well and the disease did not come up as there were so many other things to talk about.

At the end of the month the shah succumbed to cancer in Cairo. Initially there was speculation in the media his death might pave the way to an agreement for release of the hostages. It soon became clear the situation in Tehran had changed too much. While the shah remained a bogeyman while he lived and was useful for energizing crowds, it soon became clear the hostages were now pawns in an internal political struggle that had little to do with him. So the stalemate continued.

Not so good was the personal stuff. Some of it bordered on the comic while other things could have long term significance for my career. In the comic category was an issue regarding a travel voucher. I owed the Department the magnificent sum of $74.95 for the travel from Washington to Tehran as the cash advance I obtained before leaving DC ended up slightly exceeding the expenses I could claim. I submitted the paperwork to the Budget and Fiscal Office in Tehran after arrival, but for unexplained reasons the Department could find no record the check had been processed. My bank book showed I had submitted it in August, which should have been more than enough time for the check to clear before the November attack. But there was no way for me to prove payment from the records I had. So I wrote my bank, explaining the unusual circumstances, and they were able to produce a copy of the canceled check along with the necessary proof the actual payment had been deducted from my account.

The less funny stuff had to do with my evaluation report. The day before we left Washington I was handed a blank report form and asked to fill in my parts. Being new, I did not realize personnel had given me the wrong form, the one for regular officers rather than untenured newbies. Several weeks previously, I had been asked for descriptions of the jobs I did in Tehran. That was easy and I turned in a statement a few days later. But the sections I was now being asked to complete were normally done after the rest of the report was finished. They essentially ask the employee for his or her reaction to what the report contains. This should have made me suspicious but there was simply no time to ask questions.

In a bureaucracy where performance is almost by definition difficult to measure in concrete terms, careers live and die by evaluation reports. There is a tendency for these reports to be written in glowing terms so even a minor negative comment can be a killer. Because of this tendency the Department actually mandated each report contain an "area for improvement" so rating officers would have to say something negative (realistic?) about the employee. Good rating officers could turn even the "area for improvement" into a back-handed compliment. A favorite was "works too hard."

While evaluations are important for virtually all officers, they were critical for new hires who lack career status. While a less-than-stellar report may delay a promotion, for someone in my situation it could mean termination at the end of the four year probationary period. I took the process seriously and submitted my input shortly after arriving in Hong Kong.

Let's just say I was surprised when I received my evaluation. First, personnel realized its mistake regarding the form so what I filled out was not what I received. The actual evaluation had been done on the correct career candidate form. This meant some of my comments did not relate properly to what was asked for in that particular section of the evaluation. Then there was the matter of who wrote it. Normally, your boss writes your evaluation and his boss reviews it. My boss, Dick Morefield, was a hostage and had no contact with the outside world. His boss was Bruce Laingen. By this time, post Eagle Claw, Bruce also was cut off, but someone must have thought to ask for his comments while he was still able to communicate. Personnel decided to substitute Henry Precht for Morefield. This might well have been a reasonable thing to do, but certainly not without consulting me. I might have preferred to take a chance on Dick writing the report when he was able. The rules say the minimum time in service before tenure is two years, excluding training, which meant July 1982 for me. So there was plenty of time for a resolution of the hostage situation before then.

The first part of the report was reasonable, using statements from Bob Anders and from Cy Richardson, who had occasionally supervised me. But the killer was the section on "weaknesses." Henry criticized me for participating in the lawsuit against Iran. He opened by acknowledging it was "a personal decision about a personal matter," but then went on to write I should have consulted persons involved in hostage matters (i.e. Henry) before doing this. In any case by putting this into my performance evaluation he had elevated it into something rather different from a personal matter.

He also wrote that during his pre-attack visit, he sensed I was "not happy in the revolutionary conditions that prevailed." I plead guilty, but it still shocked me to find that listed as a criticism. At the risk of sounding harsh, I was tempted to write in my response that only a suicidal maniac would have been "happy" under these conditions, particularly since at the time of his visit we already knew the shah was coming to the US for medical treatment. The secret memo I referenced earlier, which Henry himself had drafted, warned of dire consequences should we admit the shah and recommended a significant upgrade of the embassy guard force before admission. That upgrade had not occurred. I did not know about the memo at the time Henry saw me in Iran, but the point remains that Henry, from the safety of Washington, was criticizing me for being less than thrilled with the personal security situation I faced. And, of course, it wasn't only me. Thanks to the unintentionally misleading information Henry had provided, my wife was also at risk. That did make me concerned if not angry, and I have to believe most people would have felt the same way.

The entire situation was unfortunate. In the end, I had to file a formal grievance to get the report changed. It was an odd situation. The people who worked in the performance evaluation section of personnel were very sympathetic to my situation but had no authority to make changes. Only the grievance board could do that so I began the process of filing a grievance. It took over two years, but in the end the changes I requested were made.

I was tenured effective in November 1982. The Commissioning and Tenure Board, as it was called, met in August, and although it was my second review, this was the first board that saw the evaluation report with the changes I had requested and the grievance board had approved. My first review was based solely on one report from Hong Kong. The board had also approved my request for an additional year of probationary status in the event I needed it. In the end, I don't think my career suffered because of this report. In those days, the first promotion was automatic after 18 months in service. By the time an earned promotion was a reasonable prospect I had achieved tenure. All in all, the system worked. But I couldn't help once again think of the disconnect. The President called me a hero (again, not deserved but you'd think it would count for something as far as being able to remain employed), but I had to spend two years in bureaucratic battle in order to make sure I didn't get bounced from the service.

Some months after I started the grievance I received a letter from Precht. He said the comment about my being "unhappy" was not intended as a criticism, but rather to indicate I was doing a good job under difficult circumstances. As for the lawsuit, he explained his reasoning. I had to admit he made some valid points. Even in hindsight, it is not clear. President Carter made the decision to create a commission on hostage compensation the day before he left office, making it one of his last official acts. The commission report makes reference to the lawsuits and notes their dismissal was an unconditional Iranian demand. One can make a good argument the existence of those suits gave our side another bargaining chip as the Iranians were adamant they would not pay compensation to the hostages. The President therefore issued an executive order that effectively terminated the suits.[1] The report does note the question of the suits was considered by the panel and it heard testimony regarding them. So it is certainly reasonable to argue the existence of the suits might have affected both the President's decision to create the commission as well as the commission's deliberations. It is worth noting some of the hostages even now are continuing a legal battle against the US government for the right to sue Iran.

The tone of Henry's letter was conciliatory and I do think

---

[1]. The President's Commission on Hostage Compensation, The Final Report and Recommendations of the President's Commission on Hostage Compensation, September 28, 1981, 7-10. Document in possession of the author.

he understood why I had to file the grievance. To my knowledge he made no objection to the changes ultimately ordered by the grievance board. His letter ended with the note he had been proposed for the position of ambassador to Mauritania but the nomination was being held up by Senator Jesse Helms of North Carolina. The senator was unhappy with our Iran policy and did not believe Henry's performance merited an ambassadorship. If and when the nomination was approved and were we ever in the neighborhood, he invited us to visit.[2] As I have written previously, I considered Henry a friend and a very capable officer even though we disagreed on some things.

The President's Commission also recommended some administrative changes in the way the US government should deal with persons in a "missing" status, which was the general administrative category into which we and the hostages were placed during our time in Iran following the takeover. The most immediate impact for us was income earned during this period became tax exempt and we were able to file amended tax returns and receive a refund. Six years later Congress passed unrelated legislation that authorized a $50 per day payment to employees in that status. So once again we received a benefit earned by the hostages.

In September of 1980 Cora and I were contacted by Les Harris, a Canadian film producer. I think he was technically a British national at the time but resident and working in Canada. Actually, our first contact with Les had taken place before we left Washington. He was interested in making a film, a docudrama, about the exfiltration. I am not sure why we agreed to cooperate, but he seemed like a decent sort and genuinely interested in the story. Les asked to interview us for a documentary he was producing for the Canadian Broadcasting Corporation. He was prepared to come to Hong Kong and was also planning to interview Bob in Oslo and the Staffords in Palermo. Skeptical as we had become about the media, we asked the Department to confirm he really was working for CBC and the Canadian side was also planning to cooperate. The

---

2. Henry Precht, letter to the author, November 14, 1980. In possession of the author.

Iran Working Group confirmed Les was legitimate and Ken Taylor would be involved. The intent was to broadcast the documentary on the one year anniversary of our exfiltration, but the CBC accepted the Department's argument the actual broadcast date should be determined by the status of the hostage negotiations. In the end four of the six of us (the Staffords excepted) agreed to be interviewed. The result was a documentary called *Escape from Iran: The Inside Story*. Of course it told the public version, excluding the CIA angle, but it was well done. It was the first Canadian-made documentary to be shown in prime time in the US market, while in Canada it was the highest rated documentary of 1981. I still have my original copy on commercial ¾ inch Sony tape. The timing could not have been better with the hostages themselves being on the news at the same time.

The docudrama also made it to TV on CBS later in 1981. It was titled *Escape from Iran: The Canadian Caper* and it too told the sanitized version. I thought a few parts of it were corny, but overall it was a good film and still shows up on late night cable from time to time. Many years later, I tried to interest Les in doing a remake with the CIA role included, but he had moved on to other things. Les became a friend and has remained an honorary member of the exfiltration alumni, coming to our reunions when he can.

# 19. The Hostages Come Home

Several things happened near the end of 1980 that were good omens for the hostages. The first, in mid-October, was a telephone call from a man named Mark Kramer. He identified himself as a producer with CBS news and said they were potentially interested in hiring me as a "spotter" in the event the hostages were released. Of course my first response was to ask whether he had any information this was likely to happen soon. He claimed not; his boss had asked him to call me and work out an arrangement for when the release did occur. He also said they would be interested in an interview.

I replied I would have to think about the offer, as well as obtain permission from the Department to enter into an arrangement. We agreed he would call me back in a couple of days. While the offer was certainly beguiling, as a practical matter I wondered whether I could do the job adequately. While I knew most of the hostages, some better than others, I also realized from the Christmas videos and even Rich Queen's appearance at the time of his release they did not look very much like I remembered them. The obvious candidate was Queen himself, assuming his health permitted. When the subsequent call came, I had already decided I should share my concern with Kramer. I didn't need to, however, as he told me they were withdrawing the offer. Although I didn't know at the time, Rich was the person they chose. As far as the interview, he said they were still interested. I was as well. I thought once the hostages were out I could speak with more freedom about everything except the CIA's role in our exfiltration. But nothing ever came of that offer either, which in the big picture was probably a good thing.

A second omen was the election of Ronald Reagan. I remember my boss pulled me into his office that morning, closed the door, and took a bottle of Johnnie Walker Black from his desk drawer. We toasted Reagan's victory and the hope the hostages would be home soon. Some have argued Reagan's tough talk intimidated the Iranians and made them want to settle while Carter was still President. While

I believe there is some truth there, I think it might be as much the case Carter's defeat had become an end in itself for the Iranians and the hostages the means. Once the defeat was accomplished there was less reason to retain them. The Iranian hatred for Carter is difficult to comprehend. It may come down to the fact his human rights rhetoric gave them hope which made his later enthusiastic embrace of the shah seem more like a personal betrayal rather than foreign policy realism.

Another development was the September 22 Iraqi military attack on Iran. The Iranian forces were poorly prepared. The majority of Iran's weapons systems were US-manufactured, and of course the US was no longer providing training or logistical support. Many other nations were reluctant to supply Iran, at least openly, in the face of UN sanctions and continuing general condemnation of Iran for holding the hostages. The war made Iran's isolation from the world community potentially far more costly.

Lastly, the domestic political reasons for holding the hostages were becoming less important. During the first months after the takeover, the terrorists and their political allies discovered the hostage crisis could be used as a tool to strengthen the Islamic radicals at the expense of the pro-Western democrats. As the takeover progressed, embassy staff made efforts to destroy sensitive documents but many had to be put through ribbon shredders for lack of more effective equipment. The terrorists eventually brought in teams of students to spend thousands of hours reassembling the documents. Some of these contained the names of Iranians who had contacts with embassy officers. The contacts were usually benign in the sense it is the job of diplomats to meet with host country officials and also opposition leaders. But the Iranian people were not well versed in the nature of diplomacy and it was all too easy to portray any contact as sinister. As one might expect, many of our contacts were with secular democrats opposed to the shah, people who now stood in the way of an Islamic theocracy. The terrorists and their allies used these files to discredit and in some cases prosecute their political opponents. As the Islamist revolutionaries strengthened their grip on power and developed the political infrastructure for their Islamic republic, this process became less critical to their success.

As I wrote at the outset, this book is not intended as history and there is no way to boil down the complex negotiations between the US and Iran to a couple of paragraphs. But in the interest of a coherent narrative, I will try. The first real break was the Iranian decision to appoint Algeria as an intermediary in negotiations, which was seen as an opportunity by the American side. Warren Christopher, the Deputy Secretary of State, made a secret trip to Algiers following Carter's election loss. He brought with him the US response to the latest set of Iranian demands. Unlike in past exchanges the Iranian reply this time was specific and focused, seeking clarifications and additional details rather than making ritual denunciations.[1] Christopher provided the answers via the Algerians, and the US side waited. On December 19, the Iranians replied with a demand for $24 billion.[2]

While the administration's initial reaction was one of shock and anger at the seeming step backward, Christopher studied the document closely and looked for areas of possible compromise. As the hostages were "celebrating" their second Christmas in captivity, Christopher was putting together yet another counter proposal. This time it included the idea the US side would develop a financial guarantee acceptable to the Algerians. The US and Iran would each sign a separate agreement with Algeria; this was more satisfactory to many Iranian hard-liners than a direct deal with the great Satan. Iranian funds frozen in the US would be transferred to Algeria but only after the hostages were out of Iran. The US would freeze the shah's assets in the US and permit the Iranians to go after them in US courts. Claims against Iran pending in US courts would be canceled (including, not surprisingly, ours), although some of the larger commercial ones could be pursued through an international tribunal that would be established under the agreement.[3]

Meanwhile, the terrorists had grown increasingly tired of their jobs as jailers. Even those who knew of the plan to extend the takeover beyond the sit-in anticipated by the real students never expected the situation would continue into a second year. In early

---

1. Doyle McManus,198
2. Ibid, 202
3. Mark Bowden, 576-7

November they officially turned over control of the hostages to the Iranian government, but were told there was no one to replace them so they had to carry on for the time being.[4] But while the government was initially slow in taking control of the hostages, eventually it happened and at last they were put on a plane to Algiers. From there US Air Force aircraft took them to Rhein-Main Air Force Base and then they were transferred to a hospital in Wiesbaden. In a final act of cruelty to President Carter the aircraft were not allowed to take off from Iran until 30 minutes after his term as President had ended.

Their stay in Germany was longer than ours, as unlike us they did need real medical attention as well as a longer decompression time. Meantime, we were peppering Sheldon Krys with cables requesting our promised travel orders for the trip back to DC, as we did not know how long they would be in Germany and we wanted to be in Washington for their arrival. We got our orders on January 23 and left two days later. Thanks to the international date line we arrived in DC late on the same day.

We also did not know the hostages would go first to the US Army Military Academy at West Point, NY, where they would spend three days getting reacquainted with their families as well as becoming more aware of the welcome they could expect over the coming weeks. They arrived in New York on January 25th, the same day we hit Washington. As it turned out our frantic efforts to secure travel orders were unnecessary. But on the other hand, these days presented an opportunity to reconnect with the previously released hostages, both the thirteen and, especially, for us to see Richard Queen, whose multiple sclerosis seemed to have gone into remission following his release by the terrorists. As I mentioned earlier, Rich had been hired by CBS to be the spotter and color commentator for their coverage of the arrival ceremony in Washington. Who better? The Department had not told anyone how long the former hostages would remain at West Point so Rich was prepared to move on a moment's notice.

The big day turned out to be January 28, fittingly the one year anniversary of our own departure from Iran. The Department was planning to follow the same paradigm as with us, using Metro buses

---

4. Doyle McManus, 194

to caravan from Andrews Air Force Base. But this time there was to be no intermediate stop at the State Department. The buses were going directly to the White House.

We were allowed to ride the buses on their outgoing journey and even at this early time we could see people already standing along the route (which had been publicized) with their welcome signs. This was clearly going to be something quite different from our trip; the only thing in common really was that both we and they rode on city buses. They had nine; we had one. There were an estimated 500,000 people greeting them along their route to the White House.[5] We had none, although we did get an enthusiastic welcome at the State Department which was not available to them.

These comparisons are not intended seriously. There is no way in the world I would have traded our experience for theirs. They deserved every bit of the wonderful welcome they received. We were happy just to be there, to be spectators at their event. And that is what we were. The situation at Andrews was awkward. While we wanted to be there and to be seen and noticed by the former hostages, it was in my mind more a matter of us showing our respect to them than anything else. Of the fifty-two hostages, there were some we hardly knew, some we knew quite well, while the largest group, probably thirty-five or forty, we knew as acquaintances but the takeover interrupted the process of becoming friends. Meantime, although close family members were taken to West Point and had already been given an opportunity to reacquaint themselves with the former hostages, most of them had more distant relations who had come only to Andrews. We did not want to get in the way of those reunions. So we watched carefully, and when there was an opportunity, we approached and gave whatever greeting seemed appropriate, from a hug to a handshake. Those who knew us were pleased to see us and happy we had managed to escape. Going in, I was particularly curious about the reaction of the other six who had been with us in the consulate but had not managed to make it out. To a man they congratulated us on not being captured.

The greetings on the tarmac could have gone on for hours, but

---

5. Ibid, 225

as I was to learn very well in working Presidential visits later in my career, where the White House is concerned the clock is critical. So at the appointed hour we were shepherded into the buses for the drive to the White House. The buses traveled slowly, giving the hostages the opportunity to acknowledge the many well-wishers lining the routes. It was an unforgettable experience. Of course we understood these people were not there for us, but it did not matter. They were there for our friends and colleagues. I felt privileged just to be able to see the well-deserved outpouring of affection for them.

The White House reception was also unforgettable. I do not know how many people were there; I have read 6,000 were invited.[6] The reception was necessarily held outdoors, and considering it was the end of January the weather was very cooperative. The fifty-three ex-hostages (Rich Queen was rightfully included) entered the White House separately from the rest of the crowd. They went through a receiving line where they met the President and Mrs. Reagan. The rest of us were milling around on the south lawn and when the time came the former hostages took their places at a horseshoe-shaped table set just for them. Bruce Laingen gave a short address thanking the President and the nation for the welcome.

The former hostages overnighted at a hotel in the Virginia suburbs, near the Pentagon as I recall, and the next day went to New York for the traditional ticker tape parade down Broadway. After the White House reception we did not see them again, except as individuals in the course of our mutual normal lives. The one exception was a monthly luncheon group Bruce Laingen organized while an instructor at the National Defense University at Fort McNair in Washington. During the two and a half years I spent in Washington between Kathmandu and Warsaw in the mid-eighties, Cora and I were regular attendees.

The former hostages went through a process of accommodating to their new status. I did read some of their remarks in the press. It appeared they started out with many of the same reservations we did but before long most of them seemed accepting of all the attention

---

6. Katherine Koob, Guest of the Revolution (Nashville, Thomas Nelson, 1982), 226

they were getting. On one level it continued to feel strange we were not part of them. We had started out together. While no one was happier than me we had not ended together, I had subconsciously assumed we would have some special relationship to them, perhaps because of the closeness and sense of community we had felt in Tehran before the takeover. We did not. They had been through too much. Those who were our friends before the takeover continued to be our friends, but the ex-hostages as a group shared a unique bond. We were outsiders as much as if we had never set foot in Tehran. But that was as it should be, and I was in a great mood when we departed Washington on January 30. We stopped in Hawaii for three days and then returned to Hong Kong to pick up our new lives where we left off. But of course there was one huge difference: our friends were home and able to restart their lives as well. I could pick up a newspaper without dreading the headline. For a while at least the world seemed like a much nicer place.

# 20. Living the Little Lie

After working with Les Harris on the documentary and the television movie, our lives became progressively more detached from the Iran drama. Once in a while something would come up. The Young Presidents Organization, a group of under-forty corporate CEO's, invited me to Singapore to give a speech at their annual meeting. The Hong Kong Chamber of Commerce made me a luncheon speaker. I had long ago lost any fear of public speaking and I enjoyed these opportunities to tell the sanitized story, say nice things about the Canadians, and usually, I would get a question or two that would allow me to give my opinion of the Carter administration's handling of the crisis. The publication of memoirs by some of the major players in the making of Iran policy, along with access to all of the classified documents the terrorists had reassembled, had done nothing to change my assessment this was an administration in over its head.

The Algiers agreement also called for the Iranians to return the property of the hostages to the US. We had long forgotten this part of the agreement when just before leaving Hong Kong an unexpected package arrived. It contained printed invitation cards with the Majidi Street address. Apparently it was the only thing our landlady decided wasn't worth stealing.

After Hong Kong we transferred to Kathmandu, Nepal. At that time it was still isolated and exotic. It was almost impossible to make a telephone call in or out and that was fine with us. From there it was back to Washington, although we spent October and November of 1985 in Kuwait on a temporary assignment primarily focused on cleaning up the bomb damage from the terrorist attack on our embassy earlier that year. A truck bomb had obliterated half of the annex building. The other half was still standing and occasionally I would take a walk through the remnant. The view from the roof was nice; our compound was close to the water so the Persian Gulf was visible. On the other side was Iran. This was as close as I cared to get.

But I didn't need to see Iran to see Islamic terrorism. It was all around me. One of my jobs was taking inventory of the furniture that had been inside the annex. The usable stuff had been transferred to the temporary pre-fabricated buildings in which the former annex offices were now housed, but I had several large tents full of damaged but still identifiable items. I particularly remember a black leather desk chair which had several large, dagger-shaped pieces of glass embedded in it. The employee to whom the chair belonged told me he would normally have been sitting in it at the time of the explosion, but he'd received a phone call a few minutes earlier to come pick up papers in another section. That call saved his life. I told him I could relate to the idea of a small thing making a huge, unexpected difference.

After the temporary stay in Kuwait, we continued on to Cairo where Joe and Kathy Stafford had gone after Palermo. Undeterred by our Iran experience, Joe was rapidly becoming a middle-east specialist. He had taken Arabic training, a two-year long program which entailed study first at the Foreign Service Institute in Rosslyn and then a second phase of training in Tunisia. He was also starting the process of switching cones from administrative to political. He was working as a political officer at the embassy and I understood he had the best Arabic of anyone in the section. That did not surprise me at all given Joe's facility with languages, incredible work ethic and great interest in the Middle East. Cora and I spent a week cruising the Nile and visiting many of the spectacular tourist sites Egypt offers, then accepted the Staffords invitation to stay with them for a few days. We had a good opportunity to catch up. It had been almost four years since the release of the hostages. We spent the holidays with my parents. My father had retired from Northrop and they were living temporarily in a small house on an island not far from Seattle.

We bought a car in Washington state and made a leisurely trip back to Washington for some training and my first assignment to the Department. Our first stop was California, where we had lunch with Richard Sewell. He was assigned to the New Zealand consulate in Westwood near Beverly Hills and seemed to be enjoying himself greatly. Then we were supposed to drive to San Diego to have dinner with Massoud, the former chief local employee in the American services section. Unfortunately, the less than 100 mile journey ended up taking close to six hours in traffic that was horrible even by Southern California standards. We eventually got there and managed a late supper.

Like many former embassy employees, Massoud had taken advantage of the opportunity to apply for a special immigrant visa upon completion of fifteen years service. He did not have enough time in before the takeover. For a while he worked for the Swiss Embassy, which as I mentioned earlier had become the protecting power for US interests. This included helping US citizens so it was a natural fit for him. Although now on the Swiss payroll, Massoud's continued involvement with issues involving American citizens did not endear him to Iranian authorities. It finally came to the point he became concerned about his own safety as well as that of his family, so he left Iran. Thanks to Sheldon Krys, who made similar arrangements for other employees, he was allowed to work at one of the US posts in Canada until he reached the fifteen year point and was permitted to immigrate. He went to San Diego where there was a large Iranian community. Although we communicated from time to time, I eventually lost touch with him after we transferred to another overseas posting.

Meantime, life went on for our Canadian rescuers as well, although we heard rumors of discord among the Canadians. My understanding was the government of Canada wished to award the Order of Canada, the nation's highest civilian decoration, to Ken Taylor, John Sheardown, Roger Lucy, Laverna Dollimore, Ken's secretary, and Mary O'Flaherty, a communicator. John was unhappy with the exclusion of Pat Taylor and his wife Zena. As a foreign national, Zena was technically not eligible. The website of the Department of Foreign Affairs and International Trade, as the Ministry of External Affairs is now known, in its summary of the "Canadian Caper" states "Foreign Service spouses were outraged that Pat Taylor and Zena Sheardown were not similarly honoured."[1]

---

1. Foreign Affairs and International Trade Canada, Department of History, Ken Taylor and the Canadian Caper, p 4 <www.international.gc/history-histoire/people-gens/ken_taylor.aspx> October 21, 2011

As a British national, Zena was the first honorary appointment to the order. Flora MacDonald was her advocate, to the point of obtaining unanimous consent from the House of Commons to gain serious consideration for the appointment. By the time she had succeeded, 1986, Zena had become a Canadian national so her honorary status was withdrawn.[2]

The version I heard informally was John believed Zena in particular deserved the recognition because she had been our caretaker. When we needed her she was always available and she was the person answering the door and the telephone. She made sure we got fed and had our creature comforts met. And had there been some kind of problem, an effort to enter the house by Iranian thugs, for example, Zena would have been the one to try to stop it. I know it was stressful for her. We all shared the luck that no serious episode took place, but that in no way minimizes her role.

Apparently Ken thought John's campaign was in some way in-appropriate, with the result the two men were not on speaking terms for many years. In fact, when Roger Lucy and I began planning for our first reunion to take place twenty years after the exfiltration, we worried whether it would be possible to invite both. As it turned out, the Taylors were not available (or at least said so) and the issue did not arise. By the time of the 25th anniversary reunion the matter did not come up and both the Taylors and the Sheardowns attended. I heard them speaking cordially and it seemed like old times again.

I was not involved in the Order of Canada controversy or even aware of it until many years after. For what it's worth, though, I would tend to give John the benefit of any doubt. After the Yankees/Blue Jays game in 1980, we did not see John and Zena again until 1991 when we visited Ottawa while on leave from Warsaw. The Sheardowns took us to their cottage on a lake in Quebec several hours drive from Ottawa. John was largely building it on his own and the indoor plumbing was yet to come. We had ample opportunity for conversation and I never once heard John complain about not getting his share of the credit. Zena was quite willing to discuss the

---

2. Honorary Appointments to the Order of Canada, Note 4, Wikipedia, The Free Encyclopedia. Wikimedia Foundation Inc. April 24, 2011. Web. July 10, 2012, <http://en.wikipedia.org/wiki/Order_of_Canada>

point but John was not concerned. I learned only recently he had turned down an offer from Mayor Ed Koch of New York to receive the keys to the city, on grounds that Ken Taylor's receiving of the keys was on behalf of the entire group.[3] But as Zena was dedicated to John, he was to her, and he felt strongly she was an integral part of our rescue team.

After the public relations mission finally came to a close, Taylor needed an onward assignment like the rest of us. He became the Consul General in New York. As seemed typical with Ken, anything he did generated controversy. In this case, there was some sniping he had taken the position away from the previous incumbent who had been there only a year. On the other hand, while it was an ideal job for Taylor who was a trade promotion type by specialty, it was also undeniably a boon for Canadian trade promotion in the commercial center of the US. Ken had entre like no one else. Besides, I am reasonably sure the man he replaced was taken care of properly.

Ken did not occupy the position for long. He was made an offer he could not refuse and left government service in 1984 to become vice-president of government relations for RJR Nabisco. He remained in New York and in late 1985 became a permanent US resident. I was invited to the ceremony by the director of the former Immigration and Naturalization Service office (now part of Homeland Security) in New York. Afterward Ken treated me to lunch at the posh 21 Club. We were riding over in his gray Cadillac limousine, but the traffic was so heavy Ken was afraid we'd miss our reservations. The driver stayed with the car and we walked the last mile. During a wonderful lunch, Ken made clear his allegiance to Canada was as strong as ever. It was the hassle of entering the US as a foreigner that had caused him to seek a green card. As a frequent international traveler, when processing through immigration he could now use the line for US citizens and permanent residents which was generally much shorter and faster.

I saw Taylor twice that year. Bob Anders and I were invited to Kansas City, MO, to represent the Department of State at a ceremony

3. Richard Brennan, "Key player in Tehran Rescue needs rescuing this time," thestar.com, July 29, 2010,<www.thestar.com/news/canada/article/842132> October 21, 2011

during which Ken would receive the Harry S. Truman Good Neighbor Award. This award was the invention of a foundation set up to honor President Truman. It had been in existence for thirty-three years, and since 1973 had annually recognized an individual who best exemplified the former President's values in public life, including good citizenship, patriotism, public service and courage. Ken was the first recipient who was not an American citizen, but this award almost seemed custom made for him, especially as his acceptance speech made clear he considered the recognition to be intended for the Canadian embassy staff and the nation of Canada rather than for himself. Canada was indeed the quintessential good neighbor at least as far as I was concerned.

For me, the highlight of the event occurred after it was over, when Ken invited Bob and me to fly back to DC aboard the RJR Nabisco corporate jet that brought him there from New York. He had business in Washington and room on the aircraft so we happily accepted the opportunity to experience again what it was like to travel as a VIP. I did discover one down side, however. After all the beverages served during the flight, I found myself needing the toilet. But the toilet was configured in such a manner it could not be used once the aircraft began its descent into Washington's National Airport. Thankfully, the jet was given prompt clearance to land and we were able to exit immediately after reaching the parking area. Apparently even the rich and famous have to put up with some hardships.

Our relationship with the Canadians receded over the years as we each pursued our daily lives. With the Taylors and the Sheardowns it became pretty much an exchange of Christmas cards. Roger Lucy and I exchanged letters from time to time in the days before the Internet. We visited Roger once in the mid-eighties while he was posted to Ottawa, and I mentioned earlier our 1991 trip when we saw the Sheardowns. We were not doing reunions in those years. We were all still active Foreign Service with the exception of the Taylors who even so probably traveled more than the rest of us. It would have been unlikely to find us all on the same continent. Lee left the Foreign Agricultural Service to pursue an opportunity with a private firm but he was traveling also. He did return to FAS eventually, but in a job that did not involve overseas assignments.

# 21. Five More Minutes of Fame

If one assumes Andy Warhol was right about everyone having fifteen minutes of fame, we used more than our quota during the weeks following the exfiltration. But there was to be a second, much shorter round. In September 1997, the CIA announced what it called Trailblazer Awards, recognizing fifty employees who had made exceptional contributions during the agency's fifty year history. Several of the names were secret: Tony Mendez' name was not. Along with his name, the CIA released information explaining why he was among the Trailblazers, including details of his role in the exfiltration. With the usual sensitivity our government shows its northern neighbor, the Canadians received no advance notice. It probably would not have mattered except as a courtesy, however, as the real reaction was in the press and among the Canadian people. Much to my surprise, Ken Taylor was being widely denounced as a fake who had perpetrated a fraud.

I first learned of the agency announcement when a Philadelphia news reporter called and asked for my comments. I was stunned, both that the CIA would reveal so much of its tradecraft (presumably exfiltrations are still done from time to time) and because the news was being so thoroughly misunderstood. After verifying the CIA press release was genuine, I called the reporter back and said Tony was a true American hero and I was pleased we could finally thank him publicly for what he had done for us. But this did not in any way diminish what the Canadians had done. John Sheardown's warmly welcoming response to Bob Anders' exploratory phone call remained, in my view, the single most important step in our journey from the consulate building to the airport in Zurich. Of course there were many critical actions along the way and picking one is necessarily arbitrary. But if we had not been convinced we were truly welcome at the Sheardown's home, we most likely would have continued trying to survive on our own. I doubt we would have lasted another week.

Ken's wholehearted endorsement of John's action, as well as that of Joe Clark and his government, sealed the deal. They bought us the time for Tony's plan, brilliant as it was, to be conceived, developed, approved and implemented. The Canadian passports were key as well. The reporter then asked about Ken's very visible presence during the period when it seemed virtually every American wanted to thank Canada. I replied it was a critical part of the plan. As long as Iran held the hostages, it was necessary for Ken to claim credit, on behalf of his staff and his government as well as himself. Did he do it too well? As I have written previously, the Sheardowns, Zena in particular, may have thought so. But it was necessary for Ken to be convincing.

I did not say it to this particular reporter, but the press was at least as responsible for Ken's visibility as he was. As I noted earlier, they were fascinated by this young, dashing, stylish, handsome, daring, debonair (I could go on, but this is just a sampling of the terms used by the media to describe him) diplomat. They were certainly familiar with the other names. Although Roger Lucy felt no great desire to grant media interviews, the Sheardowns would almost certainly have cooperated if asked. They generally were not asked, despite the fact Cora and I, Bob and Lee were putting their names out there repeatedly in those early days following our return to the US. If anything, we were focusing more on the Sheardowns in an effort to counterbalance what we perceived as too much media focus on Ken. Having convinced themselves Taylor was the second coming of Sir William Stevenson, they were now upset he had a previously silent partner.

Over the next two years, we participated in four or five documentaries that focused on Tony. It was fun to be able to discuss the real story in full detail, because aside from the opportunity to praise and discuss a brilliant plan, it was a chance to thank Tony and say good things about the CIA. Over my years in the Foreign Service, I had worked with many CIA officers and with very few exceptions had found them to be selfless, hard-working and honorable people. Sure, there were some who thought they should have nicer houses, but even in that department they were pikers compared to the employees of the US Agency for International Development.

In all of these interviews, Cora and I made sure to emphasize the importance of the Canadian role. At one point, I was asked whether I believed the Canadians could have smuggled us out of Iran on their own without any CIA assistance. I think the answer is yes, and said so, primarily because the Canadian government was the source of the all-important passports. Of course the CIA made the passports look real by providing the entry and exit stamps for other countries that made them look used as well as the Iranian visas and entry stamps. I do not know whether the Canadians could have done any of that work themselves or found others to help them with it. I do not really know what a Canadian-only plan might have looked like and how well it would have worked. I have never asked in part because the US government would have been worse than foolish not to use its expertise on our behalf, but also because the question is not really relevant. The Canadian contribution was to keep us safe until the CIA was ready to act. In that role they performed superbly.

Speaking of superb performances it was very satisfying to Cora and me when we were finally given an opportunity to discuss what John and Zena did for us in a documentary focused exclusively on them. In late 1999 we were contacted by a company producing a show called *Courage*. It ran for a couple of years on one of the US cable channels and it focused, as one might expect, on stories of ordinary people showing extraordinary bravery. While I hesitate to call anyone who agrees to go gallivanting around the world in the service of his or her country ordinary, the point was we finally had an opportunity to talk about what John and Zena had done for us without the expectation the important parts would end up on the cutting room floor. The show was broadcast in the spring of 2000 and I hope it quieted some demons for Zena.

Our five minutes of second round fame ended with that *Courage* episode, although Iran resurfaced occasionally. In 2004 there was a proposal for another made-for-TV movie, but for a variety of reasons it died. In 2006 we were interviewed by a journalist, Joshuah Bearman, who was writing an article for *Wired* magazine. I was only vaguely aware of the magazine, but Tony indicated he was cooperating so I agreed also. In 2007 we were interviewed by a Washington-based reporter for the German magazine *Der Spiegel*.

He was a complete gentleman and took the trouble to translate his article for our collection. In 2008, Roger Lucy contacted me on behalf of Robert Wright, who was writing a biography of Ken Taylor. Cora and I had an opportunity to provide information for the manuscript and it was pleasant to work with someone who understood the importance of the Canadian role.

In the summer of 2010 we finally made it to the International Spy Museum in Washington. We heard about it first from Tony, who I recall was involved in setting it up and served on the board. Friends told us we should see it but living so far away made it difficult. I enjoyed the museum and was impressed with the collection, although the display about our adventure was smaller than I had been led to expect. We participated in a couple of podcasts about the exfiltration, one with Tony and the other just Cora and me with the host. We also donated Cora's Molson's key chain (I still use mine) and two small containers of face powder Tony had given Cora to help her change her appearance. Cora told me it was the best face powder she had ever found but the boxes were nearly empty. Of course there was no brand name. She went so far as to ask Tony if he remembered what it was. He didn't. It was fun to make a little contribution to the permanent history of the event, a small way to keep the true story alive.

A year or two after the *Wired* article ran, we heard from Tony it had been sold to George Clooney as the basis for a film. This surprised me. There was nothing wrong with the article, but there were many better sources about the Canadian Caper, and Mendez had written his own book detailing his role in 1999. I learned only in 2011 the *Wired* piece was written with the specific hope it would catch the attention of the right person in Hollywood, where the magazine is apparently popular with the movers and shakers. In addition, Bearman had an associate (I am not sure what term best applies) whose job it was to take the article around town and sell the film idea. He was successful, but Tony told us Clooney normally had a backlog of projects and there was no way to know when and if it would actually go into production.

In early 2011 we started hearing rumors there was going to be a film. Then we heard that Ben Affleck was particularly interested in playing Mendez. Before long people were sending us press items about the film, to be called *Argo* in honor of our fake movie. These indicated Affleck would direct as well as star. In late spring we were contacted by one of the executive producers and sent a copy of the script as well as "True Event Character Consent forms." In exchange for a modest payment, we agreed to be depicted in the film and also to act as consultants. The first part of the agreement was designed to keep the lawyers happy since we were public persons and could not prevent anyone from using our story. The second part did involve some work, as I, and to some extent Cora, answered quite a number of questions, including from the actors who were to portray us. We both read the script and offered our suggestions, which not surprisingly centered around the way the Canadian role was depicted. While we did understand the movie was primarily about Tony, we were disappointed the Sheardowns were not mentioned.

At the end of September 2011, we were invited to Los Angeles for several days. Mendez, his wife and several other family members had arrived earlier. We had the opportunity to visit some of the sets. A facade resembling the chancery exterior had been constructed at a partially vacant Veterans Administration facility north of the city and an empty building nearby was used for some of the interior shots. There we watched several actors rush down a hallway with a cart full of documents and begin to shred them. We watched it over and over and over again, and I wondered how it must be for the actors to have to repeat a scene endlessly. But I guess repetition pays off in terms of the final product. And as an old friend of mine would have said, it was indoor work with no heavy lifting.

We met the actors who were playing the six of us as well as several others and had lunch inside a large tent filled with rows of tables and chairs. This is where the cast and crew were fed. I had heard movie location catering was outstanding and the food more than met my expectations. I opted for New York strip steak with all the trimmings. Affleck joined us for the lunch, although as I recall he did not eat. He was dressed in jeans and an old t-shirt with some kind of logo too faded to read clearly, but from his conversation it was clear he was the man in charge. It was also evident he was committed to making the film authentic. While the events would only partly track actual history, he wanted the mood and atmosphere to be genuine. I now understood why many of the questions I received had to do with details such as the layout of the consular section or the types of signs on our doors as well as what we were thinking or feeling at a particular moment. We also learned from a producer why the Sheardowns were not in the film: money. Including them would mean two more actors, another set and camera time devoted to explaining their role. This was all avoided by housing the six of us with Ambassador Taylor, already a necessary character.

Later, another executive explained the reasoning differently. The movie was about the exfiltration. There were many angles from which the story could be told, but regardless of which angle was chosen, the nature of the film medium demands a limit on the number of characters. Despite their importance to the four houseguests they hosted, the Sheardowns did not fit within this particular version of the story. There were already more than 125 speaking roles and good storytelling required a tight focus on the primary elements of the plot. Both answers made sense to me. During this visit we also recorded interviews for the special features segment of the DVD version of the film scheduled for release in 2013.

*Argo* may well be the last gasp of our five more minutes of fame. It will almost certainly have been the most fun. In addition to the set visit, we attended the premiere and the party following. The hospitality extended to us was overwhelming and the film turned out to be terrific. While the story receives considerable embellishment for dramatic effect, it remains true to the most basic facts and mood, and the Canadians receive recognition. I hope movie audiences consider it great entertainment and at least a few will be motivated to learn more about the hostage drama, a critical event in the confrontation with Islamic radicalism that continues to this day. While I am concerned that many viewers will take the movie as complete truth, this is not the fault of Affleck or the screenwriter. We live in a society where the knowledge of history is increasingly devalued. I learned more about the DVD special features while attending the premiere, and to the credit of the producers, there will be considerable material of historical importance included. Those who want to learn the true story will have the chance.

More personally, *Argo* gave me the incentive finally to write this book. There is an old saying about truth being stranger than fiction. In our case it might be better to say the true story reads as well as good fiction. I think that is why just when we think it has finally disappeared entirely in the rear view mirror of history, someone throws the car in reverse and wants to have a better look. We don't mind. As I wrote in the beginning, we are not the heroes of the story. But we relish any opportunity to give the heroes their due. *Argo* does that, for Tony Mendez and in part for the Canadians, symbolized by Pat and Ken Taylor. This book has attempted to fill in the details, giving due credit to the many people who could not possibly have been included in a film.

Among those who have interviewed me over the years one of the more interesting was a US government team charged with helping prepare Americans who operate in circumstances that might leave them behind enemy lines. The interviewer focused on what he called decision points, critical times when choosing to do one thing rather than another could reasonably be said to influence the future course of events.

There were many decision points in our adventure, so many I have found myself repeating over and over someone up there was looking out for me as choices made with little understanding at the time turned out to be both consequential and, more often than not, correct. Yet there are two that stand out. One was the collective decision of our group to head to the British embassy by the best available route. This prevented our arrest on the first day. The second, for which we can take no credit, was the enthusiastic welcome John Sheardown extended to Bob Anders and the rest of us when Bob first called him. I realize many others took tremendous risks on our behalf and Ambassador Taylor and ultimately the Canadian government and its embassy staff stood firmly behind the message John transmitted that day, but it is clear to me from everything Bob has ever said about the call that the genuine and heartfelt,

"Why didn't you call sooner?"

was pure John Sheardown. It made all the difference.

The only photograph taken in Tehran, just prior to the departure of John and Zena Sheardown. Despite professional efforts it proved impossible to increase the clarity. From left to right, Lee Schatz, Cora Amburn-Lijek, Mark Lijek (note the traces of the alleged beard), Bob Anders, Zena Sheardown, John Sheardown and Roger Lucy.

Cora Amburn-Lijek, whose pseudonym was Teresa Harris, carried a copy of an issue of the Hollywood Reporter in which this advertisement appeared.

STUDIO SIX PRODUCTIONS
SUNSET GOWER INDEPENDENT
STUDIOS       SUITE 300
1420 NO. BEECHWOOD DR.
LOS ANGELES, CALIFORNIA 90028
TELEPHONE (213) 465-2101 - 2102

JOSEPH HARRIS
TRANSPORTATION COORDINATOR

The business cards we carried were dual purpose. Aside from strengthening the cover legend, the knowledge the phone number was real boosted our confidence.

The author descending the ladder to US soil at
Dover Air Force Base, Delaware.

Preparing the speeches at Dover Air Force Base.
From left, Lee Schatz, unknown person, Sheldon Krys (with
back to camera), Kathy Stafford, Joe Stafford, Bob Anders, Cora
Amburn-Lijek, Mark Lijek and the base commander's secretary.

At the Department of State as Bob prepares to give his speech.
From left, Bob Anders, Kathy Stafford, Joe Stafford, Mark Lijek,
Cora Amburn-Lijek and Lee Schatz.

In the background is the Memorial Plaque where names of
employees who die in the line of duty are inscribed

At the White House following our meeting with President Carter. From left, Kathy Stafford, Lee Schatz, Joe Stafford, the President, Cora Amburn-Lijek, Mark Lijek, Bob Anders.

*With best wishes to*
*Cora and Mark Lijek*          Jimmy Carter
                                              2-80

Cora Amburn-Lijek and the author with the President. Yes, the eyeglasses are enormous but the stylish Ken Taylor had an equally large pair. This photo was taken following the meeting and mailed to us later.

John Sheardown receiving the Order of Canada from
Governor General Ed Schreyer.

Ambassador Ken Taylor and Roger Lucy at the Order of Canada
Ceremony. Note the large glasses.

# Epilogue: Where Are They Now?

I am always annoyed when a book or movie ends without telling me what happened to the major characters. So here is a brief summary of what I know about the people who were particularly important to this story.

Bob Anders remained in the Foreign Service, serving in generally nice places including two tours in Vienna where he was finally able to work seriously on his German. He retired to London, England, and lived there for twelve years before returning to the DC area. He now lives in the Maryland suburbs.

Chris Beebe continued his successful diplomatic career. His last posting was as ambassador to one of the international organizations in Geneva, where he died suddenly several years ago at the age of 65.

Don Cooke married a dynamic woman fully capable of handling his BS. They had three children. Unfortunately she passed away, leaving him to raise the kids on his own. In 2012 he became the last of the hostages to retire from active government service.

Laverna Dollimore retired to Brighton, Ontario, where she hosted our 25th anniversary reunion. She passed away in 2011.

Jim Edward retired from the Canadian Forces and worked as security manager for Calgary International Airport as well as a security consultant. Cancer claimed him suddenly in 2011.

Mark and Cora Lijek served in Kathmandu following their "reward" tour in Hong Kong. After returning to Washington they subsequently were assigned to Warsaw and Frankfurt. They have two grown children. After retirement, they returned to the Pacific northwest and live in a small town on an island in Puget Sound.

Roger Lucy is retired and living in Ottawa. He is married to the wonderful Susan, who is very tolerant of his eccentricities (such as filling the basement with military gear), and has become an expert and published author on certain types of military equipment as well as ancient diplomacy.

Tony Mendez retired in 1990, and turned his avocation, painting, into his primary career. In addition, he is a successful author and consultant. He continues to live on his farm in Maryland.

Trolls Monk became the Danish ambassador in Rome, after which we lost track of him. He passed away several years ago.

Henry Precht was unable to outlast Senator Helms, who continued to block any effort to appoint him to an ambassadorial position. He became a diplomat-in-residence at the Fletcher School of Law and Diplomacy at Tufts University. This program allows senior Foreign Service officers to teach at universities and is also part of State's outreach to potential recruits. After retirement Henry became the president of the World Affairs Council of Cleveland.

Richard Queen, after being diagnosed with multiple sclerosis, had several periods of remission during which he served tours in London and Toronto. He was even able to achieve his great ambition of getting married. Cora and I met Moire several times. She was attractive and energetic, and although the marriage did not last very long, she remained a close friend to Rich. He was very proud he was the first person to convince the government to classify MS as an illness that can be caused by job-related stress. I last saw Rich in 1996, just before I retired and moved west. His short term memory was virtually gone; he had forgotten about our dinner invitation even though I had called him earlier in the day. The disease finally took his life in 2002.

Lee Schatz married his long-time girlfriend. They have two sons. He did leave government service for a while, but returned to the Foreign Agricultural Service in a position that does not entail overseas assignments. He lives in Maryland, in a place that permits him to engage his passion for sailing while still commuting to DC for work.

Richard Sewell served at the consulate in Los Angeles, after which we lost track of him. We heard about ten years ago he had passed away after a serious illness.

John and Zena Sheardown returned to their beautiful condominium in downtown Ottawa. John served at the Ministry of External Affairs for a time, following which he and Zena were assigned to Budapest, Hungary and Colombo, Sri Lanka. John then returned to Ottawa, where he worked as a trouble-shooter. He was sent on temporary duty assignments to countries where immigration operations had problems, including a stint at the Canadian embassy in Warsaw. As we were then assigned there, this gave us an opportunity to repay a tiny portion of the hospitality John had extended to us, and also to introduce him to my mother, who was visiting. He retired in 1994. At our 25th reunion in 2006, it was noticeable John's memory was failing. He was unable to attend the 30th: he had suffered a fall and been placed in a hospital. Most of the reunion group visited him there but the crowd may have been overwhelming as he seemed confused by our presence. Subsequently he was placed in a memory care facility. Only as a result of the publicity surrounding his admission did I learn his World War II service entailed numerous bombing missions over Europe and that he broke both of his legs when forced to bail out of a damaged aircraft over Britain. Like many of his generation, he did not brag. Zena has remained John's advocate and companion.

Sam (Somchai) Sriweawnetr went through some difficult times in Tehran after we separated. He had several run-ins with the authorities and had to go underground for a time, taking advantage of the network of Thai cooks and housekeepers around town. Eventually he was able to get an exit visa and return to Thailand. Thanks to Vic Tomseth who pushed for passage of a private bill in Congress, Sam was granted US citizenship and now lives in Massachusetts.

Joe and Kathy Stafford retired from the Foreign Service in 2012, although as of this writing he is still working for the Department on a contract basis. Joe achieved the rank of ambassador and continued his preference for tough posts, including Algiers during the civil war. Kathy pursued her art wherever Joe's career lands her. They have one son.

Ken and Pat Taylor continue to live in New York City. Ken works as a consultant for several energy companies and serves on some corporate boards. Pat retired in 2011 from her position as a medical research scientist.

# Afterword

I begin with a brief apology to the Foreign Service. Despite a less than auspicious beginning I enjoyed my career and would advise anyone interested to give it serious consideration. My description of the entry process is dated. Although I am not familiar with the new process in detail, I understand there is more emphasis on hiring people who already have language knowledge, medical restrictions have been relaxed and the security clearance process accelerated.

There are a number of good books available that cover different aspects of the hostage crisis.

For those who wish to learn more about the broader context of the attack on the American embassy as well as understand more fully the extent of Canadian support to the US during the crisis, including the specific role of Ambassador Ken Taylor, I highly recommend Our Man in Tehran by Robert Wright (Other Press, 2011, USA edition; Harper Collins 2010, Canadian edition). The book draws on Canadian government documents declassified over the past decade. Another bonus is that it also provides a good understanding of how Eagle Claw, the failed hostage rescue operation, was supposed to have worked. If you plan to read only one book, this should be it.

If you are interested in learning more about the experiences of the actual hostages, there are two possibilities. Guests of the Ayatollah by Mark Bowden (Grove Press, 2006) is very readable and comprehensive. 444 Days: The Hostages Remember by Tim Wells (Harcourt Brace Jovanovich, 1985) is an oral history that lets the hostages describe their experiences in their own words. Bowden's book gives more background information, while Wells allows the former hostages to speak directly to you.

Those wanting a good understanding of the overall history of US-Iran relations should consider The Eagle and the Lion by James

Bill (Yale University Press, 1989). This was one of the books used in our area studies course before we went to Iran. The current version was revised in 1989 to cover the fall of the shah and the hostage crisis. Although I have not read the updated version, I presume that Professor Bill maintained the quality of his earlier work. And though more than two decades have passed since the update, there have been no dramatic developments that would render this book seriously out of date as a history of the Iranian revolution and its initial aftermath.

Nikki Keddie's <u>Roots of Revolution</u> (Yale, 1981) was useful and comprehensive. Although I have not read the revised version, <u>Modern Iran: Roots and Results of Revolution</u> (2006), I expect she too has maintained her high standards.

Lastly, <u>Takeover in Tehran</u> by Massoumeh Ebtekar (Talon Books, 2000) is a memoir from the Iranian side. The author was known as "Tehran Mary" because she was the primary spokesman for the hostage-takers. The book contains some interesting details, but the author never manages to come to grips with the wanton and unnecessary cruelty with which the hostages were treated, in some cases denying established facts and in others serving up weak and self-serving excuses.

# About the Author

Mark Lijek was born in 1951 in Detroit to a Polish-American father and a Polish mother. They had met during World War II in Algiers where she had come as a refugee. Perhaps it was this international background that sparked Lijek's interest in the Foreign Service. He attended the Foreign Service School at Georgetown University after graduating from Seattle Preparatory School in Seattle, where his family had moved when he was six. Following graduation from Georgetown, Lijek served as an officer in the US Army. He was assigned to Washington, DC and took advantage of the location of obtain a Masters in Business Administration from American University.

Lijek's interest in the Foreign Service dated back to his high school days. He took the examination several times, passing both the written and oral portions on his second attempt. Fortunately the timing of the Department of State employment offer coincided with the end of Lijek's military service and he joined the Foreign Service in October 1978. Less fortunately, he was asked to volunteer for assignment to Tehran just as the political situation was seriously deteriorating. He nevertheless accepted the job and the possibility of a separation from his wife, Cora. Shortly afterward, family members at the Tehran embassy were evacuated because of increasing chaos and instability. Many employees were also withdrawn, including much of the consular section.

Despite the abdication of the shah and the assumption of power by the virulently anti-American Ayatollah Khomeini, the US Government was determined to rebuild relations. One aspect of the process was the return of normal tourist visa operations to Iran, which created an opportunity for Cora to accompany her husband while working in the visa unit. In late October 1979, the US admitted the shah for medical treatment, resulting ultimately in an attack on the embassy compound and the capture of most Americans. Lijek and his wife escaped, initially the compound and later Iran.

Although this was not a good beginning to a Foreign Service career, Lijek decided the law of averages should work in his favor. Future assignments to Hong Kong, then still a British colony; Kathmandu, Nepal; Warsaw, Poland and Frankfurt, Germany proved him correct. He also served several tours at the Department of State in Washington, DC. The Iran experience remained a constant in his life. While media interest came and went, Lijek never forgot the selfless help provided by Canadian Embassy personnel during the crucial months following the takeover. He remained in touch with several of the Canadians and served as the US-side coordinator for the periodic reunions hosted by the Canadian side.

Following retirement the Lijeks returned to the Pacific Northwest. Cora, who had to sacrifice her career during their Foreign Service years, went to work while Mark took care of the house and their two children. He has been treasurer of the Anacortes Sister Cities Association for twelve years and has from time to time dabbled in local politics.

Made in the USA
San Bernardino, CA
05 March 2013